THE
CRIMINOLOGICAL
ENTERPRISE

DON C. GIBBONS

Portland State University

THE
CRIMINOLOGICAL
ENTERPRISE
THEORIES AND PERSPECTIVES

Prentice-Hall, Inc., Englewood Cliffs, New Jersey 07632

Library of Congress Cataloging in Publication Data

GIBBONS, DON C.
  THE CRIMINOLOGICAL ENTERPRISE.

  Includes bibliographical references and index.
  1. Crime and criminals–United States–History.
2. Crime and criminals–History. I. Title.
HV6021.G5   364′.09   78–15736
ISBN 0-13-193615-8

Prentice-Hall Series in Sociology
Neil J. Smelser, Editor

Printed in the United States of America

10   9   8   7   6   5   4   3   2   1

PRENTICE-HALL INTERNATIONAL, INC., *London*
PRENTICE-HALL OF AUSTRALIA PTY. LIMITED, *Sydney*
PRENTICE-HALL OF CANADA, LTD., *Toronto*
PRENTICE-HALL OF INDIA PRIVATE LIMITED, *New Delhi*
PRENTICE-HALL OF JAPAN, INC., *Tokyo*
PRENTICE-HALL OF SOUTHEAST ASIA PTE. LTD., *Singapore*
WHITEHALL BOOKS LIMITED, *Wellington, New Zealand*

To Calvin F. Schmid and Clarence C. Schrag

CONTENTS

PREFACE

This book explores the major themes or theoretical viewpoints that have guided criminologists over the past 75 years, particularly in the United States. It examines the formative years of American sociological criminology, discusses the developmental period between 1930 and the present, and contemplates the implications of recent radical versions of criminological thought for the future of this area of inquiry.

This is not meant to be an introductory textbook. Introductory books must review most of the etiological theories that have been devised by scholars from a variety of fields, along with much of the research data that has been produced in criminological investigations. Also, introductory textbooks usually contain a wealth of descriptive information on the workings of police agencies, the courts and related judicial operations, and correctional systems, none of which are covered in this volume.

Throughout this book, "criminology" refers to the sociological study of adult crime and juvenile delinquency. Most contemporary criminologists exhibit a good deal of interest in both of these topics. Much of the criminological theorizing considered here deals with explanations of adult criminality. Chapter 3, however, involves a detailed examination of the research of Clifford Shaw and Henry D. McKay on delinquency, and Chapter 4 comments on more recent formulations concerning juvenile law breaking. Furthermore, many of the broad social influences that have been enumerated in sociological formulations about delinquency have appeared in nearly identical form in theories of social disorganization or "criminogenic" social structure which have been put forth concerning adult criminality. Finally, many of the research findings on delinquency, such as those of Shaw and McKay, have been incorporated into criminological accounts of differential association or other processes through which juvenile offenders are thought to be drawn into careers in adult crime.

American sociological criminology has gone off in a variety of theoretical directions, although it is fair to say that the greatest concentration of effort has been on the etiological forces that generate criminality and delinquency. The emphasis here is also on theoretical perspectives on causation, although some attention is given to other matters that have captured the interest of criminologists, such as deterrence and the organizational analyses of the police, courts, and correctional institutions.

The accent is on theory in this book, for it concentrates on the major ideas that have informed the sociological study of criminality. There is much less space devoted to the research evidence, although some of the observations about various theoretical viewpoints will at least touch on the quality of empirical support that exists for them.

The key ideas that have guided scholars in particular fields of inquiry are the life blood that nurtures inquiry and sustains those who carry it on. A volume on the major themes and perspectives that have dominated criminology may serve to correct the common notion that theory is something encountered only in sociology courses bearing that designation. This book is intended to reveal that sociological criminology contains a large body of theory, some of which is as sophisticated as any currently to be found in sociology.

Although the central focus is on sociological themes that have been employed in the study of criminality, there is also some commentary regarding the men and women who developed the ideas woven into these pages. Those figures are placed within the times in which they wrote as a way of highlighting those aspects of American life that seemed to influence the criminological perspectives that flourished at one time or another. However, this is not a full-blown sociology of criminology, in which the societal forces behind criminological activities are spelled out in great detail. There are limits to what can be said about the social climate within which criminological ideas have sprung up in the past, for although sociologists have offered a considerable quantity of commentary on the social influences that operated in the rise of European and American sociology, detailed reports on the formative years of American criminology are more difficult to come by. On the same point, while some accounts have been provided by others regarding the social backgrounds and academic careers of a few pioneering figures in American criminology, very little is known about the lives of other important scholars.

To sum up, this book deals mainly with the key perspectives and themes that have dominated American sociological criminology and secondarily with the social context within which those notions developed and the social backgrounds and careers of those who shaped those theories. It touches only tangentially on criminological hypotheses that have arisen in other disciplines, such as biological contentions about genetic influences in criminality or psychiatric claims about psychopathy or other psychological malfunctioning thought to be operating in law breaking. The volume presents a selection of what I feel are the most important ideas in the development of sociological criminology. Doubtless some will quarrel with the choices, holding that some of those included are relatively insignificant while other, more influential ideas have not been mentioned.

A number of people have contributed advice and criticism concerning earlier drafts of this book. I wish to thank my colleagues at Portland State University for their help: Jan Hajda, Joseph F. Jones, Nanette J. Davis, and R. Kelly Hancock. I also want to acknowledge the advice and critical comments of a number of people who read the manuscript for Prentice-Hall: Jon Simpson, Peter G. Garabedian, Donald Black, Gresham M. Sykes, Neil Smelser, and Adrian J. Marriage. I want to single out Adrian Marriage for special mention, for he provided a great deal of trenchant criticism of the first draft of this book, drawing attention to a number of major flaws in the manuscript. I have tried to revise the material in the directions suggested by him and hope that I have succeeded in these efforts. I have also tried to respond to many of the points raised by other reviewers, but I probably have not managed to deal with all of them to their satisfaction. Finally, I could not have completed the book without the highly skilled secretarial assistance of Ms. Kathy Grove.

D. C. G.

THE NATURE
OF CRIMINOLOGY

INTRODUCTION

This is a book about criminology in which many of the more important themes and ideas that have guided criminological inquiry, particularly in the United States during the present century, are outlined. The story that unfolds in these pages is richly textured and involves a large cast of characters, many of whom are employed in universities as criminologists. But what is criminology? What is a criminologist? Although most adults probably have some sense of what these labels mean, the fact is that opinions differ, even among social scientists, concerning these terms. Thus, before beginning the story, some boundary markers that indicate the major purposes of this volume need to be set, along with the major topics and directions to be pursued in detail in the chapters that follow.

OBSERVATIONS ON CRIMINOLOGY

The search for the meaning of unfamiliar words often starts with the dictionary. Consider its definition of criminology: "the scientific study and investigation of crime and criminals." [1] This definition is not very useful because it doesn't tell us much about the nature and content of that study. A leading American criminology textbook is more helpful. Sutherland and Cressey have written that "Criminology is the body of knowledge regarding delinquency and crime as social phenomena. It includes within its scope the processes of making laws, of breaking laws, and of reacting toward the breaking of laws." [2] They also identified the three divisions of

[1] *Webster's New World Dictionary* (New York: World Publishing Co., 1959), p. 180.
[2] Edwin H. Sutherland and Donald R. Cressey, *Criminology,* 9th ed. (Philadelphia: Lippincott, 1974), p. 3. Throughout this book, "American" will usually be employed

1

criminological study as the sociology of law, criminal etiology, and penology.

Is Criminology a Scientific Discipline?

Most lists of the major social science disciplines include sociology, anthropology, geography, economics, political science, and often history as well. Criminology appears much less frequently in such inventories of the major disciplines. The attributes used to identify scientific disciplines or fields are often only implicit in discussions of this sort. But for people who are concerned about disciplinary identities and boundaries, a relatively distinct subject matter is the major criterion used in singling out areas of intellectual endeavor. For example, concerning sociology, Alex Inkeles has contended that it "is the study of systems of social action and of their interrelations." [3]

A somewhat different approach would be to say that sociology is a discipline because it attempts to answer certain distinctive questions such as "What are the relatively enduring effects of social structure on human behavior?" These conceptions of sociology mark it off from the discipline of economics, which is concerned with the production of goods and services, and from political science, which deals with political power and government administration.

Although it is possible to sort out the various social science disciplines according to their central concerns and subject matter, there is a good deal of pulling and tugging at the edges of these fields of inquiry. For example, it is difficult to see a great deal of difference between much of the day-to-day activity of some anthropologists and sociologists and the research activities of many political scientists and those sociologists who specialize in political sociology. Even more important, new candidates for disciplinary status are pushed forward from time to time. As a case in point, American sociology arose in large part through the efforts of people

---

as a substitute term for "United States." Although this is a somewhat questionable practice given the fact that America includes Canada, Mexico, and a number of Central and South American countries, it is the case that writers do often equate America with the United States. There is a further problem when speaking of criminology in the United States as American criminology, namely that there are criminologists actively involved in this work in Canada and elsewhere. Let it be understood that "American" is used in this book as shorthand for the United States and that the existence of other American nations is acknowledged, as well as the existence of American criminologists outside the United States.

[3] Alex Inkeles, *What Is Sociology?* (Englewood Cliffs, N.J.: Prentice-Hall, 1964), p. 16. See pp. 1–27 for a detailed attempt to identify the central concerns of sociology and to mark off boundaries separating it from the other social sciences.

who had broken away from economics. More recently, urban studies and criminal justice have arisen as contenders for disciplinary status.[4]

Criminology, now a subdiscipline of sociology, has also been nominated as a fledgling social science in its own right. Marvin Wolfgang has argued that criminology should be identified as an autonomous discipline because it has accumulated its own set of organized data and theoretical perspectives. He has also suggested that the label "criminologist" be given to people whose professional training and occupational role center around the study of criminality and whose main source of income derives from that activity.[5] Thus, all individuals who devote most of their scholarly activity to the study of crime and its control ought to be regarded as criminologists, whether they began their studies as sociologists, psychologists, political scientists, or the like.

Daniel Glaser's views regarding criminology as a discipline seem close to those of Wolfgang.[6] Glaser has observed that although criminology is not a clearly distinct and integrated science, it does collect and assimilate the contributions of various sociologists, psychologists, psychiatrists, and others who specialize in the study of criminality. At the same time, he implied that criminology can properly be regarded as a synthesizing discipline.

The practical consequence of these arguments regarding criminology is to locate it as a specialty within academic sociology. The plain fact is that, until recently, there have been few economists, geographers, or other social scientists who have devoted much attention to the study of criminality.[7] Similarly, there have been few psychologists who have con-

---

[4] For some commentary on the disciplinary status of criminal justice, see Don C. Gibbons and Gerald F. Blake, Jr., "Perspectives in Criminology and Criminal Justice: The Implications for Higher Education Programs," *Criminal Justice Review*, 2 (Spring 1977):23–40.

[5] Marvin E. Wolfgang, "Criminology and the Criminologist," *Journal of Criminal Law, Criminology and Police Science*, 54 (June 1963):155–62. Wolfgang quite correctly pointed out that nearly all criminologists have received their scientific training in some field such as sociology, rather than in criminology. There has only been one graduate program in the United States that has awarded a doctoral degree in criminology, the School of Criminology at the University of California, Berkeley. That program is no longer in existence.

[6] Daniel Glaser, "Criminology," *Encyclopaedia Brittanica*, Vol. 6 (Chicago: Encyclopaedia Brittanica, 1965), p. 773.

[7] For some recent cases of economic analyses of crime, see Gary Becker, "Crime and Punishment: An Economic Approach," *Journal of Political Economy*, 76 (March–April 1968):169–217; Sheldon Danziger and David Wheeler, "The Economics of Crime: Punishment or Income Redistribution," *Review of Social Economy*, 33 (October 1975):113–30; Llad Phillips, Harold L. Votey, Jr., and Darold Maxwell, "Crime, Youth, and the Labor Market," *Journal of Political Economy*, 80 (May–June 1972):491–503. For some recent geographical inquiry, see Keith D. Harries, *The Geography of Crime and Justice* (New York: McGraw-Hill, 1974).

centrated their scholarly attention on lawbreaking or lawbreakers. Thus, Wolfgang's definition of the criminologist as a full-time specialist in the study of criminal behavior would apply to relatively few individuals outside the discipline of sociology, at least in the United States.[8]

Richard Quinney, Sue Titus Reid, and others were on the mark in emphasizing that criminology in the United States has been centered on sociological criminology for the most part, with criminology courses most often being offered in departments of sociology by people who identify themselves as sociologists specializing in criminology.[9] Moreover, virtually all of the criminology textbooks written in this country have been authored by sociologists.[10]

However, to acknowledge that criminology has developed as a specialty or field of interest within the discipline of sociology is not necessarily to applaud that fact. A number of critics have pointed out that American sociological criminology has given little attention to the work of legal scholars. American criminologists have been woefully ignorant of even the rudimentary principles of criminal law and criminal procedure. Other commentators on the criminological enterprise have taken note of its ahistorical character, its silence on the question of psychological forces in criminality, and other signs of academic provincialism. The succeeding chapters of this book examine some of these alleged deficiencies of criminology in considerable detail.

Criminology in the United States

Because people have been fascinated by sin, wickedness, and crime for many centuries, one should not be surprised to find the roots of modern criminology in the work of scholars long since dead. One likely candidate for the title "the first criminologist" is J. Baptiste della Porte (1535–1615), who tried to find links between bodily forms and types of lawbreakers by studying the cadavers of criminals.[11] Paul Topinard, an anthropologist, should perhaps be nominated as an early criminologist for coining the term "criminology." [12] However, the most frequently men-

---

[8] European writers and researchers in criminology have much more frequently come from the ranks of university faculties in law or medicine; see Glaser, "Criminology."

[9] Richard Quinney, *Criminology* (Boston: Little, Brown, 1975), pp. 7–9. A brief and relatively superficial account of the development of American criminology from about 1920 to 1970 is contained in Walter C. Reckless, "American Criminology," *Criminology*, 8 (May 1970):4–20. Sue Titus Reid, *Crime and Criminology* (Hinsdale, Ill.: Dryden Press, 1976), p. 21.

[10] One exception was Robert H. Gault, *Criminology* (Boston: Heath, 1932). Gault was a psychologist, and his book was written from that perspective.

[11] Stephen Schafer, *Theories in Criminology* (New York: Random House, 1969), p. 113.

[12] Reid, *Crime and Criminology*, p. 21.

tioned "pioneers in criminology" are Cesare Beccaria (1735–1795), Jeremy Bentham (1748–1832), and a number of other members of the classical school. These men were followed by Cesare Lombroso (1835–1909), Enrico Ferri (1856–1928), and Raffaele Garofolo (1852–1934), who were major figures in the Italian positivist school.[13] American sociological criminology is only tenuously linked to the criminological heritage represented by the works of these and other early figures.[14] As Chapter 2 indicates in detail, criminology in the United States dates from the early 1900s and is largely an indigenous intellectual product, not a derivative of the writings of European scholars.

The first full-scale textbook in American criminology was published in 1918, followed by several others in the next half-dozen years.[15] American criminology textbooks have customarily included a chapter on the early schools of criminology, which includes a brief mention of the perspectives of the classical school, the cartographic or geographic school, early socialist theorists, and the Lombrosian or positivist arguments.[16] However, that commentary usually appears as an historical appendage, for few if any connections have been drawn between these European writings and contemporary American criminological viewpoints.

There were only a handful of people teaching criminology courses at the time that the first textbooks appeared, but the field expanded markedly in the intervening period. The American Society of Criminology, founded in 1941, currently has over 1,000 members. Most of the members of this organization live in the United States, but its roster also includes people in Canada, Brazil, Japan, Australia, Germany, and a number of other countries. Many of those who belong to this association are correctional employees and other individuals whose activities fall outside of academic sociological criminology. A clearer indicator of the growth of academic criminology is provided by the criminology section of the American Sociological Association. That section was founded in 1966 with an initial membership of 433 persons, while the 1977 roster listed

[13] George B. Vold, *Theoretical Criminology* (New York: Oxford University Press, 1958), pp. 14–40. The term, "pioneers in criminology" comes from Hermann Mannheim, *Pioneers in Criminology* (Chicago: Quadrangle Books, 1960).

[14] Sawyer F. Sylvester, *The Heritage of Modern Criminology* (Cambridge, Mass.: Schenkman Publishing Co., 1972). Sylvester's anthology includes excerpts from the writings of Beccaria, Quetelet, Mayhew, Lombroso, Tarde, Ferri, and Bonger, as well as Americans Healy, Sellin, and Sutherland.

[15] Maurice F. Parmelee, *Criminology* (New York: Macmillan, 1918); Edwin H. Sutherland, *Criminology* (Philadelphia: Lippincott, 1924); John L. Gillin, *Criminology and Penology* (New York: Century, 1926); Philip A. Parsons, *Crime and the Criminal* (New York: Knopf, 1926).

[16] For example, see Sutherland and Cressey, *Criminology*, pp. 48–61; Don C. Gibbons, *Society, Crime, and Criminal Careers*, 3rd ed. (Englewood Cliffs, N.J.: Prentice-Hall, 1977), pp. 125–53.

631 individuals. Sociological criminologists thus constitute a substantial constituency within the professional organization of sociologists.

Criminology and Sociology

Criminology is only one of many special fields or areas within sociology. Social psychology, medical sociology, industrial sociology, political sociology, and a number of others come quickly to mind as other concentrations of interest. As special fields, each ought to exhibit reciprocal relations with the basic discipline, drawing many key concepts and theoretical arguments from general sociology at the same time that they yield empirical findings and conceptual refinements that feed into sociological theory. Accordingly, one might inquire about the extent to which criminological theory has been informed by theoretical viewpoints that exist within sociology on such matters as social structure, social conflict, social stratification, political–economic organization, and kindred phenomena. One might also like to know whether the research activities have in turn made significant contributions to basic sociological theory.

The chapters that follow are concerned with this reciprocity between sociology and its subsidiary field, criminology. In brief, criminologists have frequently been somewhat isolated from mainstream sociology. As a result, they have failed to develop formulations about the causes of crime that have reflected elements of general sociological theory as fully as might have been the case if closer intellectual ties had been forged. On the other hand, theorists in the parent discipline have borrowed generously from the research findings of criminologists when seeking illustrative support for social disorganization theory, including broad arguments concerning the deleterious effects of urbanization on certain population groups. Then, too, a substantial part of contemporary deviance theory has been constructed on a foundation of criminological findings. In short, linkages between general sociology and criminology have been neither total nor nonexistent.

KEY QUESTIONS IN CRIMINOLOGICAL INQUIRY

Returning to the nature of the criminological enterprise, recall that Sutherland and Cressey specified that it includes the study of lawmaking, lawbreaking, and reactions to criminality. These broad categories put some order into the day-to-day activities of criminologists as they go about poking into a bewildering assortment of specific topics having to do with crime and the behavior of criminals. However, it might be well to broaden the list of core questions in criminology, to capture more fully the central issues around which criminological inquiry is organized.

One expanded listing of key questions involves the nature and origins of criminal laws, the extent and distribution of crime, the sociology of criminality, the social psychology of criminal acts and careers, and social reactions to crime.[17]

The Nature and Origins of Criminal Laws

How is crime different from sin, wickedness, deviance, or other forms of disapproved behavior? How do criminal laws differ from other social rules? How are criminal laws created? Do the statutes serve the interests of all of the members of a particular society, or do they favor the interests of some groups over others? Although a compelling case can be made that the discovery of answers to questions such as these ought to be the first order of business, in actual fact, American criminologists have had relatively little to say about them. A number of critics of sociological criminologists have argued that they have been inordinately concerned with the behavior of criminals and much less curious about the criminality of behavior, that is, the nature of law-making processes through which particular kinds of conduct become singled out as crimes.

These commentators are clearly correct in stressing the concentration of criminological efforts on etiological or causal questions. Still, American criminologists have occasionally struggled mightily over debates about the criminal laws. For example, much discussion was heard at one time about the merits of a legalistic definition of crime as opposed to one that would single out conduct norms for study. At another juncture, a lively argument broke out between those who wanted to bring white-collar crime within the scope of criminological study and those who wanted to exclude this activity from scrutiny. More recently, a vigorous quarrel has raged between those who favor a pluralistic account of the origins of criminal laws and more radical scholars who contend that the statutes are designed solely to serve the narrow interests of a national ruling class. These differing perspectives on criminal laws are examined at greater length in the chapters ahead. A recurring concern of this book is to examine how different cohorts of criminologists have dealt with the criminal statutes, their origins, their relationships to other forms of social rules, and related questions.

The Extent and Distribution of Crime

Explanations of lawbreaking nearly always begin with epidemiology: the available facts regarding the incidence of criminality, spatial distribution of offenses, social characteristics of offenders, and associated

---

[17] These distinctions appeared in somewhat different form in Gibbons, pp. 6–13. Also see Don C. Gibbons and Joseph F. Jones, *The Study of Deviance* (Englewood Cliffs, N.J.: Prentice-Hall, 1975), pp. 30–39.

facts.[18] However, the factual building blocks of criminology are much less clear cut and more open to argument than is the case in such fields as demography, where relatively objective statistics on birth rates, death rates, and other population measures are readily available, or urban sociology, where a generous supply of uncontested data is at hand.

American criminologists have usually based etiological arguments about lawbreaking on various statistics compiled by official agencies, particularly the F.B.I.'s *Uniform Crime Reports,* after some perfunctory acknowledgement of the various pitfalls and shortcomings of these data. The usual assumption has been that these official statistics represent relatively accurate indicators of actual criminality and that the biases and gaps within them do not warrant their rejection.

Even while making this assumption, some criminologists have been struck by the disquieting hypothesis that the official figures may be as much an indicator of the behavior of the officials as they are of actual levels of crime. Enough reports of police tampering with statistics and other activities that distort the official data are on hand to dramatize this possibility. Moreover, even if it is assumed that official statistics are reasonably accurate measures of crimes known to the police, one would be on very shaky ground in speculating about "the dark figure" of undetected and/or unreported crime from these data.[19] Virtually nothing can be asserted with much confidence about the extent of total crime on the basis of official reports of lawbreaking.

At least two major departures from the practice of relying on official statistics have occurred: first, in the form of theories of white-collar crime that have been predicated on unconventional indicators of crime; and, second, in the investigations of self-reported or hidden crime and delinquency. These are taken up in detail at later points in this book, along with some other observations about the kinds of data on lawbreaking that have been utilized by criminologists.

The Sociology of Criminality

Crime statistics and other indicators of the amounts and distribution of crime across nations and within different social structures within a particular society provoke the question: "What is it about social struc-

---

[18] The term, epidemiology, was employed in Gibbons, *Society, Crime, and Criminal Careers,* pp. 8, 101–23, to refer to the matter of extent and distribution of crime, crime statistics, etc. In medicine and public health, that term is used to designate studies of the incidence and prevalence of diseases. However, the term was employed in a slightly different manner by Donald R. Cressey, "Epidemiology and Individual Conduct: A Case from Criminology," *Pacific Sociological Review,* 3 (Fall 1960): 47–58. His discussion of epidemiology emphasized explanations that have been offered for the observed facts concerning criminality.

[19] Sutherland and Cressey, *Criminology,* p. 25.

tures—their organization, their cultures, their histories—that accounts for differences [in crime] within and between them?" [20] The criminological literature contains a large number of theoretical formulations that are concerned with the sociology of criminality and delinquency, that is, with attempts to account for particular distributions and concentrations of law-breaking within American society or across several nations. Many would argue that articulation of theories of this kind is the central task of sociological criminology. A sampling of these arguments includes such notions as hedonistic youth culture, which is claimed to be related to middle-class delinquency; legitimate and illegitimate opportunity structures, along with social disorganization or differential social organization that allegedly generate garden-variety crimes on the part of inner-city residents; and other criminogenic features of societal structure that are thought to exert pressures on particular population segments and to which criminality is sometimes a response.

The Social Psychology of Criminal Acts and Careers

Criminological explanations have often been directed toward providing social-structural accounts that make sense out of particular crime patterns that have been observed. An example is the various arguments that have been put forth to account for the apparent concentration of garden-variety felonies in certain ecological areas within urban communities. But not all of the etiological formulations of sociologists or other social scientists have been directed at the sociological level of explanation. Instead, criminological curiosity has often been centered on questions such as: "How did they get that way?" or "Why do they do it?" As Albert Cohen has indicated, the problem of explanation that is reflected in these queries is: "How do people become the kinds of people who commit deviant acts?" [21] Cohen designated these questions, which concentrate on the processes by which particular individuals become involved in criminal or deviant acts, as the psychological level of explanation.

Theorists have not always been sensitive to this distinction between the sociological and psychological levels of inquiry. Cohen underscored the importance of distinguishing between them in the following passage:

> Much that travels under the name of sociology of deviant behavior or of social disorganization is psychology—some of it very good psychology, but psychology. For example, Sutherland's theory of

[20] Albert K. Cohen, *Deviance and Control* (Englewood Cliffs, N.J.: Prentice-Hall, 1966), p. 46.
[21] *Ibid.*, p. 43. See also Gibbons and Jones, *The Study of Deviance*, pp. 34–35.

differential association, which is widely regarded as preeminently sociological, is not the less psychological because it makes much of the cultural milieu. It is psychological because it addresses itself to the question: How do people become the kinds of individuals who commit criminal acts? A sociological question would be: What is it about the structure of social systems that determines the kinds of criminal acts that occur in these systems and the way in which such acts are distributed within the systems? In general, a sociological field is concerned with the structure of interactional systems, not with personalities, and the distribution and articulation of events within these systems.[22]

A number of etiological formulations in the psychological genre are examined in the chapters that follow, including differential association theory, social control arguments, and contentions about positive self-images and other so-called insulators against delinquency. All these are accounts of the processes through which specific individuals become drawn into criminal misconduct rather than social-structural theories regarding crime rates and concentrations of criminality. However, in this book those theoretical contentions are identified as instances of the social psychology of criminal acts and careers, rather than as cases of the psychological level of explanation.

Social psychology is usually defined as the study of the impact of social environment on the behavior of individuals, as well as of the mediating influence of the behavior of individuals on group functioning. Socialization processes through which humans come to acquire behavior patterns, social attitudes, self-images, and other social attributes are the stuff of social psychology. In turn, the social psychology of criminal acts and careers refers to those etiological constructions that probe into the socialization processes through which specific individuals acquire deviant motives, pro-crime attitudes, and lawbreaking behavior patterns. This term has the advantage of avoiding the connotations of idiosyncratic personal characteristics or psychological malfunctioning that are carried by the psychological label. It may well be that many offenders are psychologically normal individuals who have acquired criminal motivations through socialization processes, while certain other lawbreakers may be aberrant individuals. Both possibilities remain open for investigation at the social psychological level of investigation.

Social Reactions to Crime

From the first volumes written in the early 1900s up to the present, criminology textbooks have nearly always been divided into two virtually independent parts, the first dealing with the extent of crime and etiological

---

[22] Albert K. Cohen, "The Study of Social Disorganization and Deviant Behavior," in Robert K. Merton, Leonard Broom, and Leonard S. Cottrell, Jr., eds., *Sociology Today* (New York: Basic Books, 1959), p. 462.

questions and the second with punitive methods of crime control, a subject often known as penology. This division implies that, in the real world, the causes of criminal deviance only operate prior to the onset of initial acts of lawbreaking, after which the legal and correctional machinery is set in motion in an effort to rehabilitate, resocialize, or in some other way redirect the errant individual back to conformity.

In this traditional division of criminology into causal and penological categories, penology was often reduced to dreary descriptive accounts of how police agencies, courts, probation agencies, prisons, or parole organizations are intended to function in the eyes of those who designed or manage these people-processing bureaucracies. In short, penology involved an abundance of administrative and descriptive commentary and a paucity of sociological analysis.

The lack of sociological inquiry regarding societal reactions to crime is not a reflection of a shortage of meaningful sociological problems for examination. On the contrary, questions about societal attitudes regarding public policies for the control of crime; the organizational dynamics of law enforcement, judicial, and correctional structures; and the impact of correctional intervention experiences on offenders who have been processed through correctional agencies, are all preeminently sociological in form.

Subsequent chapters take note of some instances in which sociological scrutiny has begun to be given to these topics. In particular, Chapter 5 reports at length on the rapid and impressive growth of interest in the sociology of correctional organizations, which began to take place during the 1960s, while Chapter 6 examines a number of contentions about social control agencies that have become prominent in labeling arguments regarding various forms of deviance. In particular, labeling theorists have recently conjectured that many of the intervention activities that are directed at apprehended delinquents and criminals have the unintended and unanticipated effect of driving them further into careers in criminality rather than diverting them out of misbehavior. Such hypotheses assert that correctional experiences operate as career contingencies, exacerbating the difficulties that offenders experience in their attempts to extricate themselves from nonconformity. If that line of argument is correct, the view that causal influences only operate prior to the onset of criminality would need to be revised.

Criminological Theories and Images of Society

The theoretical constructions of criminologists that have been developed in response to these key questions do not exist in isolation. Specific theories and hypotheses about law making, lawbreaking, and reactions to lawbreaking are predicated on broader perspectives on the nature of social order and human behavior, even though those underlying images of society are often implicit and unspoken.[23] For example, most of the accounts offered by social scientists in the United States at about the turn of the nineteenth century assumed that biologically based mental defects and pathology weighed heavily in criminality. These arguments of the early criminologists and social pathologists were derived from social Darwinism and other biological perspectives on societal order that dominated this period of history.[24] By contrast, most contemporary criminologists have little patience with hypotheses that locate the well-springs of crime in biological forces, nor do they give much credence to psychological elements in lawbreaking. Instead, most current sociological accounts contend that offenders are psychologically normal individuals who have motivations toward lawbreaking that have been engendered by a variety of criminogenic social conditions. In turn, these formulations show the influence of the overarching theories to which most contemporary criminologists owe allegiance, in which biological and psychological factors receive scant mention.

Although biological forces are absent from most current criminological theories, some people have questioned the adequacy of explanations that make no room for these influences.[25] This criticism of criminology for its inattention to biologically related factors is linked to a much more far-reaching criticism of sociological portrayals of human behavior and social order that holds that sociologists must "bring beasts back in." [26] Critics of this persuasion have argued that sociological explanations of social action will continue to be incomplete and inadequate unless the biological bases of behavior are acknowledged and incorporated into them. In the same way, some observers have contended that sociological criminology is flawed because it slurs over the importance of individual personalities and psychological forces in deviance and criminality. That criticism does not stand alone, but is instead, part of a much broader indictment of sociology for its failure to "bring men back in." [27] This argument holds that theories

---

[23] For a detailed and insightful discussion of the sociological imagery involved in theories of deviance, see David Matza, *Becoming Deviant* (Englewood Cliffs, N.J.: Prentice-Hall, 1969). Also see Gibbons and Jones, *The Study of Deviance*, pp. 14–27.

[24] For an analysis of the underlying ideology and perspectives of early social pathologists, see C. Wright Mills, "The Professional Ideology of Social Pathologists," *American Journal of Sociology*, 49 (September 1943):165–80.

[25] Saleem A. Shah and Loren H. Roth, "Biological and Psychophysiological Factors in Criminality," in Daniel Glaser, ed., *Handbook of Criminology* (Chicago: Rand McNally, 1974), pp. 101–73.

[26] Pierre Van den Berghe, "Bringing Beasts Back In: Toward a Biosocial Theory of Aggression," *American Sociological Review*, 39 (December 1974):777–88.

[27] George C. Homans, "Bringing Men Back In," *American Sociological Review*, 29 (December 1964):809–18. Also see Dennis Wrong, "The Oversocialized Conception of Man in Modern Sociology," *American Sociological Review*, 26 (April 1961): 183–93.

that speak only of social structure, social organization, social roles, role players, and the like, are not conceptually sensitive enough to capture the richness and variability of human conduct. In this view, a truly adequate sociology will exist only when sociological arguments based on an underlying imagery that includes individual differences and personality characteristics are developed.

There is much argument among sociologists over specific substantive issues such as the dividing line between working-class and middle-class social strata, the nature of subcultures of violence in modern societies, or the extent to which elderly citizens are involved in processes of disengagement. But, indictments of sociology for its failure to deal adequately with the biological or psychological dimensions of human conduct go well beyond those captious quarrels. These criticisms call into question the background and domain assumptions on which sociological theories have been constructed.[28] Background and domain assumptions refer to those taken-for-granted beliefs about human conduct that lie behind particular theoretical formulations in sociology. For example, many social-psychological accounts of socialization processes are predicated on a view that human beings are extremely malleable and totally vulnerable to social influences and thus imply that there are few if any biological imperatives that influence socialization outcomes. Those who have argued that beasts or men must be brought back in have questioned the validity of this core assumption.

This book would grow to gargantuan proportions if it were to attempt to provide a full examination and critique of the underlying images of social order that have informed sociological theories over the past three-fourths of a century in the United States. A full-scale treatment of that topic would require detailed scrutiny of the major dimensions of different sociological viewpoints on culture, social structure, and human action. Additionally, it would call for intensive study of the background and domain assumptions on which particular sociological constructions have been based. The volume might then be caught in a pattern of infinite regress, in which probing into the underlying structure of criminological thought would become an unending task. However, the chapters that follow do include some commentary on the sociological perspectives and core assumptions that have lain behind criminological viewpoints, even though these viewpoints themselves remain the principal interest of this book.

---

[28] Alvin W. Gouldner, *The Coming Crisis in Western Sociology* (New York: Basic Books, 1970), pp. 29–60. See also Robert Dubin, *Theory Building* (New York: Free Press, 1969); Charles W. Lachenmeyer, *The Language of Sociology* (New York: Columbia University Press, 1971); Arthur L. Stinchcombe, *Constructing Sociological Theories* (New York: Harcourt Brace Jovanovich, 1968).

Because formulations or theories are nearly always evaluated in terms of how well they make use of key sociological concepts, one can speak of the literary merits of a particular set of theoretical contentions. Indeed, newly developed conceptual formulations are often greeted with enthusiasm or disdain, depending on critical judgments about the degree to which they are truly sociological in their use of concepts and terminology.

Sociological theories must be judged in terms of another set of criteria as well, if sociology is to be properly regarded as a scientific enterprise. In the final analysis, the acid test of a scientific theory is testability, that is, the extent to which it can either be verified or disproved by appropriate empirical evidence.[29] And, if a theory is to be subjected to empirical confirmation or disconfirmation, it must be stated with sufficient rigor and clarity that investigators can agree on the research implications of the argument. A testable theory is one that is sufficiently explicit for the specific hypotheses and empirical data relevant to it to be identified. In short, different scholars must be able to reach some agreement on the research observations that, if undertaken, would either lend credence to the theory or raise doubts about its accuracy.

These remarks about scientific theories are straightforward and uncontroversial, largely because they are little more than general platitudes. They do not reflect the widespread disagreement regarding testability and allied criteria among sociologists. Although nearly all would agree that theories must be testable, there is little consensus on precisely what that proposition implies.

Robert Merton has had much to say about the nature of sociological theories. In one discussion, he asserted that "the term *sociological theory* refers to logically interconnected sets of propositions from which empirical uniformities can be derived." [30] In this same commentary, Merton stated his preference for *theories of the middle range,* which he identified as explanatory formulations that lie between specific working hypotheses and all-inclusive systems of general theory. Merton's observations are useful, but his discussion concentrated on the content of sociological theory rather than its form, so that he said relatively little about how a testable theory might be recognized.

Other sociologists have had much more to say about the nature of

---

[29] For detailed discussions of these matters, see Karl R. Popper, *The Logic of Scientific Discovery* (New York: Science Editions, 1961); Abraham Kaplan, *The Conduct of Inquiry* (San Francisco: Chandler, 1964).

[30] Robert K. Merton, *On Theoretical Sociology* (New York: Free Press, 1967), p. 39.

verifiable theories and hypotheses. For example, Hubert Blalock has made an emphatic case for the formalization of theories, that is, articulation of the basic assumptions of a theoretical argument so that testable propositions can be generated from them. This sort of formalization also involves the construction of theoretical arguments with sufficient logical rigor for the internal consistency of the entire formulation to be assessed.[31] Jack Gibbs has enunciated even more stringent requirements for sociological theorists, arguing that they are obliged not only to develop clear, precise, and logically tight theories, but also to spell out in great detail the particular kinds of studies and data that would be required for verification purposes.[32]

Most of those who have urged sociologists to work toward rigorous statements of their theories have acknowledged that existing explanatory schemes vary markedly in these terms. While there is an abundance of very fuzzy, ambiguous theorizing to be found in contemporary sociology, some instances of relatively explicit, logically coherent formulations can be identified. Formalization is a matter of degree, rather than an absolute that is found in some theories but is totally absent from others.

It would be pointless to try to evaluate existing criminological formulations with the most stringent measuring rod enunciated by advocates of formalized theory. Rather, a more relaxed standard is in order. These arguments should be scrutinized and criticized insofar as they contain glaring omissions, inconsistencies, and ambiguities of expression. Clarence Schrag has put the case well for relaxed criteria of theoretical adequacy in sociology.

> Few if any sociological theories satisfy the criteria used in evaluating the formalized research activities of some of the more mature physical sciences. Undeveloped disciplines like sociology lack the abstract and powerful vocabularies, the precise rules of grammar, and the technical dictionaries that are necessary for translating the philosophy of science into viable procedures for handling their distinctive problems. This means that there are no authenticated methods for resolving controversies over the definition of concepts, the acceptability of assumptions and theories, or even the identification of problems that are unique to sociology as a specialized field of inquiry. It may therefore be unwise for most sociologists to devote their energies to the attempted construction of abstract and comprehensive theories such as those found in the more advanced sciences. Perhaps the greatest need in sociology

[31] Hubert J. Blalock, Jr., "The Formalization of Sociological Theory," in John C. McKinney and Edward A. Tiryakian, eds., *Theoretical Sociology* (Englewood Cliffs, N.J.: Prentice-Hall, 1970), pp. 271–300. Walter Wallace has written a brief but useful volume that stresses formalization of theories, *The Logic of Science in Sociology* (Chicago: Aldine, 1971).

[32] Jack Gibbs, *Sociological Theory Construction* (Hinsdale, Ill.: Dryden Press, 1972).

today is for more of the modest "inference chains," "explanation sketches," and embryo theories that aim primarily at organizing selected research findings and suggesting further avenues of inquiry.[33]

One can identify formulations, such as the opportunity theory of Richard Cloward and Lloyd Ohlin, that are fairly impressive in the clarity with which they are stated and for the number of researchable propositions that they contain,[34] but even so, critics have noted some ambiguities in those theoretical arguments.[35] Other theories that are considered in the chapters ahead are more defective in terms of rigor of statement. Much of what follows is a critique of these criminological formulations as well as simply a report on the turns and twists that have occurred in sociological criminology over the past three-quarters of a century.

CONCLUDING COMMENTS

This chapter has established some of the boundaries within which the remainder of this book is located. This volume is an examination of the major conceptual problems and explanatory theories that have engaged the attention of sociologist-criminologists, particularly in the United States, from the beginning of this field of inquiry to the present. No attempt is made to provide a detailed review of all of the varied ventures into criminological analysis that began with the classical school in the 1700s and that involved large numbers of European scholars in the 1700s and 1800s. For one thing, summaries of the perspectives of various "pioneers in criminology" are already available, and, for another, there is little continuity between the criminological writings of the eighteenth and nineteenth centuries and those that have been produced in this century.

A comprehensive inventory of all of the contributions to criminological understanding that have been made in recent years by historians, psychologists, geographers, economists, political scientists, anthropologists, and other social scientists has yet to be produced.[36] This volume is

---

[33] Clarence Schrag, "Elements of Theoretical Analysis in Sociology," in Llewellyn Gross, ed., Sociological Theory: Inquiries and Paradigms (New York: Harper & Row, 1967), p. 244.

[34] Richard A. Cloward and Lloyd E. Ohlin, Delinquency and Opportunity (New York: Free Press, 1960).

[35] For a critique of the Cloward and Ohlin theory, see Clarence C. Schrag, "Delinquency and Opportunity: Analysis of a Theory," Sociology and Social Research, 46 (January 1962):167–75.

[36] As stated earlier, this book omits any detailed consideration of biological arguments about criminality. For a summary discussion of biogenic viewpoints, see Gibbons, Society, Crime, and Criminal Careers, pp. 125–53. For a masterful review

restricted largely to the intellectual products of sociological criminologists. At the same time, it does involve a good many critical observations about the ahistorical character of much contemporary criminology, the inattention of sociological criminologists to economic forces in criminality, and the failure of criminologists to deal adequately with psychological factors in lawbreaking.

The chapters are organized chronologically, beginning with Chapter 2, which takes up the birth of an American brand of sociology in the late 1800s and early 1900s. Although criminology in the United States began at about the same time, both of these developments were largely divorced from the significant developments in European sociology and criminology that had already occurred.

The unsophisticated and eclectic versions of criminology that first developed were soon replaced by the sociological investigations of gang delinquency by the Chicago sociologists, Clifford Shaw and Henry McKay, and by Edwin Sutherland's many contributions to criminology. These efforts are the topic of Chapter 3. Chapters 4 and 5 comment on an assortment of criminological endeavors in the period from about 1955 to 1970 that fleshed out the structure of mainstream criminology that had been sketched earlier by Shaw, McKay, and Sutherland.

Although it is difficult to locate specific dates that mark off different periods of intellectual activity, 1970 does represent an approximate turning point in criminology. Chapter 6 discusses the labeling and conflict perspectives to which many criminologists began to turn in the 1970s.

Chapter 7 involves a detailed presentation and critique of radical-Marxist criminology that also was thrust upon the criminological scene in the 1970s. Radical-Marxist criminological thought has been said by some to be a wholly new paradigm, rather than a variation or permutation on mainstream criminological themes.

There is no single, best way in which to organize a review and critique of the major interests and perspectives of criminologists. For example, it might be revealing to organize this book around major issues such as the sociology of law or the sociology of criminality, in order to see the varied ways in which those problems have been attacked by sociologists. The main thing to be said about a chronological format is that it may illuminate the processes of theoretical development, drawing attention to the extent to which the growth of theoretical insights within a field of inquiry has been cumulative or discontinuous. As the pages ahead indicate, it is no simple matter to chart out the twisting course sociological criminology has taken in its meanderings across the theoretical terrain.

---

and assessment of the evidence on biological correlates of criminality, see Shah and Roth, "Biological and Psychophysiological Factors in Criminality."

THE EARLY
YEARS

2

INTRODUCTION

As criminological inquiry in this country is one of the progeny of the discipline of sociology, the most appropriate place to begin probing into its development is with the geneology of its parent field of study. A number of works that identify the major events giving rise to sociology and sketch the contours of the emerging discipline are already available.[1]

Modern sociological inquiry represents the accretion of centuries of social thought. Thus, it is exceedingly difficult if not futile to attempt to identify the putative fathers of the discipline. Some analysts contend that it had its beginnings in the musings of Socrates (471–399 B.C.) or Plato (427–347 B.C.), while others regard ibn Kalduhn (1332–1406), a Muslim historian and statesman, as a major progenitor of sociology.[2] However, the most frequently identified creator of modern sociology is Auguste Comte (1798–1857), a French social philosopher. Comte coined the term "sociology" and also developed a systematic conceptualization of the social sciences (with sociology placed at the apex of a hierarchy of disciplines).[3] Even so, Comte must share parentage of the discipline with a long list of other distinguished thinkers of the nineteenth century, including Karl Marx

[1] See, for example, Harry Elmer Barnes, ed., *An Introduction to the History of Sociology* (Chicago: University of Chicago Press, 1948); Roscoe C. Hinkle and Gisela G. Hinkle, *The Development of Modern Sociology* (New York: Random House, 1954); Raymond Aron, *Main Currents in Sociological Thought,* 2 vols. (New York: Basic Books, 1965, 1967); and Howard W. Odum, *American Sociology: The Story of Sociology in the United States through 1950* (New York: Longmans, Green, 1951).

[2] For a useful summary of ancient and medieval social philosophy, and for a discussion of social thought in modern times, see Barnes, *Introduction,* pp. 3–78.

[3] Comte's life and writings are discussed in detail in Lewis A. Coser, *Masters of Sociological Thought* (New York: Harcourt Brace Jovanovich, 1971), pp. 3–41.

(1818–1883), Herbert Spencer (1820–1903), Emile Durkheim (1858–1917), and Max Weber (1864–1920).[4]

Examination of the history of sociology in America also fails to turn up a birth certificate indicating that the discipline sprung up at some precise moment in the past. Instead, its origins are clouded and subject to some disagreement. For example, publications dealing with sociological topics began appearing in the United States in the 1880s, and courses labeled as sociological offerings began to be included in university curricula in the 1890s.[5] The American Sociological Society, created largely by dissident members of the American Economic Association, was founded in 1905. Leon Bramson has noted the difficulty of assigning a precise birthdate to American sociology: "Periodization is always somewhat arbitrary, but several writers agree that the appearance in 1883 of Lester Ward's *Dynamic Sociology* marks the beginning of sociology in this country. The first period in American sociology ends, according to the perspective of the writer, in 1915, with the publication of Robert Ezra Park's essay on the city, or in 1918, with the end of the First World War." [6]

THE NATURE OF EARLY AMERICAN SOCIOLOGY

Whether one chooses to locate the birth of American sociology in the 1880s, 1890s, or early 1900s, the infant discipline showed little resemblance to sociology as it has developed in the second half of the twentieth century. As Anthony Oberschall has remarked, "a striking feature of U.S. sociology was that it was institutionalized before it had a distinctive intellectual content, a distinctive method, or even a point of view." [7] A number of accounts of the early years of American sociology have presented generally the same characterization of the major forces that gave birth to this amorphous discipline and of its ill-formed nature.[8]

The rise of sociology was part of the broader historical sweep of events in the United States during the first two decades of the twentieth century, which historians have identified as the Progressive Era. The pro-

[4] For analyses of the works of Marx, Spencer, Durkheim, and Weber, see *ibid.*, pp. 43–174, 217–60.

[5] Hinkle and Hinkle, *Development,* p. 1. For another brief and useful account of the major developments in American sociology from around 1895 to the period of dominance by the University of Chicago from 1920 to 1932, see Robert E. L. Faris, *Chicago Sociology—1920–1932* (San Francisco: Chandler, 1967).

[6] Leon Bramson, *The Political Context of Sociology* (Princeton, N.J.: Princeton University Press, 1961), p. 84.

[7] Anthony Oberschall, "The Institutionalization of American Sociology," in Oberschall, ed., *The Establishment of Empirical Sociology* (New York: Harper & Row, 1972), p. 189.

[8] *Ibid.,* pp. 187–251; Hinkle and Hinkle, *Development,* pp. 1–17; Bramson, *Political Context,* pp. 73–95.

gressive movement expressed reformist concerns about the harsh social consequences of rapid industrialization and urbanization which were overtaking the country.

Recruits to progressivism were appalled by the stark contrasts between the unbridled power and immense wealth of industrial plutocrats such as J. P. Morgan, Andrew Carnegie, E. H. Harriman, and a handful of others, on the one hand, and the abject misery of industrial workers, agricultural laborers, miners, and the great mass of other workers, on the other. The inequities of industrial capitalism at the turn of the century have been described by Ernest May.

> In 1904, in a book entitled *Poverty*, Robert Hunter added up the meager statistical data in existence and estimated that in 1900 at least 10 million of America's 76 million people were so poor they could not "obtain *those necessaries which will permit them to maintain a state of physical efficiency.*" Clinging to the old notion of America as a land of limitless opportunity, many reviewers found his figure incredible. Within two years, however, John A. Ryan, an economist, concluded that 60 per cent of the adult male workers earned too little to maintain a family. Although this meant that as many as 50 million Americans could be classified as poor, the evidence was now too clear to be denied. While industrialism had made a few families fantastically rich, it had reduced millions of Americans to a state in which, as Hunter wrote, they lacked "a sanitary dwelling and sufficient food and clothing to keep the body in working order"—the "standard that a man would demand for his horses or slaves." [9]

Who were the advocates of progressivism? They were middle-class farm owners, storekeepers, clergymen, lawyers, doctors, and others who stood between the small band of extraordinarily wealthy industrialists and financiers and the teeming masses of the working poor. Although these solid and industrious middle-class citizens were enjoying relative affluence, many of them were displeased with the economic trends they saw occurring in the United States. The progressive movement drew into its ranks prohibitionists, advocates of women's rights, small businessmen who were incensed about competition from the giant trusts, and an assortment of other individuals who saw advantages to themselves in progressive proposals. Although progressivism attracted diverse groups of citizens, it represented an effort to remake the United States into a homogeneous, classless society.

Progressivism stood for the conservation of the nation's resources, regulation of the rapacious activities of corporate giants, honest and efficient government, and other changes in American life. Progressive thought

---

[9] Ernest R. May, *The Progressive Era* (New York: Time-Life Books, 1964), p. 33.

also stressed the intrinsic worth of all citizens. Thus, progressives advocated rehabilitation of criminals, assistance for the poor, and humane treatment for the insane. Progressivism also contained a spirit of optimism born of the conviction that people could solve most or all of their problems simply through the application of reason and sincere effort. Accordingly, progressives supported programs for creating healthy work conditions, decent housing, public ownership of utilities, and scientific administration of cities, as well as efforts to deal positively with social problems. The rise of American sociology must be viewed against this background of progressive thought.

Hinkle and Hinkle have enumerated four core elements that dominated sociology up to the 1930s: belief in natural laws governing social relationships, faith in progressive social change, emphasis on social reformism, and an individualistic conception of society. Additionally, they have argued that "sociology emerged largely as a response to the industrialization and urbanization of the post–Civil War era." [10] More specifically, they have contended that sociology was in considerable part a response to the social dislocations generated by industrialization and urbanization.

Hinkle and Hinkle also drew attention to several features of early American sociology that showed its sources in the concomitants of urbanization and industrialization around the turn of the century. First, Lester Ward, Franklin Giddings, William Sumner, Edward Hayes, Albion Small, and most of the other eminent sociologists in the first two decades of the twentieth century were all from rural and religious backgrounds. Second, although programs in sociology were initially established in Eastern universities located in urban centers, Midwestern sociologists were most prominent in the emergence of sociology. Hinkle and Hinkle have speculated that the economic expansion and development then being experienced in the Midwest provided a fertile climate for reformism and sociology.

The third and probably the most crucial indicator of the link between urbanism, industrialization, and the birth of sociology in America, according to Hinkle and Hinkle, was sociology's roots in the social science movement. Throughout its history, between 1840 and 1890, this movement centered on social reform. [11] The social science movement gave rise in 1865 to the American Social Science Association, out of which the American Economic Association grew in 1884 and the breakaway American Sociological Society developed in 1905. Finally, Hinkle and Hinkle have pointed out that most of the sociology courses offered in colleges and universities at the turn of the century were centered on pauperism, child

[10] Hinkle and Hinkle, *Development,* pp. 2–3.
[11] *Ibid.,* p. 4. See also Luther L. Bernard and Jessie Bernard, *Origins of American Sociology: The Social Science Movement in the United States* (New York: Crowell, 1943).

labor, poverty, crime and juvenile delinquency, and other social ills held to be generated by urbanism and industrialization.

A parallel but more detailed discussion of these events has been presented by Oberschall, who also stressed the social reform movement background of American sociology. He placed the earliest strivings of the embryonic discipline in the 1800s and noted that

> the novel and amorphous discipline of sociology received the backing at this opportune time of groups in favor of social reconstruction: the Protestant clergy (especially its social gospel wing); the municipal reformers; the various groups and organizations active in the areas of philanthropy, charities and correction, social settlement, and social work; and the backers of other Progressive causes, all of whom were seeking an academic foothold and scientific justification.[12]

For example, the ties of early sociology to the National Conference of Charities and Correction, later called the National Conference of Social Work, included the presidency of that organization by Charles Richmond Henderson, one of the founding members of the sociology department at the University of Chicago. Also, substantial numbers of early sociologists belonged to this organization or the American Prison Congress.

Oberschall also commented on the eclectic but reform-oriented character of early sociology, indicating that

> perhaps the clearest link of sociology with social reform can be gleaned from the content of the early sociology courses, the manner in which departments of sociology were established, the purposes for which sociologists were hired, and what they were supposed to add of value to the existing curriculum. Sociology made its entry into the competing universities without any intellectual or scientific program or content, in completely opportunist fashion, in order to cater to students', reformers', philanthropists', and social workers' demands for vocational training before professional schools of social work were established.[13]

Oberschall also indicated that early sociologists were often people who had broken away from economics and had taken over "the 3 Ds": the study of the defective, dependent, and delinquent classes.[14] Indeed, the title of Charles Richmond Henderson's seminal 1893 text was *Introduction to the Study of the Dependent, Neglected, and Delinquent Classes.*

But it was not solely the sponsorship and active backing by organized and influential reformist groups who viewed the new field favorably

---

[12] Oberschall, "Institutionalization," pp. 187–88.
[13] *Ibid.,* p. 210.
[14] *Ibid.,* p. 196.

that lead to the emergence of American sociology. In order for sociology to become firmly established in institutions of higher education, recruits to staff these new programs had to be found, and opportunities for this new breed of academics to gain access to colleges and universities had to open up. According to Oberschall, the emergence of sociology coincided with and was encouraged by the rapid expansion of the higher education system in the United States in the late 1800s and early 1900s.[15]

The formation of the American Sociological Society in 1905, comprised in large part of dissidents from the American Economic Association, has already been noted. This event was part of a broader trend taking place in economics, involving the rapid professionalization and institutionalization of that discipline in the late 1800s. One facet of the movement toward professionalization was that many economists began to disassociate themselves from a concern with social problems, particularly "the 3 Ds," regarding these matters as alien to their professional field of study. The withdrawal of academic economists from social reform interests created a void, which neophyte sociologists rushed to fill. According to Oberschall, the recruits to the new discipline of sociology were drawn heavily from the ranks of intellectually dissatisfied and socially concerned scholars from other fields such as economics and a group of upwardly mobile individuals who would have been unable to pursue academic careers through the more firmly established academic specialties.[16]

The interests of Protestant reformism joined the expansionist developments in American colleges and universities and the individual aspirations of early sociologists in supporting a new field of inquiry responding to social problems. Protestant reformism and the organizational network associated with it provided a public forum in which sociological topics were articulated, courses taught, and textbooks written and widely sold. Most important, it encouraged the development of opportunities for intellectually inclined individuals with ministerial backgrounds to enter this new field. The leaders of Protestant reformism also operated as a powerful pressure group supporting the introduction of sociology into universities. For its part, the emerging discipline filled a void created by the withdrawal of economics from the Christian reform movement. These events accounted for the presence of large numbers of former ministers, including George Vincent, J. P. Lichtenberger, John Gillin, and J. M. Gillette in the ranks of early American sociologists.

Early American sociology bears little similarity to the present version of the discipline, for it focused heavily on social problems of one kind or another, often viewing them as individualistic and pathological

---

[15] Oberschall, "Institutionalization," pp. 188–89.
[16] *Ibid.*, p. 188.

by-products of urbanization and industrialization. The nascent discipline was often greeted with skepticism and hostility from the established disciplines and consequently faced a pressing question of academic legitimacy, as a result of the previous intellectual backgrounds of sociologists in the ministry, political economy, philosophy, and charities and corrections. The influence of the social reformers was also felt on the sociologists' choice of subject matter, techniques of study, and presentation of results. Because sociology was pulled and tugged by this dual constituency, early sociologists showed an obsessive concern with becoming legitimate scientists at the same time that they were at pains to demonstrate that their field had practical usefulness. The first of these pressures often led them into arid, abstract system-building endeavors, while the second pushed them in the direction of popularized, reform-oriented, atheoretical investigations of social ills.[17]

Robert Faris's account of the development of the University of Chicago department of sociology between 1920 and 1932 has provided some additional information about the formative years of American sociology. He briefly traced the major developments in the growth of the field from about 1895 to the domination of American sociology by the University of Chicago department, beginning around 1920. He observed that the academic writings of such European giants of nineteenth-century sociology as Spencer, Maine, Tarde, Durkheim, and Simmel were usually identified as moral philosophy until Comte coined the term "sociology." The pioneers of American sociology, such as Lester Ward, William Graham Sumner, E. A. Ross, Franklin Giddings, and Charles Horton Cooley drew upon these European figures for many of their sociological viewpoints. But, Faris also indicated that Ward, Sumner, Giddings, and Ross

> all saw the assignment as large and conceived that they needed to give definition to the field, to systematize it and point out the major applications to human welfare and survival of the always imperiled civilization.... These American pioneers had a strong disposition to discover, mainly by reflection, one or a few fundamental and simple principles that would serve as an explanation of all human behavior.[18]

The history of American sociology indicates that these architects of grand systems of sociological thought all failed to construct lasting sociological edifices. Indeed, the only one of these pioneers whose works are still read for their contemporary relevance is Cooley, a diffident and scholarly figure who shied away from attempts at synthesizing all knowledge.

Many of these early figures in American sociology were single-

---

[17] *Ibid.*, p. 189. Also see Edwin M. Lemert, *Human Deviance, Social Problems, and Social Control*, 2nd ed. (Englewood Cliffs, N.J.: Prentice-Hall, 1972), pp. 3–13.
[18] Faris, *Chicago Sociology*, pp. 3–4.

mindedly devoted to their own careers or ideas or were abrasive figures, so that they failed to become the foci of large and active departments of sociology. It was at the University of Chicago, under the chairmanship of Albion Small, that institutionalized sociology first flourished. Small was recruited to Chicago in 1892 and was given a strong mandate from the university president to build a sociology department. His original colleagues in the department were George Vincent, W. I. Thomas, and Charles Richmond Henderson. Faris has described Henderson as "a former minister whose interests were mainly in applied humanitarianism, [and who] left little lasting mark on the history of sociology." [19]

However, Henderson did author a forerunner of the first American criminology textbooks. This original band of Chicago sociologists was later joined by Robert Ezra Park, Elsworth Faris, and Ernest Burgess, who quickly began to create a new and distinctive brand of "Chicago sociology," which stressed objectivity and an empirical orientation to the study of social behavior, rather than armchair theorizing. Chicago-style sociology ultimately became the model around which most American sociology developed.

Faris's account of the early days of Chicago sociology placed much stress on the research in social ecology that was stimulated by Park and Burgess, including studies of the morphology of cities, investigations of urban "natural areas," and the delinquency area studies carried on by Clifford Shaw and Henry D. McKay. As Faris has written, "empirical American sociology was perhaps popularized and transmitted to all corners of the world by the Shaw monographs more than by any other examples of this brand of social research." [20] On this point, the delinquency area studies that came out of the Institute for Juvenile Research in Chicago contributed heavily to the intellectual foundations upon which mainstream American criminology was constructed.

This brief history of the origins of American sociology has proceeded from the first stirrings of sociological activity in the 1880s to the beginning of the modern era of intellectual development. The stage is now set for a discussion of the first gropings toward construction of sociological criminology in the United States.

EUROPEAN ROOTS AND AMERICAN CRIMINOLOGY

Like American sociology more generally, American criminology did not spring up instantaneously as the product of native seeds. It, too, had some tenuous connections to the work of European scholars of the

[19] *Ibid.,* p. 12.
[20] *Ibid.,* p. 76.

19th century.[21] Richard Quinney has provided a useful, brief analysis of the European roots of American criminology.

> Criminology as the "scientific" study of crime grew in reaction to the turmoil and disorder in the European countries. The early theorists in criminology and the social sciences in general were disturbed by many rebellions and revolutions in the eighteenth and nineteenth centuries. It was their hope that the new sciences could discover the natural laws on which society had grown and provide a program for social tranquility.[22]

Quinney traced the rise of European criminology from the writings of members of the classical school, including Bentham, Beccaria, and Romilly, to the work of Quetelet, Guerry, and others in the so-called cartographic school in the mid-1800s. He also devoted attention to the biologically based work of Lombroso in the late 1800s, as well as to the theories of his followers, Enrico Ferri and Raffaele Garofalo. Lombrosian positivism, which emphasized the employment of a natural science stance toward the study of crime, as well as deterministic views of crime causation, had considerable influence on the writings of many American criminological pioneers.[23]

Crime and delinquency became major targets of nineteenth-century reformism in the United States and central topics of the emerging discipline of sociology. According to Quinney,

> Americans were inclined to equate crime with sin, pauperism, and immorality. Even when they recognized crime as a distinct phenomenon, they usually thought of it as an ill that should not be a part of social life. Crime was therefore one of the problems that fell into the embrace of nineteenth-century reformism in America. . . . That social science could supply knowledge to be used for reform became an important idea in the American academic community. Criminology became one of the first courses in the curriculum of the newly established social science departments.[24]

---

[21] Detailed reviews and critiques of European criminological endeavors can be found in George B. Vold, *Theoretical Criminology* (New York: Oxford University Press, 1958); and Stephen Schafer, *Theories in Criminology* (New York: Random House, 1969).

[22] Richard Quinney, *Criminology* (Boston: Little, Brown, 1975), p. 4.

[23] These eighteenth- and nineteenth-century European endeavors are also reviewed in Don C. Gibbons, *Society, Crime, and Criminal Careers*, 3rd ed. (Englewood Cliffs, N.J.: Prentice-Hall, 1977), pp. 125–53.

[24] Quinney, *Criminology*, p. 5.

There is no one event that signaled the emergence of American criminology. Books dealing with crime and delinquency began to appear in some number around 1895, including Henderson's volume on the 3 Ds. A number of exposés on the urban crime problem by Charles Loring Brace, Edward Crapsey, and others made their appearance in the late 1800s. American criminological works containing a heavy stress on Lombrosian hypotheses about congenital criminality were also published around the turn of the century.[25]

These early emphases on biological and evolutionary theories of criminality continued for a number of years in the writings of early criminologists. As Quinney has said, "the *sociological* study of crime moved very slowly in the United States during the first part of the century. With today's hindsight, we can see that the study of crime by early sociologists was filled with questionable assumptions and was not specifically aimed at social matters." [26] He observed that Frances Kellor's *Experimental Sociology* was actually a study of hypothesized physical differences between women offenders and female students, while Arthur Hall's *Crime and Its Relation to Social Progress* analyzed crime within a social Darwinist framework.

This is not the appropriate place for a lengthy discussion of the theories of evolution put forth by Darwin and others, but a few comments are in order. Charles Darwin (1809–1882), an English naturalist, published *On the Origin of Species* in 1859, in which he outlined the elements of the processes of biological evolution. According to Darwin, animal species developed through the natural selection of superior and fortuitous variations of species, which occurred as a result of the struggle for existence. Although Darwin did not formulate a theory of social evolution, Herbert Spencer voiced independent but parallel views regarding the evolution of social organisms. Also, Bagehot, Gumplowicz, Ratzenhofer, and a number of other European scholars endeavored to bend elements of Darwin's teachings to the analysis of social life, as did also Albion Small,

---

[25] Arthur MacDonald, *Criminology* (New York: Funk and Wagnalls, 1892); August Draehms, *The Criminal, His Personnel and Environment: A Scientific Study* (New York: Macmillan, 1900); Philip A. Parsons, *Responsibility for Crime* (New York: Columbia University Press, 1909). Parsons held a Ph.D. in sociology from Columbia University and taught at Syracuse and the University of Oregon. Parsons claimed that Lombroso's criminal type was probably a fiction, but then continued on to assert that "the fact is growing daily more certain that the criminal is a being apart" (p. 27) by which Parsons meant that offenders are physically stigmatized, the offspring of degenerate parents, or in some other way defective.
[26] Quinney, *Criminology*, p. 7.

William Graham Sumner, and many other early American sociologists.[27] Evolutionary and biological beliefs, growing in considerable part out of the influence of Darwinism, were commonplace and contributed heavily to the spirit of the times. It is little wonder that vulgarized versions of biological and evolutionary theory turned up in many of the writings on criminality.

Quinney asserted that a critical event in the growth of American sociological criminology was the appearance, in 1918, of Maurice F. Parmelee's text.

> In the first American attempt at a comprehensive exposition of criminological knowledge, Parmelee in his *Criminology* analyzed the social sources of crime. Nevertheless, he found it necessary to discuss evolution, the physical environment, "criminal traits," and the "organic basis of criminality." His work, despite these faults, represents the transition in the United States from an eclectic study of crime to a sociological kind of explanation.[28]

Parmelee's book was soon followed by texts by Gillin, and Parsons.[29] Thus, academic criminology began to acquire some of the outlines of its contemporary structure in these few years after World War I. The core ingredients of some of these books ought to be examined in more detail.

Maurice F. Parmelee

Maurice Parmelee received a Ph.D. in economics at Columbia University in 1909 and was for over half a century a prolific source of books and articles in the social sciences.[30] He authored thirteen books, beginning in 1908 with *The Principles of Anthropology and Sociology in Their Relations to Criminal Procedure*. His *Criminology* appeared in 1918, and he also contributed a half dozen or more articles to the *American Journal of Sociology, Journal of Criminal Law and Criminology,* and other popular or scientific journals.

A detailed account of Parmelee's ventures into criminological

---

[27] Nicholas S. Timasheff, *Sociological Theory,* rev. ed. (New York: Random House, 1957), pp. 59–71.

[28] Quinney, *op. cit.,* p. 7.

[29] Edwin H. Sutherland, *Criminology* (Philadelphia: Lippincott, 1924); John L. Gillin, *Criminology and Penology* (New York: Century, 1926); Philip A. Parsons, *Crime and the Criminal* (New York: Knopf, 1926).

[30] Parmelee's career and criminological works have been discussed in considerably more detail in Don C. Gibbons, "Say, Whatever Became of Maurice Parmelee, Anyway?" *Sociological Quarterly,* 15 (Summer 1974):405–16. The discussion of Parmelee's book is abridged from this paper.

work appeared in Mabel Elliott's discussion of the formative years of American criminology.[31] She indicated that a National Conference of Criminal Law and Criminology was held in 1909 at the Northwestern University School of Law on the occasion of the fiftieth anniversary of the school. About 150 leaders in medicine, psychiatry, sociology, penology, and the criminal court system attended the conference. The American Institute of Criminal Law and Criminology emerged out of that conference, as did also a committee that was ultimately responsible for the publication, in translation, of nine books by noted European scholars on criminality, including Lombroso, Ferri, Tarde, Bonger, and Aschaffenburg.

American students of crime had been limited to these translated essays by European scholars, or to works such as Henderson's *The Dependent, Neglected, and Delinquent Classes,* until the appearance of Parmelee's 1918 volume. Parmelee, who attended the national conference, apparently produced his book in part as an attempt to supplement these inadequate criminological source materials.

It is difficult to know quite how to evaluate Parmelee's *Criminology* 60 years after it originally appeared in print. Although some of the commentary is quite strange by our current standards, in all likelihood, those remarks were considerably less outrageous or transparently erroneous when they first appeared.

Parmelee's text was divided into six parts, beginning with a section on the nature of crime. The three chapters in that section, which set the general tone for the entire book, portrayed criminality as an abnormal and pathological form of behavior. Parmelee enunciated an eclectic orientation to the explanation of criminality, arguing that a variety of perspectives from the biological and social sciences must be brought to bear on the crime problem. The modern-day criminologist would be put off by those remarks that stress an eclectic approach and would also find the invocation of instincts by Parmelee to be unpalatable. Then, too, most modern criminologists would quarrel with Parmelee's view that crime is made up of the more serious antisocial acts, most of which are also instances of immorality. However, Parmelee also pointed out that some laws are created by "religious, despotic, and class legislation" (pp. 32–36), a view not entirely foreign to modern conflict or radical criminologists. Indeed, the following assertion certainly has a contemporary ring: "But there has probably been even more penal legislation in the interests of classes. Whenever a class has succeeded in gaining the ascendancy politically, economically, or otherwise, it has invariably enacted more or less penal legislation in its own interest" (p. 34).

Part II, on criminogenic factors in the environment, included

[31] Mabel A. Elliott, *Crime in Modern Society* (New York: Harper, 1952), pp. 25–27.

chapters on seasonal and climatic variations, urban and rural crime patterns, and economic factors in criminality. Although there is little of current interest in the first two of these, the chapter on economic pressures and lawbreaking has a faintly modern tone. Parmelee viewed much crime as arising out of adverse economic conditions that propel the less fortunate toward involvement in theft and other antisocial acts.[32]

Part III included seven chapters on criminal traits and types. Several of those emphasized the overrepresentation of "aments," "dements," and "psychopaths" in the population of offenders, claims that have not stood the test of time. Parmelee offered a classification of criminal types (p. 198) that included criminal aments and dements, psychopaths, professional offenders, occasional criminals, and evolutive criminals.[33] The latter was his term for radicals and revolutionists who find themselves in trouble with the law because of the unpopular ideas that they espouse.

Parmelee's observations about female criminality were shot through with the prevailing biases of the day, which held that women were inherently inferior to men. However, he also took note of "extrajudicial crime" among women, by which he meant hidden criminality, and argued that females exceeded males in this kind of lawbreaking. Some of those comments are not unlike the views of Otto Pollak and other contemporary students of female crime.[34]

Part IV dealt with criminal jurisprudence, including six unexceptionable chapters on criminal procedure, principles of evidence, and related matters. Judged by contemporary standards, Part V is an undistinguished discussion of penology. However, some of Parmelee's penological observations in an earlier section are worth noting. Speaking of the impact of incarceration on juvenile offenders, he observed that

> Still another factor in the causation of juvenile criminality is the effect of incarceration in industrial and reform schools and in reformatories.

---

[32] This point should not be pushed too far. Parmelee was loath to abandon notions about personal inadequacies as factors in crime in this chapter. Then too, he was oblivious to the crimes of the wealthy individuals and corporations. Surely no one would argue that there is a direct link between Parmelee and modern economic theorists.

[33] Some criminologists have taken Parmelee to task for his typological efforts, holding that these are doomed to be unfruitful. But in defense of Parmelee, typologizing endeavors have had an enduring appeal to sociologists, and this orientation is still very much alive. For one pessimistic evaluation of contemporary work in this tradition, see Don C. Gibbons, "Offender Typologies—Two Decades Later," *British Journal of Criminology*, 15 (April 1975):140–56.

[34] Otto Pollak, *The Criminality of Women* (Philadelphia: University of Pennsylvania Press, 1950); Freda Adler, *Sisters in Crime* (New York: McGraw-Hill, 1975); Rita James Simon, *Women and Crime* (Lexington, Mass.: D. C. Heath, 1975). A large share of the contemporary theory and research on female crime is summarized in Gibbons, *Society, Crime, and Criminal Careers*, pp. 439–63.

> Sometimes the immediate effect of such imprisonment is very bad. But even when these institutions are well administered, so that their inmates benefit on the whole from their life within them, these inmates are likely to suffer from difficulties of reinstatement after leaving these institutions. Even when the boy or girl has been sent to the institution more on account of the faults and failings of the parents than of himself or herself, there is usually a stigma attached to the ex-inmate of one of these institutions which makes reinstatement difficult, and the boy or girl may become confirmed in a life of crime and vice (pp. 229–30).

One might argue that this passage is an early version of "labeling theory," which stresses the deleterious effects of "people-changing" institutions on the people processed through them (see Chapter 6).

The last section of Parmelee's book, which discussed crime and social progress, stressed that political and evolutive crimes are functional because they serve the needs of progress. According to Parmelee, political offenders often provided the initial impetus for needed social changes. Parmelee also observed that

> it also happens that some of the alleged evolutive and political crimes are committed as a result of the activities of *agents provocateurs*, . . . unscrupulous police officials will sometimes try to incite members of these groups to crime in order to secure the financial rewards and glory resulting from the repression of these crimes (pp. 466–67).

Those remarks have a contemporary ring, in view of recent disclosures about law violations carried on by the Central Intelligence Agency, Federal Bureau of Investigation, and other agencies of the federal government.

Although Quinney credited Parmelee with a considerable measure of influence in moving criminology toward sociological analysis and away from eclecticism and biological notions, other commentators have given him little recognition as a founder of criminology. For example, Marshall Clinard gave him short shrift in his analysis of the development of sociological criminology. Reckless and Caldwell made only two brief references to Parmelee in their texts, and only a few scattered citations were made to his pioneering work in several, more recent discussions of criminology.[35] On balance, it is clear that Parmelee has become one of the

---

[35] Marshall B. Clinard, "Criminology as a Field in American Sociology," *Journal of Criminal Law, Criminology and Police Science,* 41 (January–February 1951):549–77; Walter C. Reckless, *The Crime Problem,* 5th ed. (Englewood Cliffs, N.J.: Prentice-Hall, 1973); Robert G. Caldwell, *Criminology,* 2nd ed. (New York: Ronald Press, 1965); Herbert A. Bloch and Gilbert Geis, *Man, Crime, and Society,* 2nd ed. (New York: Random House, 1970); Harry Elmer Barnes and Negley K. Teeters, *New Horizons in Criminology,* 3rd ed. (Englewood Cliffs, N.J.: Prentice-Hall, 1959.)

forgotten men of early American criminology and sociology.[36] His failure to establish a lasting niche in the discipline may have been due, in considerable part, to the fact that he did not have an academic base during most of his career. Moreover, he failed to carry out a sustained program of criminological theorizing or research, probably because of his governmental career as well as a certain dilettantism in his interests.

John L. Gillin

Another early criminological text, *Criminology and Penology,* was authored in 1926 by John Gillin, who held a Ph.D. in sociology from Columbia University. Something of the tenor of that volume can be gleaned from its Introduction, penned by E. A. Ross, who averred that "the secret of our excessive criminality should be sought *in our manner of dealing with the ill-disposed element in our society"* (p. ix).

Gillin's book comprised 36 chapters. Thirteen dealt with causation, and 23 discussed punishment and control of crime. The etiological portion involved only 289 pages, while the second part of the volume consumed 565 pages. This division of criminology books into two relatively unrelated parts, in which the commentary on crime control stands apart from the analysis of causation, continues to characterize such textbooks even today. Many contemporary criminology texts still give greater space to correctional and control topics than to causal analysis.[37]

Gillin's text began with chapters on the nature of crime, the statistics on crime (lamenting their deficiencies), and observations on spatial and temporal dimensions of lawbreaking, as well as such hypothesized factors as climate and other aspects of the physical environment. He also introduced a crude typology of the forms of crime, listing crimes against property, public peace and order offenses, crimes against religion, the family, morals, and the conservation of the resources of society (pp. 19–23).

Gillin's treatment of causation paralled Parmelee's in that he was relatively supportive of Lombrosian notions about physical factors in crime, arguing at one point that

> in the present state of our knowledge it is impossible to say just how much weight must be given to physical factors in the genesis of

[36] As one indicator of Parmelee's decline, note that Mabel Elliott consistently misspelled his name as Parmalee throughout her book. Also, Sue Titus Reid, *Crime and Criminology* (New York: Dryden Press, 1974), p. 22, both misspelled his name and erroneously listed the publication date of his *Criminology* as 1920.

[37] For example, see Edwin H. Sutherland and Donald R. Cressey, *Criminology,* 9th ed. (Philadelphia: Lippincott, 1974), in which pp. 3–292 are devoted to "The Study of Delinquency and Crime," while pp. 295–636 discuss "The Processing of Delinquency and Crime." Also see Reid, *Crime and Criminology,* in which pp. 3–252 deal with causation, while pp. 256–718 center on law enforcement, corrections, and kindred topics.

criminal conduct. The facts at hand suggest that it varies with age, sex, type of crime, and frequency of conviction. It is clear that the physical condition of the individual is a factor which must be reckoned with in many cases (p. 103).

Gillin also concluded that mental defects are a cause of crime when joined with "bad social conditions," a claim that was paralleled by his assertion regarding mental illness: "Combine mental defect and mental aberration with evil influences and the result is quite likely to be an anti-social attitude" (p. 154). In another section, Gillin put forth an argument about hereditary factors which has long since been discredited.

Crime as such cannot be inherited. Crime is a social phenomenon produced by a combination of the bodily and mental characteristics of the individual and the environment acting upon the responding personality. Now, a part of that personality is the result of the biological characteristics inherited from the ancestors. Crime is not a unit biological characteristic. However, the natural characteristics which function in producing crime may be inherited. As a result of these characteristics which incline the individual to anti-social acts, the individual under the proper circumstances may become a delinquent (p. 159).

Although Gillin looked with much favor upon the studies by Goddard and others regarding the Kallikaks, Jukes, Nams, Zeros, and other families allegedly tainted by hereditary defects,[38] he was not entirely oblivious to the role of social factors in criminality. Chapter 10 dealt with economic factors, but it resulted in the conclusion that "poverty, by affecting conditions under which people live or *by providing conditions for the selection and reproduction of incapables,* increases crime" [emphasis added] (p. 183). In this same chapter, Gillin acknowledged the socialist arguments of Bonger, but rejected the claim that fundamental alterations in the economic system would eradicate crime (p. 187).

Chapters 11 and 12 of Gillin's book took note of a potpourri of other social factors, including the home, playground influences, schools, community factors, customs, beliefs, class hatred, religion, the courts, prisons, and civilization! Gillin reached the following conclusion regarding all of these diverse social influences: "The social conditions around [the individual] set the stage on which each of these factors plays its part and release in his conduct the good or evil in his nature. Thus is the criminal made" (p. 251).

Subsequent editions of his book were published in 1935 and 1945, in which much of this commentary centering around alleged in-

[38] These studies are summarized in Gibbons, *Society, Crime, and Criminal Careers,* pp. 144–45.

dividual defects on the part of criminals was muted or excised altogether in favor of greater stress on sociological analysis.[39] However, the initial version of Gillin's book was relatively similar to that of Parmelee. Both showed relatively little resemblance to contemporary volumes in terms of the substantive propositions they contained about criminality.[40]

Philip A. Parsons

Another, lesser known early author of criminology texts was Philip Parsons, who produced *Responsibility for Crime* in 1909, followed by *Crime and the Criminal* in 1926. In the preface to the latter volume, he acknowledged that the Sutherland and Gillin textbooks had recently appeared and that they were admirable sourcebooks, while his own text was intended both for the general public and college students. He also asserted that he had drawn heavily on Sutherland's book in writing his own.

In *Crime and the Criminal,* Parsons retreated somewhat from the arguments advanced in his 1909 work, which held that criminals are a distinct physical type. However, his withdrawal was less than complete, for at one point he claimed that "the bulk of crime is the result of a combination of pathological conditions of the individual, to a great extent hereditary, and vicious, demoralizing and devitalizing conditions in the environment" (p. 45).

Parsons also looked with favor on mental pathology hypotheses about causation, claiming at one juncture that "it has become increasingly apparent that a majority of typical criminal groups either have not the intelligence to manage their own affairs with prudence, or their mental pathology has made it practically impossible for them to adapt themselves to the requirements of normal social life" (p. 126). Although his book contained chapters on a variety of other factors presumed to be related to criminality, such as seasonal influences, economic factors, poverty, educational conditions, home backgrounds, and bad neighborhoods, Parsons remained obdurately committed to an individual pathology line of explanation, holding that individual defects were the primary causes of lawbreaking.

On balance, while these textbooks by Parmelee, Gillin, and Parsons contained a few hints of the directions ultimately to be taken by

---

[39] Another part of Gillin's analysis to which most contemporary criminologists would take exception was his analysis of female crime, in which he concluded that "most of the crimes of women are those connected with their sex functions. Naturally, all the prostitutes committed were women" p. 58. Gillin apparently was unaware of male prostitution.

[40] Interestingly, citations to Parmelee's 1918 text were sprinkled liberally throughout Gillin's book, but no mention was made there of Edwin H. Sutherland's *Criminology,* which had been published in 1924.

sociological criminology in the United States, for the most part, these were relatively nonsociological and eclectic works. They showed little similarity to the criminology textbooks that began to appear in the late 1930s and 1940s.

These three volumes were not idiosyncratic products standing by themselves. They were part of a larger body of writings by exponents of social pathology perspectives that dominated in American sociology in the late 1800s and early 1900s. These viewpoints drew on Darwinian hypotheses and stressed organic analogies between biological and social structures. When these social pathologists commented on crime, prostitution, or other social problems, they likened them to diseases or defects in physical organisms, as though they were directing attention to social abcesses or lesions in an otherwise healthy social organism. This form of analysis was heavily centered on individuals rather than upon societal organization. As Lemert has noted; "the notion of individual maladjustment figured large in discussions of social pathology, revolving about the consequences of physical illness, mental deficiency, mental disorders, alcoholism, lack of education, or incomplete socialization for the realization of life goals regarded as normal for most people." [41]

There is one important exception to this collection of presociological works, namely, Edwin Sutherland's *Criminology,* published in 1924. Sutherland's book exercised a powerful influence over several generations of criminologists. It can fairly be said that the appearance of his text inaugurated the transition to contemporary criminology. It is for this reason that this chapter closes with a few brief remarks about his book, even though chronologically, it would be more appropriately placed before the works of Gillin and Parsons.

Edwin H. Sutherland

Edwin Sutherland was one of the early Ph.D. products of the sociology department at the University of Chicago. In an essay in which he discussed his development of differential association theory (see Chapter 3), Sutherland provided an account of how he came to write the first edition of *Criminology.*[42] He reported that, as a student, he took a criminology course in which Henderson's volume was used as a text. Later, he was assigned to teach criminology, first at the University of Illinois and next at Indiana University, where he spent a good part of his academic career. According to his account, he considered the Parmelee and Wines texts available at the time he began to teach as inadequate. He was appar-

[41] Lemert, *op. cit., Human Deviance, Social Problems, and Social Control,* p. 10.
[42] Albert K. Cohen, Alfred Lindesmith, and Karl Schuessler, eds., *The Sutherland Papers* (Bloomington: Indiana University Press, 1956), pp. 13–14.

ently dissatisfied with the Parmelee book because it drew heavily on European sources for theory and evidence.[43]

Sutherland set the tone for the first and subsequent versions of his text in the Preface to the 1924 edition, where he contended that

> when this new knowledge is applied to the old problem of crime, it becomes apparent at once that labelling a criminal (as feeble-minded, psychopathic, pervert) is a very slight part of understanding him. It is necessary to become acquainted with the mechanisms and processes involved in the criminality. It becomes apparent, also, that the criminal must be dealt with as a human being rather than as a concept.

The many theoretical and empirical contributions to criminology for which Sutherland is justly famous are taken up in Chapter 3. These efforts included the development of the paired formulations of differential social organization and the more well-known theory of differential association, as well as his work on professional theft as a behavior system, white-collar crime, and certain other seminal contributions.

The first edition of *Criminology* contained only faint hints of these developments to come. For example, it was not until the third edition of his book, published in 1939, that the formal statement of differential association appeared.

The 1924 version of Sutherland's book was a relatively compact volume, containing four chapters on the nature of crime and law, the deficiencies of crime statistics, data on victims, and statistics on demographic correlates of crime. It also included four chapters on causation, reviewing the evidence on a standard list of etiological influences that had also appeared in the books by Parmelee, Gillin, and Parsons. The remaining seventeen chapters were given over to commentaries on the police, juvenile courts, prisons, parole, and assorted other correctional topics.

The distinguishing feature of this 1924 volume, which set it off from the writings of Parmelee and Gillin, was the well-reasoned but hard-hitting critiques of such arguments as those of Lombroso. Sutherland closely examined the evidence on intelligence factors and concluded that criminals do not differ in mental capacity from nonoffenders. Throughout the entire work, Sutherland carefully examined the popular hypotheses of the day, centered on alleged physical or mental pathology on the part of lawbreakers. Little enthusiasm for such notions was voiced in the pages of his text. Sutherland was a demanding scholar, a clear thinker, and a scientific analyst of crime who was not content with speculative argu-

---

[43] However, Sutherland's book contained a good many citations to Parmelee's work; indeed, his name was one of the most frequently mentioned there.

ments or fuzzy evidence. He was also the model of the true scientist, for he applied those same stringent standards of proof and scholarly excellence to his own work as well as to the research and writings of others.

Gilbert Geis recently provided a reexamination of Sutherland's book and arrived at a judgment parallel to the one here.[44] After reviewing the contents of that volume, Geis concluded: "Indeed, if it were used as a text today, the 1924 edition still would provide an undergraduate with an excellent understanding of important modes of reasoning about key matters involved in criminal behavior and responses to it." [45]

We have finished rummaging about in the records of the early days of American sociology and criminology. In Chapter 3, we begin an extended examination of the large and diverse body of sociological criminology that began to flourish after 1930 in this country.

---

[44] Gilbert Geis, "Editorial: Revisiting Sutherland's *Criminology* (1924)," *Criminology,* 14 (November 1976):303–306.

[45] *Ibid.,* p. 304. Geis qualified this judgment somewhat, as he claimed that the book was unbalanced, giving undue attention to corrections rather than causation. Also, Geis scored Sutherland for his emphasis on the unitary nature of crime, rather than paying attention to important variations among patterns of lawbreaking. A concentration of attention on the workings of the criminal justice apparatus continues to characterize criminology textbooks. This evaluation of the first edition of Sutherland's book, stressing the comprehensive and trenchant criticisms of conventional criminological theory contained in it, was also offered by Cohen, Lindesmith, and Schuessler, *The Sutherland Papers,* p. 1.

CRIMINOLOGY:
1930–1955

3 INTRODUCTION

Some clues about the directions taken by American criminology during its major growth period from 1930 to the present were provided in the preceding chapter. Mention was made of the ecological investigations and the inquiries into the social processes involved in delinquency carried on by Clifford Shaw and Henry McKay in Chicago which were of major importance in the rise of empirical sociology. The first edition of Sutherland's *Criminology,* which represented the turning point toward modern criminological thought and away from a theoretical eclecticism or biological hypotheses, was also discussed. This chapter moves into a more detailed examination of the work of Shaw and McKay and also deals with the several signal contributions to American criminology made by Sutherland, including the theory of differential association, his inquiries into white-collar crime, and his work on professional theft. A third concern of this chapter is with Robert K. Merton's formulation of anomie as a major explanation of deviance, including criminality. Finally, this chapter touches on a number of other related developments in criminological thought during this 25-year period.

Chapter 2 acknowledged the impossibility of identifying the precise date at which sociology originated and the futility of efforts to enunciate a listing of the half-dozen or so major figures in the rise of sociology. Such endeavors inevitably require that relatively arbitrary choices of dates or names be made. The same is true for criminology, in that several points of origin or putative founders come to mind.

Identification of major periods in the development of American criminology also requires some relatively arbitrary decisions. The criminological enterprise in the United States could be divided up or periodized in a number of different ways. In this book, four stages are identified: the early years from 1900 to 1930; a growth period from 1930 to 1955, in which many of the links in contemporary mainstream criminology were forged; followed by the further development and maturation of criminology between 1955 and 1970; and finally, some radically different versions of criminological theorizing that have sprung up since about 1970.

The period from 1930 to 1955 is by no means an entirely arbitrarily chosen one. Chapter 2 has already traced the emergence of American sociology in the late 1800s and early 1900s. That chapter alluded to Robert Faris's account of the emergence of the University of Chicago as the dominant center of sociological inquiry in this country between 1920 and 1932.[1] According to Faris, scientific sociology had taken a relatively firm root in the United States by about 1930, due largely to the efforts of W. I. Thomas, Robert Ezra Park, Elsworth Faris, and Ernest Burgess. On this point, Roscoe and Gisela Hinkle reported that the American Sociological Society reached an early peak in membership in 1932, with 1,567 persons belonging to the organization. Clearly, the sociological fraternity had expanded markedly by about 1930, from the handful of individuals who made up that group at the turn of the century.[2]

Hinkle and Hinkle indicated that the American Sociological Society declined in numbers during the depression period but rebounded with 1,651 members in 1946, while by 1953, the organization had expanded to 4,027 members. Their account of the development of modern sociology ended at 1954. They suggested that by that date, American sociology had grown to relative maturity. Some support for that claim can be found in the appearance in 1959 of the bulky anthology, *Sociology Today,* sponsored by the American Sociological Association (formerly the American Sociological Society) and consisting of stock-taking essays focused on various substantive areas of interest.[3] These papers had been prepared for the 1957 meetings of the sociological association. The volume exuded a congratulatory aroma in which many of the contributors commented favorably upon the accomplishments that had been achieved in their areas of sociological specialization.

One of the essays in *Sociology Today* dealt with the state of criminology.[4] The author, Marshall Clinard, began by discussing Sutherland's theory of differential association and the anomie formulation of Merton,

---

[1] Robert E. L. Faris, *Chicago Sociology—1920–1932* (San Francisco: Chandler, 1967).

[2] Roscoe C. Hinkle and Gisela G. Hinkle, *The Development of Modern Sociology* (New York: Random House, 1954), p. 44.

[3] Robert K. Merton, Leonard Broom, and Leonard S. Cottrell, Jr., eds., *Sociology Today* (New York: Basic Books, 1959).

[4] Marshall B. Clinard, "Criminological Research," in Merton, Broom, and Cottrell, *op. cit.,* pp. 509–36.

indicating that these were the most significant achievements of criminology to the point. The remainder of his chapter centered on a number of additions and revisions in criminological theory which he felt were called for, including more attention to situational factors in lawbreaking and to offender typologies. Clinard's assessment suggested that the period from 1930 to 1955 is relatively clearly marked off from the earlier stirrings of criminological interest and from a maturation period after 1955, in which many of the central themes of modern criminology were polished and burnished by contemporary criminologists.

CLIFFORD SHAW AND HENRY D. McKAY:
DELINQUENCY AS A SOCIAL PHENOMENON

Social Change, Ecological Patterns, and
Social Processes in Delinquency

It would be difficult to overestimate the significance of the delinquency studies carried on by Clifford Shaw and Henry McKay in Chicago and certain other American cities from 1929 through the 1930s. The results of their inquiries provided much of the intellectual capital on which criminologists have continued to draw, even to the present time.

Although Shaw and McKay have sometimes been identified as affiliated with the University of Chicago, in point of fact both were researchers with the Institute for Juvenile Research in Chicago, a state-supported child guidance clinic.[5] Clifford Shaw was first employed by the institute in the late 1920s and was joined soon after by Henry McKay. The major connecting link between the University of Chicago sociology department and the Institute for Juvenile Research was represented first by Ernest Burgess and a few of his students who had ties with the Chicago Area Project, a delinquency prevention endeavor directed by the Institute. In later years, a number of other sociology faculty members or graduate students at the University of Chicago worked with Shaw and McKay at the Institute.[6]

[5] James T. Carey, *Sociology and Public Affairs: The Chicago School* (Beverly Hills, Calif.: Sage Publications, 1975), pp. 84–92.

[6] Henry D. McKay's distinguished career centered about his work at the Institute for Juvenile Research, which continued through the 1960s. He served as chief of community studies there and worked on a number of projects, including the Chicago Area Project. He served as a consultant to the National Commission on Law Observance and Enforcement, popularly known as the Wickersham Commission, in the 1930s. He was also a consultant to the President's Commission on Law Enforcement and the Administration of Justice in the 1960s. He taught or lectured at the University of Illinois, University of Chicago, and Roosevelt University. For some description and evaluation of the Chicago Area Project, see Harold Finestone, *Victims of Change* (Westport, Conn.: Greenwood Press, 1976), pp. 116–50; and Anthony Sorrentino, *Organizing against Crime: Redeveloping the Neighborhood* (New York: Human Sciences Press, 1977).

In Chapter 1, a distinction was made between the two major questions about the etiology of crime and delinquency. The *sociology of criminality* focuses on crime rates and patterns for different areas and tries to provide explanations for these rate patterns or distributions. Other researchers and theorists center their inquiries on the individual or *social-psychological level* and try to uncover the processes that account for involvement in criminality or delinquency on the part of individuals.[7]

Both of these questions were addressed by Shaw and McKay.[8] In their ecologically oriented studies, they found that juvenile court referral rates varied widely in areas of Chicago and elsewhere, that the highest rates were in neighborhoods of rapid population change, poor housing, poverty, tuberculosis, adult crime, and mental disorders.[9] Moreover, these rates showed a gradient pattern. They were highest in inner-city or core areas and declined with distance from the city center. Delinquency rates for particular ethnic groups also showed this gradient tendency. High rates occurred near the city center, and low rates were observed toward the city periphery.

Shaw and McKay reported that delinquency rates differed markedly among specific neighborhoods. In all 15 cities studied, none of the boys in some areas had been arrested, while in other neighborhoods, which Shaw and McKay called "delinquency areas," more than one-fifth had been apprehended in a single year.[10]

High delinquency rates were usually found near the industrial areas and deteriorated community sections around the city center. Areas of high delinquency also showed high truancy rates and high rates of commitment of adults to county jail. Finally, the areas of high delinquency in 1930 also had high rates in 1900, even though the nationality composition of the populations had changed markedly. In other words, delinquency rates remained stable or consistently high in certain neighborhoods, even though the populations of those areas changed completely over a 30-year

[7] These two levels or kinds of inquiries are discussed in Don C. Gibbons and Joseph F. Jones, *The Study of Deviance* (Englewood Cliffs, N.J.: Prentice-Hall, 1975), pp. 32–35; Gibbons, *Society, Crime, and Criminal Careers,* 3rd ed. (Englewood Cliffs, N.J.: Prentice-Hall, 1977), pp. 8–12; Donald R. Cressey, "Epidemiology and Individual Conduct: A Case from Criminology," *Pacific Sociological Review,* 3 (Fall 1960):47; and Albert K. Cohen, *Deviance and Control* (Englewood Cliffs, N.J.: Prentice-Hall, 1966), pp. 41–47.

[8] The work of Shaw and McKay is summarized and evaluated in Harold Finestone, "The Delinquent and Society: The Shaw and McKay Tradition," in James F. Short, Jr., ed., *Delinquency, Crime, and Society* (Chicago: University of Chicago Press, 1976), pp. 23–49. Also see Finestone, *Victims of Change.*

[9] Clifford Shaw and Henry D. McKay, *Social Factors in Juvenile Delinquency,* Volume II, National Commission on Law Observance and Enforcement, Report on the Causes of Crime (Washington, D.C.: U.S. Government Printing Office, 1931), pp. 60–108; Shaw and McKay, *Juvenile Delinquency in Urban Areas* (Chicago: University of Chicago Press, 1932), p. 11.

[10] Clifford Shaw, Henry D. McKay, Frederick Zorbaugh, and Leonard S. Cottrell, Jr., *Delinquency Areas* (Chicago: University of Chicago Press, 1929).

period. It was this observation that led Shaw and McKay to conclude that delinquency and criminality represented a cultural tradition in some urban neighborhoods.

Finestone has offered the judgment that [Shaw and McKay] became pathfinders in the study of delinquency because they succeeded in formulating its central sociological issues in such a manner as to continue to stimulate and challenge subsequent generations of investigators.[11] One indication of this impact can be seen in the large number of ecological investigations of delinquency that have continued up to the present.[12] On balance, these studies have not produced any major revisions in the conclusions arrived at by Shaw and McKay in the 1930s.

Turning to the social psychological level of analysis, Shaw and McKay developed their account of the processes through which youths become lawbreakers in delinquency areas principally through examination of a number of life history documents on youthful offenders.[13] They concluded that delinquents were psychologically normal youngsters whose involvement in misconduct occurred within a network of interpersonal relationships that included family, gang, and neighborhood influences. Young offenders were perceived as moving into engagement in adolescent misconduct as they came under the influence of criminogenic conditions in the area, that is, the delinquency tradition that existed in their neighborhoods.

Finestone has explicated the structure of the Shaw-McKay position in detail.[14] He argued that they were particularly influenced in the development of their ideas by the formulations of W. I. Thomas regarding

---

[11] Finestone, "The Delinquent and Society," p. 23.

[12] For example, see Bernard Lander, *Toward an Understanding of Juvenile Delinquency* (New York: Columbia University Press, 1954); Roland J. Chilton, "Continuities in Delinquency Area Research: A Comparison of Studies for Baltimore, Detroit, and Indianapolis," *American Sociological Review,* 29 (February 1964):71–83; David J. Bordua, "Juvenile Delinquency and 'Anomie': An Attempt at Replication," *Social Problems,* 6 (Winter 1958–1959):230–38. These and other ecological studies are summarized in Don C. Gibbons, *Delinquent Behavior,* 2nd ed. (Englewood Cliffs, N.J.: Prentice-Hall, 1976), pp. 105–14. For a parallel evaluation of these studies, see Judith A. Wilks, "Ecological Correlates of Crime and Delinquency," in The President's Commission on Law Enforcement and Administration of Justice, *Task Force Report: Crime and Its Impact—An Assessment* (Washington, D.C.: U.S. Government Printing Office, 1967), pp. 138–56. Also see Harwin L. Voss and David M. Peterson, eds., *Ecology of Crime and Delinquency* (Englewood Cliffs, N.J.: Prentice-Hall, 1971).

[13] Clifford R. Shaw, *The Jack Roller* (Chicago: University of Chicago Press, 1930); Shaw, in collaboration with Maurice E. Moore, *The Natural History of a Delinquent Career* (Chicago: University of Chicago Press, 1931); Shaw, Henry D. McKay, and James F. McDonald, *Brothers in Crime* (Chicago: University of Chicago Press, 1938).

[14] Finestone, "The Delinquent and Society," pp. 26–29; also see Finestone, *Victims of Change,* pp. 77–115.

the cyclical processes of social change involving social organization, disorganization, and reorganization. Shaw and McKay viewed the movement of successive waves of immigrants first into inner-city neighborhoods and later to outer-city areas as a graphic case in point of the processes identified by Thomas. Finestone has indicated that "to Shaw and McKay this conceptualization appeared to be highly appropriate to their subject matter. The processes of social disorganization and reorganization could be meaningfully applied to the passage of successive nationality groups through the spatial grid of the city." [15] Shaw and McKay viewed delinquency as a part of the natural history of the settlement process experienced by newly arrived groups in the urban community. Also, they took as their task the investigation of traditional institutional efforts to control the conduct of the younger generation and the responses of the latter to those endeavors.

Shaw and McKay described the process through which youngsters became delinquent in these neighborhoods as growing out of or taking place against the backdrop of social disorganization experienced by immigrants as they and their children encountered the influences of the new culture into which they had moved. This disorganization was manifested through alienation of children from their parents and adult institutions, so that these youths became detached from customary social controls that normally produce conformist conduct. In turn, these detached and alienated juveniles drifted into association with other like-minded youngsters who collectively turned to delinquent acts. As Finestone described it, "the process of becoming delinquent was characterized by the gradual severance of relationships between the adolescent and conventional institutions and his increasing identification with similarly situated street corner boys." [16]

Although this social disorganization–reorganization view seemed to make a good deal of sense out of many aspects of delinquency observed by Shaw and McKay, it did not provide an adequate explanation for the persistence of a delinquency tradition in these inner-city neighborhoods, particularly in the 1930s. Finestone observed that the coming of the Depression and the slackening of immigration reduced residential mobility and gave greater salience to the issues of poverty and unemployment. He noted that "social change began to appear a less cogent premise for sociological theory than stable and structural features of society, such as social stratification." [17]

As a consequence, Shaw and McKay were ultimately compelled to develop another argument to account for the relatively stable delinquent

[15] Finestone, "The Delinquent and Society," p. 27.
[16] *Ibid.,* p. 30.
[17] Finestone, *Victims of Change,* p. 91.

value system they observed in delinquency areas. They eventually con-
trived a functionalist interpretation that sought to explain the tradition
of crime and delinquency in city core areas as a response of many of the
residents to local economic pressures, which were made particularly stress-
ful because of the economic and social values of the larger society. In
other words, Shaw and McKay viewed crime and delinquency as responses
to the social strains experienced by economically deprived people in a
society that encouraged all citizens to aspire to success goals, which were
measured almost entirely in monetary terms. Thus, they ultimately shifted
from a social change perspective on inner-city delinquency to a viewpoint
that anticipated Merton's anomie theory of deviance.[18] Merton contended
that deviance is one possible response when culturally structured success
goals cannot be secured because there are socially structured limitations on
approved means to their achievement. Shaw and McKay did not venture
beyond a preliminary formulation along these lines, and it remained for a
subsequent generation of criminologists to spell out these relationships in
greater detail.

Shaw and McKay's Impact
on Criminology and Sociology

The impact of Shaw and McKay's studies continued to be felt for
many years after their publications appeared in the 1930s. Empirical
sociology, which was emerging in the United States in the 1930s, was
popularized and diffused to other countries in considerable part through
the example of the Shaw and McKay monographs.

Donald Taft and Ralph England drew attention to the major role
played by Shaw and McKay's writings in criminology when they asserted:
"Perhaps no more effective criminological literature of its type exists than
[Clifford Shaw's] books, now considered to be classics, *The Jack Roller,
The Natural History of a Delinquent Career,* and *Brothers in Crime.*" [19]
Taft and England claimed that the Shaw and McKay monographs lent im-
portant support to the delinquency area thesis. However, an even more
basic conclusion is that Shaw and McKay's findings were incorporated

---

[18] Robert K. Merton, *Social Theory and Social Structure,* rev. and enl. ed. (New
York: Free Press, 1957), pp. 131–94. Merton's theory and a large number of other
critical essays dealing with that formulation are discussed briefly in Gibbons and
Jones, *The Study of Deviance,* pp. 84–111. Also see Marshall B. Clinard, ed.,
Anomie and Deviant Behavior (New York: Free Press, 1964).

[19] Donald R. Taft and Ralph W. England, Jr., *Criminology,* 4th ed. (New York:
Macmillan, 1964), p. 159. However, Taft and England also took Shaw and McKay
to task for some deficiencies in their arguments. For one, Taft and England claimed
that a "drift hypothesis" may account, in part, for the concentration of deviants in
slum areas. In other words, it may be that socially inadequate people gravitate to
these neighborhoods, rather than being the product of deleterious social conditions
existing there.

into the background assumptions on which various sociological theories of crime and delinquency were subsequently constructed. Most criminologists in the 1940s and 1950s embarking on criminological inquiry were guided by the basic premise that crime is more a matter of normal people in abnormal situations than it is of disturbed individuals acting out their pathology.

Thus, the writings of Shaw and McKay were a powerful influence in directing a subsequent cadre of criminologists, including Sutherland, Taft, Reckless, and others, toward various etiological formulations that amplified the basic theme that criminality is carried on by normal individuals who are enmeshed in criminogenic life circumstances.[20]

The findings of Shaw and McKay also became important building blocks from which the theoretical edifice of social disorganization and social problems arguments was constructed. During the 1950s, a generation of undergraduate sociology students was introduced to formulations that attributed a variety of socially undesirable behavior, including delinquency and criminality, to social disorganization, commonly defined as involving the breakdown or disruption of effective social bonds, primary group relations, and social controls in neighborhoods, communities, or nations.[21] A central hypothesis of this perspective was that particular individuals are drawn into suicide, mental disorder, lawbreaking, or other forms of disapproved behavior because they are surrounded by conditions of social disorganization, rather than because they are psychologically aberrant.

Social disorganization interpretations waned in influence over the past two decades and were gradually replaced by social problems orientations or by perspectives that speak about deviant behavior.[22] However, the influence of Shaw and McKay can often be discerned in textbooks that have been constructed around these latter viewpoints.[23] In summary, there is little indication that the Shaw and McKay tradition will soon be consigned to the sociological archives where obsolete contributions are stored away.

[20] For a succinct version of this position, see Arthur Lewis Wood, "Social Disorganization and Crime," in Vernon C. Branham and Samuel B. Kutash, eds., *Encyclopedia of Criminology* (New York: Philosophical Library, 1949), pp. 466–71.

[21] Herbert A. Bloch, *Disorganization: Personal and Social* (New York: Knopf, 1952); Robert E. L. Faris, *Social Disorganization,* 2nd ed. (New York: Ronald Press, 1955); Mabel A. Elliott and Francis E. Merrill, *Social Disorganization* (New York: Harper, 1950).

[22] The deficiencies of social disorganization arguments are discussed in Gibbons and Jones, *The Study of Deviance,* pp. 18–22.

[23] For example, see S. Kirson Weinberg, *Social Problems and Modern Urban Society,* 2nd ed. (Englewood Cliffs, N.J.: Prentice-Hall, 1970); and Marshall B. Clinard, *Sociology of Deviant Behavior,* 4th ed. (New York: Holt, Rinehart and Winston, 1974). The influence of Shaw and McKay was also apparent in Edwin M. Lemert's important volume, *Social Pathology* (New York: McGraw-Hill, 1951).

EDWIN H. SUTHERLAND: DIFFERENTIAL ASSOCIATION
AND OTHER CRIMINOLOGICAL CONTRIBUTIONS

As Chapter 2 noted, Edwin Sutherland's *Criminology,* which appeared in 1924, was the first attempt by an American sociologist to present a systematic and sociological examination of criminological thought.[24] This chapter examines the works of this major architect of criminological thought in much more detail, beginning with his development of the theory of differential association and the companion notion of differential social organization.

Development of the Theory of Differential Association

The authors of sociological theories have often presented them in their most favorable light, without any indication of their possible gaps or deficiencies. Additionally, developers of theoretical statements have rarely described the developmental processes involved in the work of converting inchoate ideas into mature theories. However, a detailed account of the genesis of the differential association perspective has been provided by Sutherland.[25]

Sutherland made it abundantly clear that the formal statement of the differential association viewpoint was preceded by a lengthy gestation period during which his ideas underwent considerable revision. The collection of essays produced by Sutherland during his scholarly career document the claim of Cohen, Lindesmith, and Schuessler that "from these papers it will be evident that Sutherland conceived of the published versions of the theory of differential association as tentative formulations, subject to revision in the light of criticism and research." [26]

In his autobiographical account, Sutherland indicated that his criminological work began in an organized fashion in 1921 when he was asked to write a textbook on criminology. He had been teaching criminology courses for a half-dozen years and had become dissatisfied with the available textbooks. Sutherland's own report of the events that followed his decision to write a textbook included these comments.

---

[24] The social backgrounds and writings of a number of American criminological pioneers, including Sutherland, are examined in detail in Jon D. Snodgrass, *The American Criminological Tradition: Portraits of the Men and Ideology in a Discipline,* doctoral dissertation, University of Pennsylvania, 1972. Others included in Snodgrass's essay are William Healy, Clifford Shaw, Henry D. McKay, and Sheldon and Eleanor Glueck.

[25] Edwin H. Sutherland, "Development of the Theory," in Albert Cohen, Alfred Lindesmith, and Karl Schuessler, eds., *The Sutherland Papers* (Bloomington: Indiana University Press, 1956), pp. 13–29.

[26] Cohen, Lindesmith, and Schuessler, *Sutherland Papers,* p. 6.

Preliminary to writing a manuscript, I attempted to review all of the literature on criminology and especially the research studies. I organized the results topically—economic factors, political factors, physiological factors, etc.—rather than abstractly or logically. I made no effort to generalize, and consequently I had a congeries of discrete and co-ordinate factors, unrelated to each other, which may be called the multiple-factor theory. I was not aware that the relations among these factors constituted a problem, except as to the relative importance of the several factors. I took pride in my broadmindedness in including all kinds of factors and in not being an extremist like the geographic determinists, the economic determinists, the biological determinists, or the mental-tester determinists. . . .

Almost all the ideas in the 1939 edition of my criminology book are present in the 1924 edition, but they are implicit rather than explicit, appear in connection with criticisms of other theories rather than as organized constructive statements.[27]

Sutherland's textbook was a commercial success, with the first edition being followed by the revised, second edition in 1934. The latter contained an embryonic version of the theory of differential association, although that fact was not clearly recognized by Sutherland at the time. On this point, he wrote that

the second edition of my criminology in 1934 shows some progress toward a point of view and general hypothesis. I was surprised in 1935 when Henry D. McKay referred to my theory of criminal behavior, and I asked him what my theory was. He referred me to pages 51–52 of my book. I looked this up and read:

The hypotheses of this book are as follows: First, any person can be trained to adopt and follow my pattern of behavior which he is able to execute. Second, failure to follow a prescribed pattern of behavior is due to the inconsistencies and lack of harmony in the influences which direct the individual. Third, the conflict of cultures is therefore the fundamental principle in the explanation of crime.

I assure you that I was surprised to learn that I had stated a general hypothesis regarding criminal behavior.[28]

Sutherland also wrote at some length about the influences that led him in the direction of differential association theory. He attributed a good deal of importance to Louis Wirth's ideas regarding cultural conflict as a general societal dynamic. Sutherland also worked with Thorsten Sellin on

[27] Sutherland, "Development of the Theory," pp. 14–15.
[28] *Ibid.*, pp. 15–16.

the Social Science Research Council monograph on culture conflict and crime, even though he did not share authorship of that volume.[29] The central thesis of that book is examined later in this chapter. The critique of criminology by Michael and Adler also prodded him to look for abstract generalizations to explain crime and to avoid multiple-factor eclecticism.[30] Finally, Sutherland attached a good deal of importance to his research with a professional thief, for at one point regarding this work he claimed: "There I seemed to see in magnified form the process that occurs in all crime." [31] These experiences, along with the urgings of a number of his colleagues, resulted in the publication of an explicit statement of differential theory in the third edition of his book in 1939.

The 1939 version of differential association theory and the subsequent revision of it represented an effort to develop an abstract explanation of criminal etiology. Sutherland has provided a clear statement of his aims.

> I reached the general conclusion that a concrete condition cannot be a cause of crime, and that the only way to get a causal explanation of criminal behavior is by abstracting from the varying concrete conditions things that are universally associated with crime.

> With the general point of view which I had acquired as a sociologist and used particularly in relation to criminal behavior, it seemed to me that learning, interaction, and communication were the processes around which a theory of criminal behavior should be developed. The theory of differential association was an attempt to explain criminal behavior in that manner.[32]

At this point, a side excursion to examine Sutherland's writings on professional thieves is in order, after which further consideration will be given to differential association theory.

The Professional Thief

Sutherland's book, *The Professional Thief,* consisted of a lengthy description of major elements of the criminal profession of theft, as related to Sutherland by a thief designated by the alias, "Chic Conwell," as well as interpretive chapters written by Sutherland.[33] The volume was one

---

[29] Thorsten Sellin, *Culture Conflict and Crime* (New York: Social Science Research Council, 1938).

[30] Jerome Michael and Mortimer J. Adler, *Crime, Law and Social Science* (New York: Harcourt Brace Jovanovich, 1933).

[31] Sutherland, "Development of the Theory," p. 17.

[32] *Ibid.,* p. 19.

[33] Edwin H. Sutherland, *The Professional Thief* (Chicago: University of Chicago Press, 1937). Page references in the discussion here are to the Phoenix Books edition of this book, printed in 1956.

of the earliest of a relatively long list of biographical and autobiographical accounts of criminal life as perceived by real-life offenders.[34] All of these works have been of considerable value in revealing some of the details about what deviants actually do in the way of rule breaking, but the Sutherland book probably had the greatest impact on criminological thinking of all of them.

The title page of the book indicated that it was written by a professional thief and annotated and interpreted by Sutherland, although Conwell's name did not appear as co-author. Sutherland reported in the Introduction that the book developed in the following fashion: The thief wrote about two-thirds of the original manuscript in response to questions prepared by Sutherland, after which the two of them discussed the thief's narrative at length. Sutherland then polished up the thief's exposition, which ran to eight chapters, and added two chapters of interpretations and conclusions.

Sutherland provided a succinct summary of the main thrust of the volume in the Introduction.

> The profession of theft is more than isolated acts of theft frequently and skillfully performed. It is a group way of life and a social institution. It has techniques, codes, status, traditions, consensus, and organization. It has an existence as real as that of the English language. It can be studied with relatively little attention to any particular thief. The profession can be understood by a description of the functions and relationships involved in this way of life. In fact, an understanding of this culture is a prerequisite to the understanding of the behavior of a particular professional thief. Also, an understanding of this culture is a prerequisite to the development of adequate policies of control of professional theft.
>
> The document in Part I should be read from this point of view. The hypothesis may well be taken that professional thieves constitute a group which has the characteristics of other groups and that these group characteristics are in no sense pathological. Also, the hypothesis may be taken that tutelage by professional thieves and recognition as a professional thief are essential and universal elements in the definition, genesis, and continued behavior of the professional thief. No one is a professional thief unless he is recognized as such by other professional thieves. Tutelage by professional thieves is essential for the development of the skills, attitudes, codes, and connections which

[34] Some of these works are Jack Black, *You Can't Win* (New York: Macmillan, 1926); Hutchins Hapgood, *Autobiography of a Thief* (New York: Fox, Duffield, 1930); Donald MacKenzie, *Occupation: Thief* (Indianapolis: Bobbs-Merrill, 1955); Bruce Jackson, *A Thief's Primer* (New York: Macmillan, 1964); Harry King, *Box Man: A Professional Thief's Journey,* as told to and edited by Bill Chambliss (New York: Harper & Row, 1972); and Malcolm Braly, *False Starts* (Boston: Little, Brown, 1976).

are required in professional theft. If this interpretation is valid, recognition and tutelage explain the professional thief in all cases, not 60 or 70 per cent of the cases (pp. v–vi).

The eight descriptive chapters of the book attributed to Chic Conwell centered on the nature of the profession of theft, the organization of crime mobs, varieties of rackets, and "the fix." Additionally, Conwell commented on thieves' attitudes toward the law and the larger society, their personal lives, and stealing as a business. Another summary statement regarding the central thesis of the book was provided by Sutherland in his interpretative chapter: "The essential characteristics of the profession of theft . . . are technical skill, status, consensus, differential association, and organization" (p. 197).

Although the term "differential association" first appeared in the book on professional theft, the concept was employed in a much narrower manner there than in Sutherland's later statements of differential association theory. That is, when Sutherland spoke of differential association among professional thieves, he had in mind interaction patterns in which thieves were restricted in their physical and social contacts to association with other thieves. Thus, differential association was a synonym for a criminal subculture or criminal group way of life. By contrast, in his mature theory of differential association, Sutherland employed the term to designate a network of associations with patterns of behavior and carriers of procrime or anticrime attitudes rather than to social contacts confined to actual lawbreakers.[35]

Two reassessments of Sutherland's volume on professional thieves have recently appeared, both of which raise doubts about the accuracy of a number of points in that work.[36] Snodgrass indicated that many sociologists have erroneously identified the book as a demonstration of differential association theory, even though it was published two years prior to the 1939 statement of the theory. Most of Snodgrass's essay centered about the nature of the friendship and joint author relationship between Sutherland and Broadway Jones, alias Conwell. According to Snodgrass, Sutherland actually wrote a large portion of the eight chapters presumably prepared by the thief, so that Conwell's description of professional theft was perhaps contaminated to some unknown degree by Sutherland's interpretations. Snodgrass also argued that Sutherland did not provide adequate

[35] This point has been made by Jon Snodgrass, "The Criminologist and His Criminal: The Case of Edwin H. Sutherland and Broadway Jones," *Issues in Criminology,* 8 (Spring 1973):2–17. This divergent usage of the term is also acknowledged in Edwin H. Sutherland and Donald R. Cressey, *Criminology,* 9th ed. (Philadelphia: Lippincott, 1974), p. 81.
[36] Snodgrass, "The Criminologist and His Criminal"; and Robert H. Vasoli and Dennis A. Terzola, "Sutherland's Professional Thief," *Criminology,* 12 (August 1974):131–54.

research support for certain claims regarding the social origins of thieves and their use of drugs.

Robert Vasoli and Dennis Terzola maintained that Chic Conwell was the "original man" in the cultural transmission school of thought on crime causation, in that this volume is frequently pointed to as a graphic demonstration of the learning process through which criminality is adopted by individuals. Also, they argued that criminologists have generally taken the book as the definitive statement on professional theft. Their revisionist essay explored a number of errors and misleading statements in the book that detract somewhat from its stature as a sociological classic. They reported that Conwell died after Sutherland's death in 1949, rather than in 1933 as claimed by Sutherland. Also, Conwell apparently continued to use drugs throughout his lifetime, contrary to Sutherland's contention that he had abstained from drug use. More important, these authors asserted that Sutherland and Conwell provided an inadequate description and analysis of certain forms of professional theft. Moreover, because certain forms of theft such as pickpocket activity and carnival grifting have become relatively uncommon, Vasoli and Terzola felt that the book had become dated. Finally, they indicated that the volume made a number of debatable assertions about crime specialization among thieves and the lesser social rank assigned to armed robbers and other "heavy" criminals.

These two reassessments of Sutherland's volume on professional theft have provided some interesting insights into his sociological work style. At the same time, these critical essays are essentially inconsequential in some ways. Professional theft is not now and never has been a common form of criminality, nor can it be said that it is one of the most socially harmful kinds of lawbreaking. Sutherland's analysis of professional theft was principally of significance insofar as it contributed to the elaboration of the theory of differential association. Seen in this light, it can be argued that most of the factual errors in the book that have been detected by Snodgrass and Vasoli and Terzola were relatively unimportant.[37]

Differential Association Theory: 1939

The 1939 version of differential association theory contained these seven propositions.

1. The processes which result in systematic criminal behavior are fundamentally the same in form as the processes which result in systematic lawful behavior.

[37] However, Snodgrass and Vasoli and Terzola have offered some valuable correctives to certain questionable claims that have become common in the sociological literature. One would hope that criminologists would discontinue making these factually erroneous statements about professional theft.

2. Systematic criminal behavior is determined in a process of association with those who commit crimes, just as systematic lawful behavior is determined in a process of association with those who are law abiding.
3. Differential association is the specific causal process in the development of systematic criminal behavior.
4. The chance that a person will participate in systematic criminal behavior is determined roughly by the frequency and consistency of his contacts with the patterns of criminal behavior.
5. Individual differences among people in respect to personal characteristics or social situations cause crime only as they affect differential association or frequency and consistency of contacts with criminal patterns.
6. Cultural conflict is the underlying cause of differential association and therefore of systematic criminal behavior.
7. Social disorganization is the basic cause of systematic criminal behavior.[38]

This initial version of the theory did not remain unscathed by criticism. For example, Korn and McCorkle claimed that this statement was a theory of contamination-by-exposure, and yet was virtually silent about the processes through which exposure operated to produce law-breaking.[39] Additionally, they charged that Sutherland failed to attend to personal or social differences in resistance to criminal influences, that is, to personality factors. In short, they judged the theory as resting upon an overly narrow and inadequate version of learning theory.

Parallel complaints about this and the subsequent version of differential association theory were voiced by Robert Caldwell. First, he indicated that, while Sutherland restricted his first formulation to systematic criminality, he did not place this stricture on the later version of his theory.[40] Caldwell also contended that the theory was a deterministic and closed system of thought that ruled out such factors as free will. Along the same line, he lamented its inattention to biological and psychological factors. Caldwell echoed Korn and McCorkle's charge that the theory provided an inadequate account of the learning processes through which both criminality and conformity are learned. Finally, he argued that it was not susceptible to empirical tests and thus could not be proved.

Sutherland was not unaware of deficiencies in the first version of

[38] Edwin H. Sutherland, *Principles of Criminology*, 3rd ed. (Philadelphia: Lippincott, 1939), pp. 4–8.
[39] Richard R. Korn and Lloyd W. McCorkle, *Criminology and Penology* (New York: Holt, Rinehart and Winston, 1959), pp. 298–301.
[40] Robert G. Caldwell, *Criminology*, 2nd ed. (New York: Ronald Press, 1965), pp. 212–13. This change in the theory has been discussed in Donald R. Cressey, "The Theory of Differential Association: An Introduction," *Social Problems*, 8 (Summer 1960):2–6. According to Cressey, Sutherland apparently regarded nearly all but the most fortuitous acts of lawbreaking as being systematic, while others interpreted the term more narrowly to refer to organized patterns of group criminality. It was for this reason that Sutherland dropped the term in the 1947 version of the theory. Also see Sutherland's own commentary on this issue: Sutherland, "Development of the Theory," pp. 21–22.

his theory. Indeed, his writings demonstrate that he was as severe a critic of his own ideas as were most of those who attacked his theory. For example, he conceded that "one of the first questions concerned the relations among the concepts of differential association, social disorganization, and culture conflict. The published statement is very far from clear." [41] This essay indicated that Sutherland employed these terms in order to focus on three levels of analysis: individual, interactional, and societal. In the 1939 formulation, "cultural conflict" referred to value conflicts related to law and crime observable at the societal level. Sutherland spoke of social disorganization or in a 1942 essay of differential group organization, in order to draw attention to the fact that modern communities are characterized by a plethora of groups, some of which are organized for criminal activities while others stress anticriminal norms. Finally, differential association was seen by Sutherland as "a statement of culture conflict from the point of view of the person who commits the crime." [42] In other words, that term referred to the particular constellation of group associations with procriminal and anticriminal groups experienced by particular individuals.[43]

There is no need to tarry longer on a discussion of the 1939 statement of differential association theory, for it was followed in 1947 by the revised and current formulation, which has continued to appear in the 1955, 1960, 1966, 1970, 1974, and 1978 editions of Sutherland's textbook.[44] The 1947 version included a number of changes in the argument, including some important alterations in the use of the terms "culture conflict," "social disorganization," and "differential social organization."

Differential Association Theory: 1947 [45]

As the differential association perspective took shape in Sutherland's mind, it began to congeal around the view that cultural conflict or complex social organization resulting from social and economic changes

---

[41] Sutherland, "Development of the Theory," p. 20. Also see Sutherland, "Critique of the Theory," in Cohen, Lindesmith, and Schuessler, *Sutherland Papers*, pp. 30–41.
[42] *Ibid.*
[43] Another problem in this version had to do with the redundancy involved in the use of the notion of consistency as a variable affecting differential association. See Donald R. Cressey, "The Theory of Differential Association: An Introduction," *Social Problems*, 8 (Summer 1960):2–6. Sutherland acknowledged this error in "Development of the Theory," p. 24: "Consistency is the same as 'differential' association and therefore is not a variable, which leaves nothing except frequency."
[44] The first edition of Sutherland's book, *Criminology*, was published in 1924. Sutherland changed the title to *Principles of Criminology* in the second, third, and fourth editions published in 1934, 1939, and 1947. Sutherland died in 1950, but his textbook continued to be revised by his former student, Donald R. Cressey. The fifth edition, co-authored by Sutherland and Cressey appeared in 1955, while the sixth and seventh editions were published in 1960 and 1966. The eighth edition, published in 1970, returned to the original title, *Criminology*.
[45] This section represents a modified version of commentary that originally appeared in Gibbons, *Society, Crime, and Criminal Careers*, pp. 221–28.

involved in the industrialization of the Western world had generated a pervasive individualism and other conditions conducive to criminality. The social influences people encounter through their lifetimes are inharmonious and inconsistent. Thus, some individuals become involved in contacts with carriers of criminal norms and become criminals as a consequence, while others may not have such contacts. This process was designated a "differential association." The elements of this theory of differential association, as stated in 1947 and in subsequent editions of the Sutherland and Cressey book, are

1. *Criminal behavior is learned.* Negatively, this means that criminal behavior is not inherited, as such; also, the person who is not already trained in crime does not invent criminal behavior, just as a person does not make mechanical inventions unless he has had training in mechanics.

2. *Criminal behavior is learned in interaction with other persons in a process of communication.* This communication is verbal in many respects but includes also "the communication of gestures."

3. *The principal part of the learning of criminal behavior occurs within intimate personal groups.* Negatively, this means that the impersonal agencies of communication, such as movies and newspapers, play a relatively unimportant part in the genesis of criminal behavior.

4. *When criminal behavior is learned, the learning includes (a) techniques of committing the crime, which are sometimes very complicated, sometimes very simple; (b) the specific direction of motives, drives, rationalizations, and attitudes.*

5. *The specific direction of motives and drives is learned from definitions of the legal codes as favorable or unfavorable.* In some societies an individual is surrounded by persons who invariably define the legal codes as rules to be observed, while in others he is surrounded by persons whose definitions are favorable to the violation of the legal codes. In our American society these definitions are almost always mixed, with the consequence that we have culture conflict in relation to the legal codes.

6. *A person becomes delinquent because of an excess of definitions favorable to violation of law over definitions unfavorable to violation of law.* This is the principle of differential association. It refers to both criminal and anti-criminal associations and has to do with counteracting forces. When persons become criminal, they do so because of contacts with criminal patterns and also because of isolation from anti-criminal patterns. Any person inevitably assimilates the surrounding culture unless other patterns are in conflict; a Southerner does not pronounce "r" because other Southerners do not pronounce "r." Negatively, this proposition of differential association means that associations which are neutral so far as crime is concerned have little or no effect on the genesis of criminal behavior. Much of the experience of a person is neutral in this sense, e.g., learning to brush one's teeth. This behavior has no negative or positive effect on criminal behavior except as it may be related to associations which are concerned with the legal codes. This neutral behavior is important especially as an occupier of the time of a child so that he is not in contact with criminal behavior during the time he is so engaged in neutral behavior.

7. *Differential associations may vary in frequency, duration, priority, and intensity.* This means that associations with criminal behavior and also associations with anti-criminal behavior vary in those respects. "Frequency" and "duration" as modalities of associations are obvious and need no explanation. "Priority" is assumed to be important in the sense that lawful behavior developed in early childhood may persist throughout life, and also that delinquent behavior developed in early childhood may persist throughout life. This tendency, however, has not been adequately demonstrated, and priority seems to be important principally through its selective influence. "Intensity" is not precisely defined but it has to do with such things as the prestige of the source of a criminal or anti-criminal pattern and with emotional reactions related to the association. In a precise description of the criminal behavior of a person these modalities would be stated in quantitative form and a mathematical ratio be reached. A formula in this sense has not been developed, and the development of such a formula would be extremely difficult.

8. *The process of learning criminal behavior by association with criminal and anti-criminal patterns involves all of the mechanisms that are involved in any other learning.* Negatively, this means that the learning of criminal behavior is not restricted to the process of imitation. A person who is seduced, for instance, learns criminal behavior by association, but this process would not ordinarily be described as imitation.

9. *While criminal behavior is an expression of general needs and values, it is not explained by those general needs and values since non-criminal behavior is an expression of the same needs and values.* Thieves generally steal in order to secure money, but likewise honest laborers work in order to secure money. The attempts by many scholars to explain criminal behavior by general drives and values, such as the happiness principle, striving for social status, the money motive, or frustration, have been and must continue to be futile since they explain lawful behavior as completely as they explain criminal behavior. They are similar to respiration, which is necessary for any behavior but which does not differentiate criminal from noncriminal behavior.[46]

In essence, Sutherland's argument is that criminal behavior will occur when individuals have acquired enough sentiments in favor of law violation to outweigh their prosocial or anticriminal conduct definitions. People get their sets of prosocial and procriminal conduct standards through associations with others in their social environment. In general, the contacts or associations that have the greatest impact on people are frequent, lengthy, early in point of origin, and most intense or meaningful. According to Sutherland, "it is not necessary, at this level of explanation, to explain why a person has the associations he has; this certainly involves a complex of many things."[47] However, he maintained that the state of differential social organization characteristic of modern societies is responsible, in general terms, for the fact that different people are exposed to varied associational ties.

[46] From *Criminology*, 9th Edition, by E. H. Sutherland and D. R. Cressey. Reprinted by permission of the publisher, J. B. Lippincott Company. Copyright © 1974.
[47] *Ibid.*, p. 77.

Sutherland's formulation has been the most popular etiological perspective in American criminology for two reasons. First, it has been the major effort by a sociologist to state a theory regarding criminality whose propositions were held to be sufficient to explain the occurrence (or non-occurrence) of all criminal conduct. The differential association argument stands in contrast to multiple-factor orientations, which have been little more than descriptive inventories of specific variables bearing some association to criminality, with few if any linkages indicated between them. Second, the propositions of differential association were stated in terms of a small group of core concepts and arguments to which nearly all sociologists owe allegiance. The sociological perspective advances an image of people as the product of their social experiences, which provide them with the definitions or standards of conduct and beliefs that stimulate and sustain their activities. Moreover, the sociological view avers that the primary groups to which people belong (Sutherland's "intimate personal groups") exert the strongest influence on them. The sociologist sees people controlled by a gyroscope that the social process has placed inside them. No wonder that Sutherland's formulation won such wide acceptance. It was stated in the rhetoric and terminology of sociology. It includes no alien language from the psychologist's or psychiatrist's bag of words.[48]

The current version of the theory of differential association is not without faults. As is true of most sociological exposition, the theory lacks clarity and precision. The problem is not that the claims are clearly false but that they are overly ambiguous; they are plausible but essentially untestable. For example, what can be said of the contention that people become criminals because of an excess of definitions favorable to law violation? In Sutherland's writings, a relationship was implied in which the sheer *number* of conduct definitions of one kind or another was thought to be the major determinant of behavior, with criminality resulting whenever the ratio of an individual's criminalistic attitudes to law-abiding ones becomes two to one, for instance.[49] However, an equally plausible argument would be that some conduct definitions are more compelling than others. Thus, a few criminalistic attitudes could, under certain circumstances, overpower a larger number of conformist preferences. If agreement cannot be reached on which of these interpretations is correct and if the relationship suggested by the theory cannot be spelled out more adequately, the argument cannot be tested.

---

[48] Although Cohen, *Deviance and Control,* discussed the theory of differential association as an example of the psychological level of explanation, it is clear that the theory differs markedly from causal arguments advanced by psychologists and psychiatrists. The latter involve a variety of claims that invoke images of criminals and delinquents as psychologically disturbed or aberrant individuals who are the products of disordered family settings and kindred influences.

[49] On this point, see Sutherland, "Critique of the Theory," p. 36.

The same point holds for other parts of Sutherland's statement. Are "associations" to be interpreted as identifiable, physical, group contacts in which individuals are enmeshed? The passages from *Criminology* rather clearly indicated that the group associations of the individual are the important forces in behavior. However, some reviewers have interpreted Sutherland's statements to mean that associations are collectivities to which individuals orient their conduct—their reference groups, in other words. Thus, some individuals may be in differential association with social units other than those with which they are in physical contact.[50] Regardless of the interpretation that is placed on associations, the question arises: What kinds of associations are intense ones? The common-sense ring to the notion of intensity implies that somehow certain groups to which people belong are more important than others. Yet it is quite another thing to operationalize the concept of intensity by settling on empirical indicators that measure the intensity of different group associations.[51]

Another relatively brief survey of criticisms of the differential association argument has been offered by Gwynn Nettler.[52] According to Nettler, the theory neglects individual differences and provides no place for variations in opportunities to engage in lawbreaking. Nor does the formulation explain crimes of passion. Finally and most crucially, the theory is impossible to falsify or prove because of its vague and subjective conceptualization.

Donald Cressey has prepared a more detailed and incisive account of the differential association controversy.[53] According to Cressey, allegations of defects in the differential association theory can be sorted into

[50] Regarding this revision of the theory, Daniel Glaser indicated that "the theory of differential identification, in essence, is that *a person pursues criminal behavior to the extent that he identifies himself with real or imaginary persons from whose perspective his criminal behavior seems acceptable.*" "Criminality Theory and Behavioral Images," *American Journal of Sociology,* 61 (March 1956):440. Although this revision made the theory more compatible with modern social-psychological thought, it did not solve the measurement problems in the formulation.

[51] James F. Short has reported on delinquency research in which he was unable to successfully operationalize certain key elements of the theory, with the result that the research findings only provided equivocal support for the theory. "Differential Association as a Hypothesis: Problems of Empirical Testing," *Social Problems,* 8 (Summer 1960):14–25. This issue of *Social Problems* also contained the paper by Cressey noted in footnote 40, as well as two other essays on differential association: Daniel Glaser, "Differential Association and Criminological Prediction," pp. 6–14; Henry D. McKay, "Differential Association and Crime Prevention: Problems of Utilization," pp. 25–37. On the issue of testability of the theory, also see Donald R. Cressey, "Application and Verification of the Differential Association Theory," *Journal of Criminal Law and Criminology,* 43 (May–June 1952):72–80.

[52] Gwynn Nettler, *Explaining Crime,* 2nd ed. (New York: McGraw-Hill, 1978), pp. 266–68. The neglect of individual differences, including personality patterns, was also discussed in Clinard, "Criminological Research," pp. 515–19.

[53] Donald R. Cressey, "Epidemiology and Individual Conduct: A Case from Criminology," pp. 47–58; Sutherland and Cressey, *Criminology,* 78–87.

two groups: those based on misinterpretations of the language of the theory or on ambiguities contained in it, and those directed at substantive claims in the argument.

One faulty interpretation holds that the theory suggests that people who associate with criminals will become criminals. But close examination of the argument shows that Sutherland maintained that criminality ensues from an *excess* of criminal associations over noncriminal ones. Another incorrect interpretation asserts that the theory says that criminality results from involvements with criminal *individuals,* while the formulation actually refers to criminal *patterns,* many of which are carried and communicated by individuals who need not be gangsters or robbers. Other objections have been raised that the theory does not specify why individuals have the associations they have, even though Sutherland did give much attention to this question at other points in his work. Still another class of erroneous judgments stems from incorrect notions about the role of theoretical frameworks.

Concerning substantive criticisms, Cressey noted that a number of criminologists who have asserted that the theory fails to account for certain forms of criminality have often failed to identify which exceptional cases they feel are outside the boundaries of differential association. He pointed out that differential association has been said not to apply to rural offenders, violators of World War II OPA regulations, naïve check forgers, and certain other types of lawbreakers who have been subjected to research investigation.[54]

Differential association theory has been criticized for ignoring personality traits or psychological variables. Sutherland wrestled at length with this objection. In one commentary, he conceded that the question of personality factors was "the most important and crucial question in criminology." [55] But, he later concluded that, even if some personality traits are associated with forms of criminality (as distinct from being the *result* of deviant careers), so that some kinds of offenders are uncommonly aggressive, introverted, or anxious, differential association would still determine which individuals with these personality patterns would become criminal

[54] Cressey, "Epidemiology and Individual Conduct," p. 51. The status of this claim is indeterminate, due to the problems of interpretation contained in the theory. While a plausible case can be made that there are kinds of criminality that lie outside the theory, an equally persuasive but qualified argument can be advanced to the effect that these alleged exceptions are not truly exceptional cases. For example, Cressey has discussed a number of ways in which the etiological processes in financial trust violation seemed to be generally consistent with the principles of differential association. See Donald R. Cressey, *Other People's Money* (Belmont, Calif.: Wadsworth, 1971), pp. 147–51. At the same time, he averred that it is "highly doubtful whether the differential association theory can be subjected to a crucial empirical test" pp. 147–48. Also see Donald R. Cressey, "The Differential Association Theory and Compulsive Crimes," *Journal of Criminal Law, Criminology, and Police Science,* 45 (May–June 1954):49–64.

[55] Sutherland, "Development of the Theory," p. 25.

and which would not. This rejoinder is reasonable as far as it goes, but criminologists are still left with the major task of specifying linkages between offender patterns and predisposed personality constellations, as well as isolating and explaining ingredients of the processes by which individuals of some type get selectively recruited and channeled by social experience along different behavioral paths. This is major, unfinished theoretical business for criminology, but Sutherland cannot be held accountable for a failure to solve this question.[56]

Another substantive, conceptual problem with the theory centers on its failure to spell out the effects that people's experiences at different age periods have on their behavior. Early life experiences may affect the meaning of later ones and thus become influential in conditioning subsequent events. Similar adult life events may be significant for some people and neutral or insignificant for other people, depending on their particular set of earlier life happenings.[57] These possibilities resemble the statistician's notion of *stochastic processes,* in which the effects of any present experience or variable depend on an earlier happening in the life histories of the individuals under examination. Further, the probabilities of future events are likely to vary among individuals, as they encounter variations in future experiences.

The theory has also been said to be defective because the ratio of learned conduct standards used to explain criminality cannot be precisely studied in specific cases. Cressey offered a number of examples in which researchers have been unable to accurately measure favorable or unfavorable definitions to violation of law. Finally, a number of critics have averred that the learning process for acquiring criminality or law-abiding behavior is more complex than the theory indicates. For example, it does not allow for the possibility that some individuals contrive their criminality apart from contact with criminal associations.[58]

There is no better summary evaluation of the dialogue on differential association than Cressey's judgment.

> It . . . seems safe to conclude that differential association is not a precise statement of the process by which one becomes a criminal. The idea that criminality is a consequence of an excess of intimate associations with criminal behavior patterns is valuable because, for example, it negates assertions that deviation from norms is simply a product of being emotionally insecure or living in a broken home, and then indicates in a general way why only some emotionally in-

[56] One essay voicing this complaint about the absence of a dynamic view of personality in the differential association theory is S. Kirson Weinberg, "Personality and Method in the Differential Association Theory: Comments on 'A Reformulation of Sutherland's Differential Association Theory and a Strategy for Empirical Verification,' " *Journal of Research in Crime and Delinquency,* 3 (July 1966):165–72.
[57] Cressey, "Epidemiology and Individual Conduct," p. 53.
[58] *Ibid.,* pp. 53–54.

secure persons and only some persons from broken homes commit crimes. . . . Yet the statement of the differential association process is not precise enough to stimulate rigorous empirical test, and it therefore has not been proved or disproved.[59]

Several efforts have been made to revise and renovate the differential association theory to make it more serviceable, in addition to Glaser's differential identification reformulation noted earlier. C. R. Jeffery criticized the argument on the grounds that it was not stated in terms of modern learning theory.[60] Robert Burgess and Ronald Akers actually rephrased the differential association formulation in terms of modern learning theory from psychology.[61] Another contribution to development of the theory was Melvin De Fleur and Richard Quinney's restatement of Sutherland's views in the language of set theory, which put the argument into a tightly logical form.[62] They turned up several points of ambiguity in the original formulation. De Fleur and Quinney's most important conclusion was that a testable version of differential association would have to be linked to an adequate taxonomy of criminal role patterns. If that were done, a number of forms of differential association that are related to different criminal patterns would be discovered.

This suggestion paralleled one offered by Sutherland and Cressey, who contended that research and theoretical labors ought to concentrate more on the study of specific orders or forms of criminality rather than on further elaboration of a general, overarching theory of crime such as differential association.[63] Such activity might begin to separate forms of

[59] *Ibid.*, p. 57. Also see Cressey, "The Theory of Differential Association," pp. 3–4.

[60] C. R. Jeffery, "Criminal Behavior and Learning Theory," *Journal of Criminal Law, Criminology and Police Science,* 56 (September 1965):294–300.

[61] Robert L. Burgess and Ronald L. Akers, "A Differential Association–Reinforcement Theory of Criminal Behavior," *Social Problems,* 14 (Fall 1966):128–47; Akers, *Deviant Behavior: A Social Learning Approach,* 2nd ed. (Belmont, Calif.: Wadsworth, 1977), pp. 42–93; Reed Adams, "Differential Association and Learning Principles Revisited," *Social Problems,* 20 (Spring 1973), 458–69.

[62] Melvin L. De Fleur and Richard Quinney, "A Reformulation of Sutherland's Differential Association Theory and a Strategy for Empirical Verification," *Journal of Research in Crime and Delinquency,* 3 (January 1966):1–22; also see Donald R. Cressey, "The Language of Set Theory and Differential Association," *Journal of Research in Crime and Delinquency,* 3 (January 1966):22–26.

[63] Sutherland and Cressey, *Criminology,* p. 279. For other detailed remarks on this direction to theoretical activities, see Don C. Gibbons and Donald L. Garrity, "Some Suggestions for the Development of Etiological and Treatment Theory in Criminology," *Social Forces,* 38 (October 1959):51–58; Gibbons and Garrity, "Definition and Analysis of Certain Criminal Types." *Journal of Criminal Law, Criminology and Police Science,* 53 (March 1962):27–35; Gibbons, *Changing the Lawbreaker* (Englewood Cliffs, N.J.: Prentice-Hall, 1965); Gibbons, *Society, Crime, and Criminal Careers,* pp. 243–63. But, also see Gibbons, "Offender Typologies—Two Decades Later," *British Journal of Criminology,* 15 (April 1975):140–56. In this review of typological efforts, considerably more pessimism and skepticism was voiced about this approach than in earlier statements.

criminality that arise out of some process akin to differential association from those that do not. Such theoretical endeavors might also introduce some clarity into the general theory of differential association by revealing the specific chains of variables or factors summed up in the general expression. Contemporary criminology needs elaborate formulations that are in agreement with the complex character of social interaction as it is played out in real life.

Differential Social Organization

It would be a mistake to assume that Sutherland was interested only in accounting for the processes involved in the adoption of criminal behavior patterns by individuals, even though an initial reading of the theory might lead to that conclusion. As Sutherland and Cressey pointed out, "students should carefully note that the theory of differential association is concerned with making sense of the gross facts about crime, rather than concentrating exclusively on individual criminality." [64] In *Criminology*, they argued that the social changes growing out of the Industrial Revolution, including marked emphasis upon individualism, great stress on pursuit of monetary wealth, increased social mobility of population groups, and cultural conflict or normative clashes due to the presence of different cultural groups within the same society, have all produced a situation of differential social organization. For example, they claimed that

> the important general point is that in a multi-group type of social organization, alternative and inconsistent standards of conduct are possessed by various groups, so that an individual who is a member of one group has a high probability of learning to use legal means for achieving success, or learning to deny the importance of success, while an individual in another group learns to accept the importance of success and to achieve it by illegal means. Stated in another way, there are alternative educational processes in operation, varying with groups, so that a person may be educated in either conventional or criminal means of achieving success. As indicated above, this situation may be called "differential social organization" or "differential group organization." "Differential group organization" should explain the crime rate, while "differential association" should explain the criminal behavior of a person. The two explanations must be consistent with each other.[65]

Sutherland and Cressey's conclusion was that, "as an organizing principle, normative conflict makes understandable most of the variations

[64] Sutherland and Cressey, *Criminology*, p. 87.
[65] *Ibid.*, p. 89.

in crime rates discovered by various researchers and observers, and it also focuses attention on crucial research areas." [66] Their chapter on differential social organization in *Criminology* examined the sources of normative conflict in considerable detail. In that discussion, they drew on a variety of theoretical statements on deviance and crime that have been offered by others, including Merton's formulation regarding anomie and deviant behavior, with the result that their writings lost some of their distinctiveness and merged into the larger body of criminological commentary. Attention turns to some of those viewpoints paralleling the writings of Sutherland and Cressey later in this chapter.

White-Collar Crime

For many years during these developmental decades of criminological thought, sociologists centered their attention almost exclusively on the garden variety criminal endeavors of working-class individuals, as though people from other social classes were free from criminal involvements. Through his extensive writings on white-collar crime, Sutherland was almost solely responsible for compelling criminologists to attend to law-breaking among the privileged and wealthy. He only began to publish on this topic about 1940.

> Sutherland began his investigations into "white-collar crime" shortly after the appearance in 1924 of the first edition of his textbook. His interest in this type of lawbreaking arose from his belief that the theories then current placed too much emphasis upon those types of crime which are prevalent among the poor, and neglected the crimes committed by members of the middle and upper classes.[67]

The discussion in this chapter regarding the development of interest in white-collar crime omits any detailed examination of the substantive findings on this form of criminality produced by Sutherland or other researchers.[68] The central concern in this section is largely with the evolution of the concept of white-collar crime as developed in Sutherland's writings.

Sutherland offered several accounts of what he meant by white-collar crime. In one place he asserted that "white-collar crime may be defined approximately as a crime committed by a person of respectability and high status in the course of his occupation." [69] In another essay, he said, "the white collar criminal is defined as a person with high socio-

[66] *Ibid.*, p. 90.
[67] Cohen, Lindesmith, and Schuessler, *Sutherland Papers*, p. 3.
[68] A generous portion of the literature on white collar crime is reviewed in Gibbons, *Society, Crime, and Criminal Careers*, pp. 321–48.
[69] Edwin H. Sutherland, *White Collar Crime* (New York: Dryden Press, 1949), p. 6.

economic status who violates the laws designed to regulate his occupational activities." [70] The first of these conceptions implied that embezzlers should be considered white-collar offenders, while the second suggested that they should not be so designated.[71] In yet another discussion, Sutherland mentioned robber barons and other rapacious figures active in American commerce and industry at the turn of the century, whose activities played a significant part in the rise of the progressive movement.

Many people who adopted Sutherland's term showed an even more cavalier attitude toward precise definitions, employing the term in a reckless and pejorative manner and without regard for whether persons so labeled had actually committed law violations. As a result, a number of critics of this concept have warned that objective analysis of criminality could deteriorate into denunciatory comments directed at business activities that fall outside the scope of the criminal law unless heed is paid to the criminal laws.[72]

Although the concept of white-collar crime has been given a variety of discordant meanings, it has most often been utilized in actual

[70] Edwin H. Sutherland, "The White Collar Criminal," in Vernon C. Branham and Samuel B. Kutash, eds., *Encyclopedia of Criminology* (New York: Philosophical Library, 1949), p. 511. Other writings by Sutherland on white-collar crime include "White Collar Criminality," *American Sociological Review,* 5 (February 1940):1–12; "Crime and Business," *Annals of the American Academy of Political Science,* 217 (September 1941):112–18; "Is 'White-Collar Crime' Crime?" *American Sociological Review,* 10 (April 1945):132–39; "Crime of Corporations," in Cohen, Lindesmith, and Schuessler, *Sutherland Papers,* pp. 78–96.

[71] There is a good case to be made for the proposal that the concept of white-collar crime be restricted to violations of laws designed to regulate business affairs and ought to exclude conventional crimes such as assault or homicide which incidentally happen to be committed by upper-status individuals. Similarly, embezzlement is not properly regarded as white-collar crime because it involves surreptitious activities by employees carried on for their own benefit and which are actually harmful to the interests of the organization. White-collar violations of regulatory provisions, on the other hand, are intended to contribute to the financial success of the organization. Also, certain "fringe" activities of professionals, such as ambulance chasing or subornation, should not be designated as white-collar crime. For a detailed defense of these views, see Gibbons, *Society, Crime, and Criminal Careers,* pp. 321–48. Gilbert Geis has also suggested that embezzlement should be separated from white-collar crime: "Toward a Delineation of White-Collar Offenses," *Sociological Inquiry,* 32 (Spring 1962):160–71. Also see Geis and Robert F. Meier, eds., *White-Collar Crime,* rev. ed. (New York: Free Press, 1977).

[72] For a good resumé of the controversy surrounding this concept, see Frank E. Hartung, "A Critique of the Sociological Approach to Crime and Correction," *Law and Contemporary Problems,* 23 (Autumn 1958):722–25. Some other important statements on this issue are Paul W. Tappan, "Who Is the Criminal?" *American Sociological Review,* 12 (February 1947):96–102; Robert G. Caldwell, "A Reexamination of the Concept of White-Collar Crime," *Federal Probation,* 22 (March 1958): 30–36. For a good discussion of the criticisms of the concept, along with rejoinders to them, see Donald R. Cressey, "Foreword," in Sutherland, *White Collar Crime* (New York: Holt, Rinehart and Winston, 1961). Critics of those who have carelessly employed the notion of white collar crime have insisted that the study of crime be restricted to acts that controvene existing criminal laws, rather than being extended to include civil violations, "immoral" conduct, "antisocial behavior," or other phenomena

research studies to direct attention to violations of such regulatory statutes
designed to control business operations as the Sherman Anti-Trust Act,
Federal Trade Commission regulations, and the like. It was this definition
that was employed by Sutherland in his investigation of the corporate life
histories of the 70 largest manufacturing, mining, and mercantile corporations in the nation. He assembled data on violations of regulations in the
categories of restraint of trade; misrepresentation in advertising; infringe-
ment of patents, trademarks, and copyrights; unfair labor practices;
rebates; financial fraud and trust violations; violations of wartime regulations; and certain miscellaneous offenses. This was also the guiding conception involved in Clinard's study of World War II black market operations, Hartung's investigation of wartime regulation violations in the meat
industry, and certain other studies.[73] In practice, then, white-collar crime
has come to mean business or economic crimes that involve violations of
regulatory statutes and that are committed at least in part for the benefit
of the business organization in question.

On the basis of the research reported in *White Collar Crime*,
Sutherland concluded that this form of lawbreaking could be accounted
for in terms of the principles of differential association and social disorganization.[74] He did not agree with Clinard, who claimed that personality
variables had to be added to differential association in order to adequately
account for white-collar crimes.[75] Most of the studies of white-collar crime
that have appeared since Sutherland's research seem in a general sense to
indicate the workings of processes broadly akin to differential association.
At the same time, these investigations appear to indicate that criminality
among businessmen and business organizations is more complex in character than is suggested in Sutherland's account.[76]

---

falling outside the purview of criminal codes. At the same time, there is another
contemporary school of thought that argues that criminologists *ought* to center attention on such matters as "violations of basic human rights," whether these happen to
be included within the criminal law or not. See, for example: Alexander Liazos, "The
Poverty of the Sociology of Deviance: Nuts, Sluts, and Preverts," *Social Problems*,
20 (Summer 1972):103–20; Herman and Julia Schwendinger, "Defenders of Order or
Guardians of Human Rights?" *Issues in Criminology*, 5 (Summer 1970):123–37.

[73] Marshall B. Clinard, *The Black Market* (New York: Holt, Rinehart and Winston,
1952); Clinard, "Criminological Theories of Violations of Wartime Regulations,"
American Sociological Review, 11 (June 1946):258–70; and Frank E. Hartung,
"White-Collar Offenses in the Wholesale Meat Industry in Detroit," *American Journal
of Sociology*, 56 (July 1950):25–32. See also Gibbons, *Society, Crime, and Criminal
Careers*, pp. 328–29.

[74] Sutherland, *White Collar Crime*, pp. 234–53, 264–66.

[75] Clinard, *The Black Market*, pp. 308–13.

[76] Sutherland's research was almost exclusively restricted to official records and the
like and did not involve direct observation of business organizations, interviews with
white-collar offenders, etc. Some of the more recent contributions dealing with ethical
standards of businessmen, the social patterning of business offenses, and related matters are described in Gibbons, *Society, Crime, and Criminal Careers*, pp. 331–36.

Final Remarks

The evidence is incontrovertible that Edwin Sutherland was the most important contributor to American criminology to have appeared to date. Indeed, there has been no other criminologist who even begins to approach his stature and importance. Moreover, it is extremely unlikely that anyone will emerge in future decades to challenge Sutherland's position in the annals of this field. Sutherland staked out many of the parameters of criminological inquiry and contributed most of the key concepts and hypotheses pursued by criminologists until recently. In many other areas in sociology, it is possible to list a considerable number of important contributors to the development of those fields, but in criminology, Sutherland stands virtually alone. Other than J. L. Gillin, he was the only criminologist to have been elected President of the American Sociological Association. We have examined the major contributions that he made to criminology, but this survey of his works has not been exhaustive. For example, Sutherland also produced one of the first sociological studies of the development of criminal laws with his inquiry into the spread of sexual psychopath statutes in this country.[77] All in all, he produced four books, nearly sixty articles, and a large number of book reviews during his scholarly career.[78] Much more difficult to measure, but of no less importance, is the impact he had on a great number of sociologists through his teaching and other forms of differential association that they enjoyed with him.

CULTURE CONFLICT, ANOMIE, AND OTHER CONTRIBUTIONS

The period from 1930 to 1955 witnessed a number of other developments in criminological inquiry, in addition to the work of Shaw, McKay, and Sutherland. It would be too large a task to identify all of the bits and pieces of theoretical activity. However, one of the more significant ventures deserves mention: the work of Thorsten Sellin on culture conflict, crime, and conduct norms.

Culture Conflict and Conduct Norms

Sellin's slim volume on culture conflict and conduct norms, *Culture Conflict and Crime* (1938), was written in response to a Social Science Research Council invitation to Sutherland and Sellin to explore

[77] Edwin H. Sutherland, "The Diffusion of Sexual Psychopath Laws," *American Journal of Sociology,* 41 (September 1950):142–48.
[78] A bibliography of all Sutherland's books and published articles can be found in Cohen, Lindesmith, and Schuessler, *Sutherland Papers,* pp. 327–30, along with a number of previously unpublished papers authored by Sutherland.

basic aspects of crime causation in order to uncover crucial research questions. In his book, Sellin arrived at the conclusion that criminal laws change from time to time as a result of changes in underlying social or conduct norms, the vicissitudes of social growth, and other factors. In turn, he concluded that this variability in definitions of crime from one time to another and from place to place renders these legal definitions invalid as the fundamental categories for inquiry. Legal categories of crime are not universal categories and therefore cannot form the basis for criminological inquiry.

> The unqualified acceptance of the legal definitions as the basic units or elements of criminological inquiry violates a fundamental criterion of science. The scientist must have freedom to define his own terms, based on the intrinsic character of his material and designating properties in that material which are assumed to be universal (p. 23).

After rejecting legal rules as the defining units circumscribing the field of criminological inquiry, Sellin proceeded to examine the nature of conduct norms and social organization. He contended that all individuals are surrounded by social groups and social norms, that cultural complexity leads to a multiplicity of conflicting norms that plays upon most individuals, and that criminological inquiry ought to center on conduct norms and violations of those norms. He maintained that

> every person is identified with a number of social groups, each meeting some biologically conditioned or socially created need. Each of these groups is normative in the sense that within it there grows up norms of conduct applicable to situations created by that group's specific activities. . . . The more complex a culture becomes, the more likely it is that the number of normative groups which affect a person will be large, and the greater is the chance that the norms of these groups will fail to agree, no matter how much they may overlap as a result of a common acceptance of certain norms. A conflict of norms is said to exist when more or less divergent rules of conduct govern the specific life situation in which a person may find himself. The conduct norm of one group of which he is a part may permit one response to this situation, the norm of another group may permit perhaps the very opposite response.
>
> For every person, then, there is from the point of view of a given group of which he is a member, a normal (right) and an abnormal (wrong) way of reacting, the norm depending upon the social values of the group which formulated it. *Conduct norms are, therefore, found wherever social groups are found, i.e., universally. They are not the creation of any one normative group; they are not confined within political boundaries; they are not necessarily embodied in law.*

These facts lead to the inescapable conclusion that the study of conduct norms would afford a sounder basis for the development of scientific categories than a study of crimes as defined in the criminal law. Such study would involve the isolation and classification of norms into *universal categories,* transcending political and other boundaries, a necessity imposed by the logic of science (pp. 29–31).

Sellin's arguments were deceptively appealing at first glance. However, a few minutes' reflection leads to the recognition of a fatal flaw in his reasoning, namely, that while conduct norms are universal, the specific content of those conduct norms is no more universal or unchanging than is the content of criminal laws. Sutherland and Cressey put the matter well.

In this respect crime is like all other social phenomena, and the possibility of a science of criminal behavior is similar to the possibility of a science of any other behavior. Social science has no stable unit, as it deals with phenomena involving group evaluations.[79]

The ultimate fate of Sellin's formulation was that the broad notions about culture conflict were incorporated into most of the discussions of crime causation offered by criminologists in the 1940s and 1950s, but the primary recommendation that criminologists turn to the study of conduct norms was rejected as an illusory proposal.

Merton and Anomie Theory

This examination of major criminological contributions would be incomplete without some mention of Robert Merton's claims regarding anomie and deviant behavior.[80] This has been the most frequently mentioned theory of deviant behavior appearing in sociology textbooks during the past several decades. The basic contention of the anomie perspective is that deviance is particularly likely to be engendered in societies such as the United States, in which all citizens are urged to strive for success at the same time that many of them are cut off from opportunities for upward mobility and monetary success. Many of those who lack legitimate opportunities for success turn to various kinds of deviant conduct, including criminality. The anomie formulation had relatively little to say about particular kinds of deviant behavior, but it has most often been applied in anecdotal form to criminality. Stated differently, Merton proposed the

---

[79] Sutherland and Cressey, *Criminology,* p. 20.

[80] Merton, *Social Theory and Social Structure.* An extended discussion and critique of anomie theory, including the anomie arguments of Durkheim from which Merton's formulation has been said to derive, can be found in Gibbons and Jones, *The Study of Deviance,* pp. 84–97. This section of this chapter has been adapted from the Gibbons and Jones book.

theory of anomie as an explanation of a large portion of the deviant conduct occurring in the United States, but he gave very little attention to the behavioral aspects of specific kinds of deviance. Nonetheless, sociologists have frequently argued that the theory makes good sense of garden-variety property crimes. Thus, according to Merton's theory, the burglar or robber can be viewed as a person who is effecting "income redistribution" through lawbreaking activities.

Merton's theory is a much more elegant argument than this brief summary has indicated. For one thing, Merton distinguished two major elements of social and cultural structures: the culturally defined goals that people are encouraged to pursue, and the social structure that regulates and controls the acceptable modes or means for the pursuit of those goals. Goals and institutionalized norms governing the means of goal striving may vary independently of each other, sometimes leading to malintegrated states, with one extreme case involving inordinate stress on goals with little concern for prescribed means of obtaining them. In this instance, a situation of "anything goes" prevails, and goal striving is governed only by considerations of technical expediency. The other extreme of goals—means malintegration involves undue stress on ritualistic conformity to norms. Between these two extremes are systems that maintain a rough balance between accent on goals and emphasis on norms, and it is these systems that constitute relatively stable societies.[81]

Merton argued that contemporary American society is anomic, for in it success goals are emphasized without an equivalent emphasis on institutionalized conduct norms.

> The emphasis upon this set of culture goals is imperfectly integrated with the organization of our society, which, as a matter of objective and generally recognizable fact, does not provide equal access to those goals for all members of the society. On the contrary, there are heavily graded degrees of access to this, in terms not only of class and ethnic origins, but also in terms of less immediately visible differentials.

> Given the composite emphasis of this uniform cultural value of success being enjoined upon all irrespective of origins, and given the fact of a social organization which entails differentials in the availability of this goal, pressure is exerted upon certain classes of individuals to engage in deviant behavior, particularly those classes or strata or groups which have the least direct access to the goal.[82]

[81] Merton, *Social Theory and Social Structure*, pp. 131–36.
[82] Robert K. Merton, "The Social-Cultural Environment and Anomie," in Helen L. Witmer and Ruth Kotinsky, eds., *New Perspectives for Research on Juvenile Delinquency* (Washington, D.C.: U.S. Department of Health, Education, and Welfare, 1955), p. 30.

Merton's central proposition was that the cultural system of American society enjoins all people to strive for success goals by means of certain normatively regulated or approved forms of activity. At the same time, opportunities to reach these goals through socially approved means are differentially distributed. According to Merton, "it is only when a system of cultural values extols, virtually above all else, certain *common* success-goals for the *population at large* while the social structure rigorously restricts or completely closes access to approved modes of reaching these goals *for a considerable part of the same population,* that deviant behavior ensues on a large scale." [83] He presented a typology of five modes of adaptation to this situation of disjunction: conformity, innovation, ritualism, retreatism, and rebellion (see Table 1).

Innovation refers to those cases in which people continue to pursue approved goals, but use deviant or illegitimate means. Armed robbers have sometimes been nominated as an illustration of innovation because they use illegal means to pursue conventional goals such as monetary success. *Ritualism* designates persistence in conformist behavior when there is no hope of realizing one's aspirations. The ritualist adaptation frequently includes blaming scapegoats for personal failure. *Retreatism* involves withdrawal from the competitive struggle and thus rejection of both the approved goals and the socially approved paths to achieve them. The retreatist adaptation may lead to passive deviance such as alcoholism, through which people demonstrate that they have ceased to hold allegiance to the conventional values of hard work and respectability presumably embraced by others. Finally, *rebellion* points to disgruntled individuals who actively reject goals, which they view as unattainable, and means, which they hold to be unworkable, and substitute new, socially unapproved

TABLE 1. A TYPOLOGY OF MODES OF INDIVIDUAL ADAPTATION

Modes of Adaptation	Cultural Goals	Institutionalized Means
I Conformity	+	+
II Innovation	+	−
III Ritualism	−	+
IV Retreatism	−	−
V Rebellion	±	±

Legend: + = acceptance; − = rejection; ± = rejection of prevailing values and means and substitution of new values and means.
Source: Robert K. Merton, *Social Theory and Social Structure* (New York: Free Press, 1957), p. 140.

[83] Merton, *Social Theory and Social Structure,* p. 146.

goals toward which they strive by nonnormative means. In his commentary on these adaptations, Merton made no systematic attempt to identify the various real-life deviants who fall within these categories. Instead, he merely offered one or two examples of deviant responses that may fit within each category, such as the alcoholic retreatists found in Skid Road. Although there are advantages to an abstract conceptualization, rather than one that is tied narrowly to particular kinds of deviant conduct, such a scheme is difficult to utilize if its developer fails to show how it applies to specific examples of deviance.

This formulation was absorbed with enthusiasm into the mainstream of sociology and was referred to in approving fashion in most criminology textbooks. However, a number of critical assessments of the Mertonian perspective have also appeared, which argue that there are a variety of conceptual and empirical deficiencies that mar it.[84] The most telling of these attacks was made by Edwin Lemert, who contended that Merton was guilty of reification when speaking of societal values, for only individuals or social groups can properly be said to exhibit values.[85] Even more important, Lemert argued that American society can more accurately be characterized by value diversity and value pluralism, that is, by a complex of different value systems exhibited by regional or other subcultural groups, than by some hypothesized set of core values. If Lemert's observations are on the mark, they point to the futility of endeavors to account for nearly all of the diverse forms of deviance or crime in terms of some society-wide set of cultural goals and values.

Theoretical formulations of the anomie kind are often difficult to evaluate. These sweeping arguments comprise the "big ideas" of modern sociology, with the result that they often have considerable influence on the field, even though they do not provoke a sizable quantity of research studies tied directly to them. Their broad sweep makes them highly attractive to sociologists, at the same time that it renders them difficult to utilize in specific research investigations.

Merton's theory of anomie and deviance has enjoyed great popularity as one of the big ideas of contemporary sociology, in spite of its defects and ambiguities. The reasons for its enduring appeal are not hard to find. The formulation is highly sociological in form, speaking as it does of cultural goals, normative structures, disjunctions, and socially structured access to opportunities for upward mobility. The argument gives little

---

[84] The critical literature dealing with the anomie argument is reviewed in Gibbons and Jones, *The Study of Deviance*, pp. 91–97. For another set of criticisms, see Clarence Schrag, *Crime and Justice: American Style* (Rockville, Md.: National Institute of Mental Health, 1971), pp. 57–71.

[85] Edwin M. Lemert, *Human Deviance, Social Problems, and Social Control,* 2nd ed. (Englewood Cliffs, N.J.: Prentice-Hall, 1972), pp. 26–61.

credence to claims that deviance is produced by psychological pathology, biological defects, or other views that are alien to the sociological perspective.

Another explanation for the popularity of the anomie argument is that it possesses considerable plausibility and is congruent with many common-sense observations about deviance in modern societies. Much of the plausibility of the anomie formulation stems from the bits and pieces of sociological research that were informed in one way or another by it. For example, the study of ethnic succession in professional boxing by S. Kirson Weinberg and Henry Arond appears to illustrate the dynamics of anomie, as do Daniel Bell's discussion of the causal roots of organized crime in the United States and Lander's ecological study of delinquency. There have been a number of other research investigations that have been guided by anomie theory, at least in a relatively general way.[86]

Merton's theory has had its most critical impact in criminology in the form of subcultural theories of delinquency, which appeared in the 1950s. These arguments are considered in detail in Chapter 4. But, for example, some threads of the anomie argument were woven throughout the pages of Albert Cohen's extraordinarily important volume, *Delinquent Boys*.[87] The Mertonian framework played an even more explicit and central role in the formulation of Richard Cloward and Lloyd Ohlin's theory which revolved around an examination of the impact of both legitimate and illegitimate opportunity structures on delinquents and non-delinquents in inner-city neighborhoods.[88]

THE TEXTBOOK EXPLOSION
AND THE MATURATION OF CRIMINOLOGY

One of the sure signs that some body of social phenomena has become firmly established as a field of study within sociology is the appearance of a large number of textbooks dealing with that area. An outpouring of textbooks indicates that a number of sociologists have come to identify themselves as specialists in that field and, more importantly, that courses have been developed in which significant numbers of students are enrolled. So it was with criminology and juvenile delinquency, which be-

---

[86] S. Kirson Weinberg and Henry Arond, "The Occupational Culture of the Boxer," *American Journal of Sociology,* 57 (March 1952):460–69; Daniel Bell, "Crime as an American Way of Life," *Antioch Review,* 13 (June 1953):131–54; Lander, *Toward an Understanding of Juvenile Delinquency;* Stephen Cole and Harriet Zuckerman, "Appendix: Inventory of Empirical and Theoretical Studies of Anomie," in Clinard, *Anomie and Deviant Behavior,* pp. 243–313.

[87] Albert K. Cohen, *Delinquent Boys* (New York: Free Press, 1955).

[88] Richard A. Cloward and Lloyd E. Ohlin, *Delinquency and Opportunity* (New York: Free Press, 1960).

came firmly established in sociology departments in the United States in the period under consideration. A plethora of criminology and delinquency textbooks appeared in the 1930–1955 period. The flow of these works has continued up to the present time, so that an even larger number of volumes of this kind have been written in the past twenty-odd years.

There is a good deal of similarity in the general tone of most criminology textbooks, for nearly all of them have revolved around a sociogenic view of criminality and have avoided biological hypotheses and the like. At the same time, these books were not entirely uniform in character or content. They range from Von Hentig's biologically oriented work to the much more sociological text of Sutherland and Cressey, and from the polemical eclecticism of the Barnes and Teeters volume to the much more heavily sociological contentions of Taft.[89] The latter devoted considerable attention to the explication of a theory of crime in the United States which centered around the dynamic quality of American society: complexity, materialism, growing impersonality, individualism, insistence upon the importance of status, restricted group loyalties, survivals of frontier traditions, racial discrimination, lack of scientific approaches to social problems, tolerance of political corruption, general faith in law in principle coupled with disrespect for specific laws, and acceptance of sharp business practices and other quasi-criminal exploitation.[90] The similarity of this line of argument to Sutherland and Cressey's claims about differential social organization should be apparent.

THE BALANCE SHEET

The theoretical contributions surveyed in this chapter, particularly those of Shaw and McKay, Sutherland, and Merton, provided the critical mass around which sociological criminology developed in the United States between 1930 and 1955. Although the theoretical formulations and research of these men varied in many details, there was much that their work shared in common.

Shaw and McKay emphasized the acquisition of criminal and delinquent behavior by people who live in urban slum areas and who are surrounded by conditions of social disorganization or normative breakdown. Sutherland's greatest fame derived from his theory of differential

---

[89] Sutherland and Cressey, *Criminology;* Donald R. Taft, *Criminology* (New York: Macmillan, 1942); Harry Elmer Barnes and Negley K. Teeters, *New Horizons in Criminology* (Englewood Cliffs, N.J.: Prentice-Hall, 1943); and Hans Von Hentig, *Crime: Causes and Conditions* (New York: McGraw-Hill, 1947).

[90] The most recent version of this argument can be found in Donald R. Taft and Ralph W. England, Jr., *Criminology,* 4th ed. (New York: Macmillan, 1964), pp. 275–79.

association, which he identified as a process of cultural transmission that occurs in societies characterized by differential social organization. Sutherland's views on differential social organization bore a good deal of similarity to many of the social disorganization themes advanced earlier by Shaw and McKay. Finally, Merton's influential essay on anomie and deviant behavior also had much to say about societal complexity in the way of variations in access to socially approved avenues to upward mobility and material success. All of these perspectives located the mainsprings of much criminality in the United States in criminogenic social conditions that push individuals into lawbreaking.

The evidence seems incontrovertible that these theoretical statements were major factors in the maturation of sociological criminology as a coherent perspective on crime and delinquency. Moreover, this sociological perspective organizes many of the specific facts about crime in American society and is surely more consistent with those facts than are alternative biological or psychological frameworks.

The growing sociological sophistication of criminological inquiry was revealed in the movement away from biological notions and mindless eclecticism that flawed the work of criminologists before 1930 toward arguments that centered on the criminogenic features of modern societies. However, during this period of criminological development, greater attention was given to questions centered on offenders and the genesis of criminal careers than to attempts to identify the social-structural root causes of criminality. As one indication of this imbalance of emphasis, Sutherland's argument about differential social organization has usually been given much less recognition than his theory of differential association, in considerable part because the former was a less detailed and less formalized statement than the latter. On this same point, the significance of Merton's essay on anomie and deviance, first published in 1938, cannot be gainsaid. But it is equally true that in the years immediately following, this theme was not pursued through sustained efforts by Merton or by supporters of the anomie perspective to develop and enrich the sociological understanding of social-structural sources of deviance and criminality. Rather, the next major steps forward did not occur until the appearance of the subcultural delinquency formulations of Cohen and Cloward and Ohlin in the 1950s, and the value-pluralism perspective advanced by Lemert as a replacement for the anomie argument, which he judged to be defective in a number of important ways.[91]

Recent critics of the sociological accounts of criminality dealt with in this chapter have argued that these theories were anchored in

---

[91] Cohen, *Delinquent Boys;* Cloward and Ohlin, *Delinquency and Opportunity;* and Lemert, *Human Deviance, Social Problems, and Social Control,* pp. 26–61.

defective imagery that viewed humans as helpless victims of deleterious life circumstances and criminogenic social forces that buffeted them about and determined their behavior. For example, Nanette Davis took issue with the portrayal of deviance by the Chicago school, which included Robert Park, Shaw, McKay, and other figures.[92] She charged that their characterization, which viewed deviance and criminality as virtually inexorable consequences of the rapid social change and social disorganization found in American cities, was defective because "an oversocialized conception of humans as the product of social disorganization is implicit in this thinking." [93] According to Davis, the Chicago sociologists slighted the influence of social interaction patterns, individual choices on the part of human actors who have a measure of control over their fates, and related factors.

David Matza has written at length about the model of man or imagery that informed the writings of Shaw, McKay, and Sutherland. According to Matza, the Chicago school emphasized a social process of "affinity" to account for deviance, in which the breakdown of community controls in areas of poverty in the city results in the release of deviant impulses on the part of those economically deprived citizens who are thrown together in those circumstances. By contrast, Sutherland was guided by implicit assumptions about human conduct that Matza designated as "affiliation." Unlike affinity, in which individuals "catch a deviance" through some kind of social contagion, affiliation involves a conversion process in which people come to acquire deviant motives through group associations and social influences.

Matza's major complaint regarding the affiliational argument contained in Sutherland's views on differential association and differential social organization was that it was not true to the real nature of social phenomena. He argued that "Sutherland nearly made his subject a captive of the milieu. Like a tree or a fox, the subject was a creature of affiliational circumstance, except that what Sutherland's milieu provided was *meaning* and *definition of the situation*." [94] In contrast, Matza argued that theories of criminality and deviance must be humanized by incorporating a view of human nature that acknowledges that individuals do possess a measure of self-determination. Humans are not hapless victims of social circumstances. Instead, "the *general* truth of affiliation and its human method of conversion is that the *subject mediates the process of becoming*." [95]

[92] Nanette J. Davis, *Sociological Constructions of Deviance* (Dubuque, Ia: Wm. C. Brown, 1975), p. 45.
[93] David Matza, *Becoming Deviant* (Englewood Cliffs, N.J.: Prentice-Hall, 1969), pp. 90–142.
[94] *Ibid.*, p. 107.
[95] *Ibid.*, p. 142.

Another charge that has often been leveled against criminologists and the criminological inquiry of this period is that these scholars and their works were almost entirely mute on the subject of lawmaking. As Chapter 1 indicated, American criminology has been almost singlemindedly concerned with the behavior of criminals rather than with the more fundamental question of the criminality of behavior. The latter asks why certain acts have been singled out as crimes while other, seemingly similar, actions have not. Insofar as criminologists endeavored to address the criminality of behavior question, their answers tended to show allegiance to a defective consensus model of society, according to the critics. The consensus view claimed that criminal laws grow out of broad societal interests and reflect the central moral values of societies, which is part of the warrant for speaking of criminals as antisocial individuals.

This line of criticism regarding criminological writings of the 1930–1955 period has merit. It has only been in the past decade or so that criminologists and other sociologists have exhibited much sustained interest in probing into the social origins of criminal laws, public support for or lack of allegiance to certain laws, and related questions.[96] In particular, the argument that criminal laws more frequently reflect differentials in social power in society and represent the victory of one group over another has become much more visible in recent years. The sociology of criminal law is an area of study that is of relatively recent origin.

At the same time, some of the strident attacks by some contemporary writers on the pioneers of criminology for their failure to perceive that criminal laws are a reflection of social conflict smack of the reinvention of the wheel. An examination of the writings of some of these pioneering figures indicates that they were not as oblivious to these matters as sometimes suggested. Furthermore, the contemporary advocates of conflict views of the law have not yet moved much beyond a call for action. Thus it cannot be said that these people have produced a large body of research on criminal laws that has been guided by a conflict perspective.

Consider an example or two of the writings of earlier criminologists regarding the origins of criminal laws. The following statements of Sellin are not unlike many of the assertions by contemporary conflict theorists.

> The criminal law may be regarded as in part a body of rules, which prohibit specific forms of conduct and indicate punishments for violations. The character of these rules, the kind or type of conduct they prohibit, the nature of the sanction attached to their violation, etc.

---

[96] A relatively brief survey of research studies on the origins of criminal laws and social attitudes toward criminal statutes can be found in Gibbons, *Society, Crime, and Criminal Careers*, pp. 27–40.

depend upon the character and interests of those groups in the population which influence legislation. In some states these groups may
comprise the majority, in others a minority, but the social values which
receive the protection of the criminal law are ultimately those which
are treasured by the dominant interest groups.[97]

Sutherland also sketched out the beginnings of a "social conflict"
perspective on the law in 1929 when he observed that

> [crime] is a part of a process of conflict of which law and punishment
> are other parts. This process begins in the community before the law
> is enacted, and continues in the community and in the behavior of
> particular offenders after punishment is inflicted. This process seems to
> go somewhat as follows: A certain group of people feel that one of
> their values—life, property, beauty of landscape, theological doc-
> trine—is endangered by the behavior of others. If the group is
> politically influential, the value important, and the danger serious, the
> members of the group secure the enactment of a law and thus win
> the co-operation of the State in the effort to protect their value. The
> law is a device of one party in conflict with another party, at least in
> modern times. Those in the other group do not appreciate so highly
> this value which the law was designed to protect and do the thing
> which before was not a crime, but which has been made a crime by
> the co-operation of the State. This is a continuation of the conflict
> which the law was designed to eliminate, but the conflict has become
> larger in one respect, in that the State is now involved. Punishment is
> another step in the same conflict. This, also, is a device used by the
> first group through the agency of the State in the conflict with the
> second group. This conflict has been described in terms of groups for
> the reason that almost all crimes do involve either the active partici-
> pation of more than one person or the passive or active support, so
> that the particular individual who is before the court may be re-
> garded as merely a representative of the group.[98]

These passages from Sellin and Sutherland, as well as a large
number of other contributions by criminologists, demonstrate more continuity in the developmental processes involved in criminological thought
than has sometimes been admitted. The next two chapters turn to the
criminological period from 1955 to the 1970s and will trace out some
other links between the past and the present.

---

[97] Sellin, *Culture Conflict and Crime*, p. 21.
[98] Edwin H. Sutherland, "Crime and the Conflict Process," in Cohen, Lindesmith,
and Schuessler, *Sutherland Papers*, pp. 103–4.

CRIMINOLOGY: 1955–1970

4

INTRODUCTION

By 1955, the skeletal structure of modern sociological criminology was largely completed. "Mainstream" criminology can be identified in terms of the small number of themes that characterize it.[1] First, it has been dominated by an interest in the behavior of criminals, rather than in the criminality of behavior. Criminological interest has focused more on the factors and influences that lead to criminal behavior than it has on the law-making processes through which criminal prohibitions are produced in the first place. Second, in mainstream criminological perspectives, the social order or societal structure is seen as relatively viable. While social-structural defects play the dominant role in crime causation, they have been viewed as amenable to social repair. However, mainstream criminology also emphasizes that the criminogenic influences that produce criminality are extremely pervasive and intimately bound up with the core institutions of modern society, with the result that the task of uncovering them requires a penetrating examination of American society.

Mainstream criminology has been labeled as cynical because contemporary criminologists often project a cynical or pessimistic stance, growing out of their awareness that crime causation is exceedingly com-

---

[1] A detailed discussion of mainstream criminology, along with observations on conservative and radical-Marxist varieties of criminological thought, can be found in Don C. Gibbons, *Society, Crime, and Criminal Careers,* 3rd ed. (Englewood Cliffs, N.J.: Prentice-Hall, 1977), pp. 187–203; Gibbons and Peter G. Garabedian, "Conservative, Liberal, and Radical Criminology: Some Trends and Observations," in Charles E. Reasons, ed., *The Criminologist: Crime and the Criminal* (Pacific Palisades, Calif.: Goodyear, 1974), pp. 51–65; Gibbons and Gerald F. Blake, Jr., "Perspectives in Criminology and Criminal Justice: The Implications for Higher Education Programs," *Criminal Justice Review,* 2 (Spring 1977):23–40.

plex and extraordinarily difficult to uncover. Contemporary criminologists are not very sanguine about the prospects for amelioration of crime, given its intricate interweaving in the fabric of society. Finally, criminologists observe that social organizations often operate in ways quite different from those shown in organizational charts. Not infrequently, mainstream criminologists are skeptical about the perfectability of the criminal justice and correctional machinery, but they do assume that this apparatus will continue to creak along, doing at least a minimal job of containing criminality. It therefore seems preferable to describe mainstream criminology more as pessimistic than as cynical.

It is probably true that most contemporary criminologists embrace liberal political views and also favor liberal reforms in the criminal justice system, but it is also possible to argue that mainstream criminology has been and continues to be relatively conservative. Adherents to mainstream criminological viewpoints have rarely called for wholesale political and economic change in American society in the name of crime control. Rather, they have been advocates of rehabilitation directed at adjusting offenders to the status quo and other relatively conservative or limited approaches to crime prevention and reduction.

This description of mainstream criminology summarizes some of the major themes contained in the work of Sutherland, Sellin, Shaw, and McKay, and other scholars examined in Chapter 3. Although the major assumptions and perspectives of mainstream criminology have remained largely unchanged, there were a number of new developments in criminological theory and inquiry during the 1955–1970 period.

One question had to do with the parameters of criminological study. This perennial issue has arisen at many points in the past and has troubled a great many criminologists. For example, in his book, Parmelee agonized over the question of whether crime is synonymous with immorality and antisocial conduct and also over whether it is appropriate to speak of crimes among lower animals. Sutherland and Sellin, as well as a larger group of other scholars, raised questions about the phenomena that ought to be included within the categories of "crime" and "criminals."

The studies of hidden or self-reported delinquency and crime that were produced in the 1950s and 1960s are linked to this continuing concern about the behavioral parameters of criminology. These investigations produced an abundance of data indicating that many youths and adults who had never been apprehended by the police had engaged in acts of lawbreaking. The reports of widespread misbehavior among nondelinquents forced sociologists to reexamine those theoretical viewpoints that assumed that delinquency was virtually restricted to working-class youths or adults.

Once a decision has been reached regarding the appropriate subject matter of criminological inquiry, a second question quickly arises: How should the heterogeneous mixture of activity gathered together under the label "crime" be divided into more sensible units for study? Classificatory activities can be traced back to Lombroso, if not further. Typological ventures that were carried on in this more modern period were predicated on the assumption that the riddle of crime causation could only be solved if criminologists would turn away from overarching theories purporting to account for the etiology of all criminal behavior. Advocates of typological approaches argued that theories and hypotheses about specific criminal behavior patterns offer much more promise. Theoretical essays and research studies dealing with particular offender patterns or roles did, in fact, generate considerable disquiet about the adequacy of formulations such as differential association to explain all lawbreaking.

These two directions were somewhat tangential to etiological theory, in that they did not deal directly with questions of causation. A third, very important collection of theorizing and research during this period was on delinquent subcultures, beginning with Albert Cohen's *Delinquent Boys* in 1955.[2] That seminal essay was followed by a number of critiques and later by a number of alternative theories of gang delinquency. During the latter part of the 1955–1970 period, empirical research on delinquent gangs began to catch up with theorizing, resulting in the production of a diverse collection of findings that indicated that all the delinquency theories that emerged following Cohen's book were flawed in one way or another. As is frequently the case in sociological inquiry, empirical investigations indicated that the real world was a good deal more complex than its representations in sociological formulations would have us believe.

A fourth form of criminological work had to do with empirical investigations of criminal justice and correctional organizations. A number of studies were produced on prisons, centering most commonly on the patterns of adjustment to confinement exhibited by inmates. The criminological literature was also enriched by a number of sociologically sophisticated inquiries on police organizations. Research investigations on the workings of the courts, the activities of public defenders, and the operation of the prosecutor's office also appeared in some number.[3] Although these inquiries are not centrally concerned with causal questions, they did have etiological implications, for they hinted at the possibility that experiences

[2] Albert K. Cohen, *Delinquent Boys* (New York: Free Press, 1955).

[3] It would be incorrect to imply that sociologists have been the only ones engaging in such studies. A good deal of interest has recently been exhibited by political scientists and other social scientists regarding these topics. Investigations of this variety have been reported in some number in *Law and Society Review*. Perusal of the authorship of papers in that journal and examination of the membership rolls of the Law and Society Association indicate the multidisciplinary nature of this area of interest.

undergone by offenders within the criminal justice machinery may significantly effect their opportunities to withdraw from deviant lines of conduct.

A fifth development during the 1955–1970 period involved renewed interest in social control arguments regarding causation. Walter Reckless's studies dealing with the hypothesis that a positive self-concept insulates youths against involvement in delinquency, as well as his writings on containment theory which grew out of his self-concept investigations, appeared during this time. Travis Hirschi's careful theorizing and research dealing with social control and delinquent conduct was an even more significant contribution to the social control literature. Another version of social control interests arose in the form of a vigorous debate on the subject of deterrence, which was accompanied by a large number of research inquiries on that topic.

This chapter and the following one deal with these five matters. Chapter 4 examines self-reported or hidden delinquency and crime investigations, typological endeavors, and subcultural theories and research. Chapter 5 discusses social control arguments and studies of the social organization of crime control structures. In addition and most important, Chapter 5 includes a social-historical examination of the major factors that helped to shape mainstream criminology. In short, Chapter 5 attempts to identify the reason why sociological criminology took the form it did.

HIDDEN DELINQUENCY AND CRIME

Who are the criminals and delinquents in American society? How many of them are there in the population of offenders? Are they members of "the dangerous classes," who live in the criminal underworld and in slum areas? Are their lawbreaking acts usually recorded in the statistics on crime that are collected by the police or other official criminal justice agencies? Do the available statistics and official records regarding criminality and delinquency provide a representative sampling of total crime? Or, do large numbers of undetected crimes occur, and can many undetected offenders be found in the United States? Most important, are these hidden or unreported lawbreakers commonly from favored social backgrounds and comfortable economic circumstances?

The answers to questions of this kind are crucial, for the ostensible facts regarding the numbers and social characteristics of offenders strongly influence the causal leads that are pursued by criminologists. The theorist who assumes that the crimes known to the police and arrest figures that are reported in Federal Bureau of Investigation publications serve as adequate indexes of criminality in the United States is likely to construct very different explanations than those that would be offered by a theorist who assumes that the "dark figure" of crime vastly outweighs reported criminality and that those who engage in unreported and undetected crimes differ in many important ways from garden-variety offenders. The former would probably formulate arguments that emphasize social class-related criminogenic influences, while the latter would search for those societal conditions that apparently generate lawbreaking at all social class levels and throughout the entire population.

Criminological attention in the 1930s and 1940s was concentrated on gang delinquency in lower-class neighborhoods and on other offenders from underprivileged backgrounds. For example, John Gillin conducted a study of prisoners in Wisconsin and found that most of them were from lower-class backgrounds.[4] Research of this kind involved an implicit assumption that incarcerated offenders constituted the real criminals and that individuals from more favored social backgrounds were untainted by lawbreaking. The first important challenge to this prevailing wisdom of criminology appeared when Sutherland published his research on white-collar crime, in which he drew attention to widespread involvement in illegality on the part of upper-status individuals. As Sutherland pointed out, his interest in white-collar crime was a result of his desire to correct class-biased theories of causation: "This book is a study in the theory of criminal behavior. It is an attempt to reform the theory of criminal behavior, not to reform anything else." [5]

Another venture into the terrain of unreported crime was conducted by James Wallerstein and Clement Wyle, who asked a sample of the adult population in New York to report the acts of law violation in which they had engaged.[6] Most of their sample admitted to one or more deviant acts that had gone unreported, but many of these self-reported incidents appeared to be relatively innocuous in character. The Wallerstein and Wyle study was methodologically unsophisticated and was significant principally because it stood virtually alone as a self-report study of adults. Almost without exception, self-report research had been restricted to juveniles.[7]

This book is not concerned with the details of all the self-report studies of juveniles that have been produced, but it would be useful to

[4] John L. Gillin, *The Wisconsin Prisoner* (Madison: University of Wisconsin Press, 1946).

[5] Edwin H. Sutherland, *White Collar Crime* (New York: Dryden Press, 1949), p. *v*.

[6] James S. Wallerstein and Clement Wyle, "Our Law-Abiding Lawbreakers," *Probation*, 25 (April 1947):107–12.

[7] Many of these studies have been summarized in Don C. Gibbons, *Delinquent Behavior*, 2nd ed. (Englewood Cliffs, N.J.: Prentice-Hall, 1976), pp. 23–34. Another detailed review and critique of these investigations is Gwynn Nettler, *Explaining Crime*, 2nd ed. (New York: McGraw-Hill, 1978), pp. 97–117.

briefly examine one of the most well-known of these studies, which was conducted by James Short and Ivan Nye.[8] Most of the other self-report investigations paralleled that one, with many of them employing the same questionnaire used by Short and Nye. Short and Nye's study involved high school students in three Washington state communities, students in three Midwestern towns, and delinquents in Washington state training schools. These youngsters were asked to complete a questionnaire regarding the acts of misbehavior in which they had engaged as juveniles and also to report whether they had committed the acts more than once. The results indicated that high school students had engaged in many relatively petty acts of delinquency for which they could have conceivably been reported to juvenile court, but the training school delinquents more frequently admitted to these same acts. In addition, and more important, the training school inmates reported involvement in other, more serious forms of misconduct not common among the students. These findings point to social class differentials in delinquency: The training school inmates were predominantly from working-class backgrounds and exhibited more extensive and more serious involvement in misconduct than did self-reported offenders.

These and parallel findings in other studies have lead to conclusions such as the following.

> A large number of youths at all social class levels and in all kinds of communities engage in acts of misconduct and lawbreaking which remain hidden or undetected. In this sense, nearly all juveniles are delinquent in some degree. However, many of the deviant acts of hidden delinquents are the kinds which would be handled informally or ignored if reported to the juvenile court.[9]

Moreover, some have concluded that there are class differentials in juvenile misbehavior. Youths from inner-city and working-class areas do engage more frequently in youthful misconduct than do juveniles from more favored backgrounds, and the most serious forms of lawbreaking are concentrated among working-class youths.

However, others have taken these self-report studies and have come to quite different conclusions about the social class distribution of delinquency. An investigation by Jay Williams and Martin Gold is often

---

[8] James F. Short, Jr., and F. Ivan Nye, "Extent of Unrecorded Juvenile Delinquency: Tentative Conclusions," *Journal of Criminal Law, Criminology and Police Science,* 49 (November–December 1958):296–302.

[9] Gibbons, *Delinquent Behavior,* p. 32. This conclusion is one with which a number of others concur. For example, see Nettler, *Explaining Crime,* p. 98; and Albert J. Reiss, Jr., "Settling the Frontiers of a Pioneer in American Criminology," in James F. Short, Jr., ed., *Delinquency, Crime, and Society* (Chicago: University of Chicago Press, 1976), pp. 64–88.

pointed to as providing evidence that youngsters from various class levels are equally delinquent.[10] These investigators conducted interviews with a probability sample of about 900 boys and girls 13 to 16 years of age across the United States. Nearly all of these juveniles admitted to committing at least one delinquent act in the previous three years, but only 20 percent had any contact with the police and only 16 youths had been sent to juvenile court. Most important, Williams and Gold found no marked relationship between socioeconomic status and reported delinquency, nor did working-class juveniles confess to more serious forms of lawbreaking than did youngsters from other social backgrounds.

How are these divergent conclusions to be reconciled? For example, how can the findings in the Short and Nye study be squared with another report by Nye, Short, and Olson which indicated that the extent and seriousness of delinquency are not related to social class?[11]

On closer examination, these contradictory claims about delinquency and social class turn out to be almost entirely artifacts of research methodology and not empirical discrepancies. In both the Williams and Gold investigation and the study by Nye, Short, and Olson, a truncated delinquency scale was employed from which the most serious acts of lawbreaking had been omitted.[12] In other words, youths from different social class levels were found to be equally involved in serious delinquency, but in terms of a measuring scale that excluded many of the forms of serious lawbreaking that are fairly common among official delinquents and incarcerated juveniles.

Little additional comment on the social-class-and-delinquency issue is required. Albert Reiss has provided an incisive review and critique

[10] Jay R. Williams and Martin Gold, "From Delinquent Behavior to Official Delinquency," *Social Problems,* 20 (Fall 1972):209–29.

[11] F. Ivan Nye, James F. Short, Jr., and Virgil J. Olson, "Socioeconomic Status and Delinquent Behavior," *American Journal of Sociology,* 63 (January 1958):381–89.

[12] The 7-item delinquency scale employed by Nye, Short, and Olson is discussed in F. Ivan Nye and James F. Short, Jr., "Scaling Delinquent Behavior," *American Sociological Review,* 22 (June 1957):326–31. The scale utilized by Williams and Gold is in Martin Gold, *Delinquent Behavior in an American City* (Belmont, Calif.: Brooks/Cole, 1970). Nine offenses were involved in that scale, with different weights assigned to them in terms of seriousness. For example, assault requiring medical attention was weighted most heavily, while petty theft, trespass, and minor property damage were assigned low weights. Two things need to be noted regarding this scale: first, some of the items seem open to differing interpretations by respondents, and second, most of these items are drawn from the lower end of a serious-non-serious scale. On the first point, it is possible that some juveniles might report engaging in assault requiring medical attention because they were engaged in a fist fight resulting in a bloody nose, while other respondents might react quite differently to this question. On the second point, Gold found in his study in Flint, Michigan, that relatively few self-reported delinquents had scores on this index indicating involvement in "serious" delinquency as defined by this truncated scale. See Gold, *Delinquent Behavior in an American City.*

of the evidence on which sociologists have arrived at the two contradictory conclusions concerning this matter. His essay focused on two major conclusions from the work of Shaw and McKay: "that delinquency is endemic in certain neighborhoods and that the probability of becoming delinquent is greater for persons in lower- than high-income status groups." [13] Reiss argued that self-report studies have not markedly altered the validity of Shaw and McKay's claims, pointing to the use of truncated scales and other measurement problems that have plagued self-report investigations. Reiss also demonstrated that "the findings on self-reported delinquency are inconsistent with what is known about patterns of delinquent and criminal offending, the relationship between victim and offender, and the relationship of both victim and offender with agents of social control." [14]

This burst of energy devoted to self-report studies of delinquency has apparently been exhausted. This work constituted a criminological fad that has waned, probably because such studies have not fulfilled their early promise. These inquiries have indicated that most youths engage in transitory, episodic acts of petty misbehavior, but they have not generated major revisions in delinquency theory. As Nettler has written: "An evaluation of these unofficial ways of counting crime does not fulfill the promise that they would provide a better enumeration of offensive activity." [15]

At the same time, the question of the extent of unreported acts of law violation among adults has remained largely unexplored territory for criminological research. It is probably true that sophisticated studies along this line directed at adult citizens would be more difficult to conduct than were the hidden delinquency investigations. Nonetheless, those inquiries are surely needed.[16] This ought to be a high-priority agenda item for criminology.

---

[13] Reiss, "Settling the Frontiers," p. 65.

[14] *Ibid.*, p. 66.

[15] Nettler, *Explaining Crime,* p. 117.

[16] One relatively large-scale study of self-reported crime among adults has been completed. See Charles R. Tittle and Wayne J. Villemez, "Social Class and Criminality," *Social Forces* 56, (December 1977):474–502. This research involved a survey carried out in 1972 among approximately 2000 citizens in New Jersey, Iowa, and Oregon. The respondents were asked to indicate whether they had committed thefts, gambled illegally, violated income tax regulations, physically harmed anyone, or smoked marijuana. No social class relationship with hidden criminality turned up for the total sample even when age, size of place of residence, and neighborhood/personal status consistency were controlled. Also, no significant social class pattern was observed when the frequency of illegal acts was examined. However, there is reason to wonder what results might have been observed had the investigators employed an offense scale with a wider range of items in terms of seriousness, e.g., burglary, armed robbery, automobile theft, embezzlement, assault with a dangerous weapon, rape, and so on. In short, this research employed a relatively truncated offense scale similar to the ones that have been utilized in investigations of unreported delinquency.

THE DEVELOPMENT OF OFFENDER TYPOLOGIES

Introduction

During the 1950s, a major criminological focus grew up around offender typologies.[17] A number of sociologists pointed out that adult and juvenile lawbreaking involves a heterogeneous collection of activities that must be broken down for study into more homogeneous units. According to this view, typologies or classifications of offender patterns, types, syndromes, or role careers are required if progress is to be made toward the discovery of causal factors. Typological ventures were launched on the premise that no single theory can be uncovered to account for all of the diverse types of lawbreaking and lawbreakers. Instead, separate but perhaps interrelated causal hypotheses must be developed for each distinct offender type.[18] There are important differences between typologies of crimes and offender classifications. Criminologists have paid relatively little attention to typologies of crime.[19]

The roster of individuals who have offered offender typologies of one kind or another is a long one. It includes Albert Cohen and James Short, who argued that the delinquent population is made up of a number

[17] This discussion of typological efforts is an abridged version of Don C. Gibbons, "Offender Typologies—Two Decades Later," *British Journal of Criminology,* 15 (April 1975):140–56.

[18] An early, influential typological study of delinquents, directed by a sociologically oriented psychiatrist, Richard L. Jenkins was Jenkins and Lester E. Hewitt, "Types of Personality Structure Encountered in Child Guidance Clinics," *American Journal of Orthopsychiatry,* 14 (January 1944):84–94.

[19] One typology of crime was by Marshall B. Clinard and Richard Quinney, *Criminal Behavior Systems,* 2nd ed. (New York: Holt, Rinehart and Winston, 1973). They listed nine categories of crime, defined in terms of the criminal career of the offender, group support of criminal behavior, correspondence between criminal behavior and legitimate behavior patterns, and societal reaction. These authors identified such types as occasional property crime, conventional crime, and political crime. However, these categories are very broad ones, including forms of criminality within them which do not seem very similar, as for example, political crime which includes everything from political protest behavior to espionage. Also, the classification is somewhat ambiguous, for it is not entirely clear as to whether they had in mind a classification of crime or of criminal persons.

Other crime typologies include a mathematically complex scheme by Shoham, Guttman, and Rahav. See S. Shoham, L. Guttman, and G. Rahav, "A Two-Dimensional Space for Classification of Legal Offenses," *Journal of Research in Crime and Delinquency,* 7 (July 1970):219–43. Another crime typology is contained in Paul H. Gebhard, John H. Gagnon, Wardell B. Pomeroy, and Cornelia V. Christenson, *Sex Offenses* (New York: Harper & Row, 1965). In this study, sexual offenses were classified in terms of the age of the victim or co-participant, and also in terms of whether the acts were forced or consensual in nature, as well as whether the victims or co-participants were children, minors, or adults. Combinations of these dimensions yielded 12 possible types of behavior. In all likelihood, individual offenders often engage in two or more of these activities and other forms of criminality as well, over time.

of types of misbehaving adolescents, and Richard Cloward and Lloyd Ohlin, who contended that lower-class, subcultural delinquents fall into several distinct types. Essays by John Kinch, Sethard Fisher, and Theodore Ferdinand, along with the National Clearinghouse for Mental Health Information are other instances where types of delinquents have been identified.[20]

One call for the development of typologies of adult offenders was uttered by Donald Garrity and the author and was followed by a tentative criminal typology, spelling out some of the dimensions along which offenders might be classified.[21] Further arguments about offender typologies in correctional therapy were presented in a book designed to serve as a primer on differential treatment for correctional workers.[22] A number of criminolology textbooks have been based on a typological perspective, including my own book, as well as those by Herbert Bloch and Gilbert Geis and Marshall Clinard and Richard Quinney.[23]

---

[20] Albert K. Cohen and James F. Short, Jr., "Research on Delinquent Subcultures," *Journal of Social Issues* 14, No. 3 (1958):20–37; Richard A. Cloward and Lloyd E. Ohlin, *Delinquency and Opportunity* (New York: Free Press, 1960); John W. Kinch, "Continuities in the Study of Delinquent Types," *Journal of Criminal Law, Criminology and Police Science,* 53 (September 1962):323–28; Sethard Fisher, "Varieties of Juvenile Delinquency," *British Journal of Criminology,* 2 (January 1962):251–61; Theodore N. Ferdinand, *Typologies of Delinquency* (New York: Random House, 1966); and National Clearinghouse for Mental Health Information, *Typological Approaches and Delinquency Control: A Status Report* (Washington, D.C.: U.S. Department of Health, Education, and Welfare, 1967).

[21] Don C. Gibbons and Donald L. Garrity, "Some Suggestions for the Development of Etiological and Treatment Theory in Criminology," *Social Forces,* 38 (October 1959):51–58; and "Definition and Analysis of Certain Criminal Types," *Journal of Criminal Law, Criminology and Police Science,* 53 (March 1962):27–35.

[22] Don C. Gibbons, *Changing the Lawbreaker* (Englewood Cliffs, N.J.: Prentice-Hall, 1965).

[23] Gibbons, *Society, Crime, and Criminal Careers;* Herbert A. Bloch and Gilbert Geis, *Man, Crime, and Society,* 2nd ed. (New York: Random House, 1970); Clinard and Quinney, *Criminal Behavior Systems.* Psychodynamic and psychological typologies of offenders have also been developed in some number. The most influential contemporary typological effort of this kind is the Interpersonal Maturity Levels (I-Levels) system developed originally in California. See Marguerite Q. Warren, "Intervention with Juvenile Delinquents," in Margaret K. Rosenheim, ed., *Pursuing Justice for the Child* (Chicago: University of Chicago Press, 1976), pp. 176–204. For some critical commentary on this typology, see Jerome Beker and Doris S. Heyman, "A Critical Appraisal of the California Differential Treatment Typology of Adolescent Offenders," *Criminology,* 10 (May 1972):3–59; Don C. Gibbons, "Differential Treatment of Delinquents and Interpersonal Maturity Levels Theory: A Critque," *Social Service Review,* 44 (March 1970):22–33; Edgar W. Butler and Stuart N. Adams, "Typologies of Delinquent Girls: Some Alternative Approaches," *Social Forces,* 44 (March 1966):401–407; Roy L. Austin, "Construct Validity of I-Level Classification," *Criminal Justice and Behavior,* 2 (June 1975):113–29; Austin, "Differential Treatment in an Institution: Reeaxamining the Preston Study," *Journal of Research in Crime and Delinquency,* 14 (July 1977):177–94.

Who would be so foolish as to claim that all offenders are alike? Clearly, there are important differences between acts of violent rape, embezzlement, arson, organized racketeering, or kindred other kinds of lawbreaking and between the people who carry them out, even though precisely what those differences are may not be clear. It seems plausible to argue that groups of offenders differ from each other, with some specializing in one kind of lawbreaking while others concentrate upon other forms of criminality. Reports on the lives of individual offenders seem to lend support to the notion that offender types or careers in crime exist.

However, it is one thing to discover a few cases of individual offenders who seem in some intuitive fashion to constitute a criminal type and quite another to develop explicit offender typologies into which the majority of lawbreakers can be reliably sorted. What has been the yield from formalized typological ventures during the past several decades? How successful have criminologists been in devising explicit offender classifications? Unfortunately, typological efforts have not entirely lived up to the early expectations voiced for them.[24]

Some Existing Typologies

One typological scheme dealing with adult offenders is the classification of inmate types in prison. As outlined by Schrag, prisoners exhibited patterns of social role behavior identified by the inmates as "square John," "right guy," "ding," "outlaw," and "politician." [25] In general, these roles were centered around an inmate's loyalty attachments to other prisoners, with the "right guy" being a loyal member of the inmate subculture, while the "square John" was an alien in that system. Schrag's observations were relatively impressionistic ones, drawn from firsthand experiences during his employment in a state penitentiary, but his contentions about inmate types were closely paralleled by the observations of Gresham Sykes regarding "argot roles" in the New Jersey State Prison.[26]

One indication of the relationship between typological characterizations and the real world can be found in a study by Peter Garabedian, conducted in the same prison where Schrag had done his research. Garabedian identified incumbents of prisoner social roles through inmate

---

[24] An excellent discussion of different kinds of typologies, criteria for good typologies, and a number of illustrative cases of typologies appears in Roger Hood and Richard Sparks, *Key Issues in Criminology* (New York: McGraw-Hill, 1970), pp. 110–40. Also see Gibbons, "Offender Typologies," pp. 141–44.

[25] Clarence C. Schrag, "A Preliminary Criminal Typology," *Pacific Sociological Review,* 4 (Spring 1961):11–16.

[26] Gresham M. Sykes, *The Society of Captives* (Princeton, N.J.: Princeton University Press, 1958), pp. 84–108.

responses to a series of attitude items on a questionnaire.[27] About two-thirds of the prisoners fell into the Schrag types but, equally important, about one-third were unclassifiable. Additionally, although the social correlates that were said to accompany the role types—such as prior offenses, participation in prison programs, and attitudes toward the penitentiary—were observed, many of the associations were much less marked than implied in some of the writings on prisoner types. Garabedian's research did document the existence of inmate social roles, but it also indicated that Schrag's classification implied that inmate behavior was considerably more regular and predictable than it actually was.

Another typology, which was inductively generated in an institutional setting by Julian Roebuck, dealt with inmates in the District of Columbia Reformatory.[28] Roebuck's scheme centered on legal categories of offense behavior, studied within the framework of criminal careers. Prisoners were sorted into classes on the basis of their total crime record as indicated in official records. Types such as "Negro armed robbers" and "Negro jack-of-all-trades offenders" were identified, with 13 types being specified in all. This typology was based on prison inmates and was restricted to black prisoners, and thus cannot be considered comprehensive.

One common occurrence when people begin to examine some specific type of offender in detail is the proliferation of subtypes, as they attempt to capture the variability of behavior within the type. For example, Charles McCaghy's research on child molesters identified six separate types of child molesters, including the "high interaction molester," the "incestuous molester," the "career molester," and the "spontaneous-aggressive molester." [29] Similarly, John Conklin found it necessary to distinguish four types of robbery offenders: professional, opportunist, addict, and alcoholic robbers.[30]

In still another typology, Daniel Glaser identified ten criminal patterns, including such types as "adolescent recapitulators," "subcultural assaulters," "vocational predators," and "addicted performers." [31] Although

---

[27] Peter G. Garabedian, "Social Roles in a Correctional Community," *Journal of Criminal Law, Criminology and Police Science,* 55 (September 1964):338–47.

[28] Julian B. Roebuck, *Criminal Typology* (Springfield, Ill.: Charles C. Thomas 1966).

[29] Charles H. McCaghy, "Child Molesters: A Study of Their Careers as Deviants." in Marshall B. Clinard and Richard Quinney, eds., *Criminal Behavior Systems,* 1st ed. (New York: Holt, Rinehart and Winston, 1967), pp. 75–88.

[30] John E. Conklin, *Robbery and the Criminal Justice System* (Philadelphia: Lippincott, 1972), pp. 59–78.

[31] Daniel Glaser, *Adult Crime and Social Policy* (Englewood Cliffs, N.J.: Prentice-Hall, 1972). Glaser's book, as well as Conklin's, was published after 1970, while this chapter deals with criminological developments only through 1970. However, these works are included here because they belong to a long-standing criminological tradition. Inclusion of these works reinforces a point made early in this book, namely that the periods identified here are somewhat arbitrary.

Glaser drew on research findings, his typological scheme was relatively speculative in character. More important, Glaser did not specify the identifying characteristics of each offender type in sufficient detail for the typology to be applied with much precision to actual lawbreakers. It is doubtful that other observers would be able to sort offenders reliably into Glaser's categories. While the notions of adolescent recapitulation, crisis vacillation, and so on, employed by Glaser make some intuitive sense, they were not explicitly spelled out in such a way that they can be observed among real-life offenders.

The thrust of these examples is that general and abstract typologies that identify a relatively small number of offender types can be formulated. At the same time, these abstract typologies have been deficient in terms of clarity or explicitness, and/or they have involved too few types, so that a markedly increased number of categories has been required in order to capture the variability among actual offenders.[32]

Role-Career Typologies

I have been involved in one of the more ambitious typological ventures. In that effort, the characteristics that identify particular offender types were explicitly spelled out, making the typology amenable to research scrutiny.

The key feature of this typological framework is the stress on role careers as an attempt to specify criminal behavior patterns that describe the lawbreaking careers of individuals. It makes little sense to speak of types such as "receivers of stolen property" or "second-degree burglars," because many lawbreakers engage in a number of different crimes. But, by using general rather than specific offenses, it may be possible to identify patterns, such as "semiprofessional property offenders," which would be made up of individuals who specialize in a collection of related predatory acts. This role-career perspective also assumes that there are sequential stages through which deviants proceed, that a career is made up of related episodes of behavior that unfold over time.

The typologies of delinquents and criminals revolve around five defining dimensions or definitional variables. Types have been identified in terms of various configurations of characteristics hypothesized to be exhibited by offenders, within the categories of offense behavior, interactional setting, self-concept, attitudes, and role career. The last category

---

[32] This point is illustrated in the San Francisco Project, in which the present offenses of probationers, along with their ages, prior record of offenses, and their scores on the California Personality Inventory So (Socialization) Scale were trichotomized, yielding 54 possible types of probationers! See William P. Adams, Paul M. Chandler, and M. G. Neithercutt, "The San Francisco Project: A Critique," *Federal Probation*, 35 (December 1971):45–53.

is one in which the overall career pattern of lawbreaking activity is described. The typologies offer descriptions of such types as the "naïve check forger," in which the forgery behavior of the person is described, along with the interactional setting in which it occurs. The check forger is also described in terms of self-concept and crime-related attitudes, as are the other types.

Nine delinquent role careers and 21 adult offender types have been developed out of these assumptions and the existing data on criminality and delinquency.[33] The criminal typology includes "naïve check forgers," "semiprofessional property offenders," "white-collar criminals," certain sex offender types, and a number of other hypothesized types.

How valid are these typologies? How closely do actual offenders fit within the types? How comprehensive are the typologies? Attempts to sort actual offenders according to some typological scheme have been quite rare, but some efforts to do so have been made with the role-career scheme. One of the more telling of these took place in a California county probation department.[34] In that study, a small group of probation officers attempted to classify probationers, sorting them into the types of adult and juvenile offenders described in Changing the Lawbreaker, as well as into two types added by the officers, "alcoholic delinquents" and "marijuana hippies." The probation officers employed abridged profiles or typological descriptions of offenders, with groups of three probation officers acting as independent judges who read case files of actual probationers in order to determine to which type, if any, the person belonged. A specific probationer was assigned to a particular offender category if at least two judges agreed.

Slightly less than half of the probationers fell within a type in the typologies, even when relatively relaxed classificatory rules were used. Subsequently, Clayton Hartjen sifted through the records of the probationers who had not been assigned to the typology. Using offense records, he managed to place most of these individuals into seven types, such as "nonsupport offenders" or "petty property offenders." However, those ad hoc types did not differ markedly from each other in terms of commitment to deviance, social backgrounds, or other variables. Hartjen concluded that most of these offenders were involved in "folk crime," which is Laurence Ross's term for forms of lawbreaking arising out of laws introduced to solve problems related to the increased complexity of modern society.[35] Such offenses usually draw little public attention and involve

---

[33] Gibbons, Changing the Lawbreaker; and Society, Crime, and Criminal Careers.
[34] Clayton A. Hartjen and Don C. Gibbons, "An Empirical Investigation of a Criminal Typology," Sociology and Social Research, 54 (October 1969):56–62.
[35] H. Laurence Ross, "Traffic Law Violation: A Folk Crime," Social Problems, 9 (Winter 1961):231–41.

little social stigma. People of relatively high status often engage in them, and offenders are frequently dealt with in a variety of administrative ways.

James McKenna also carried out an empirical investigation of the role-career criminal typology.[36] Inmates in a state correctional institution were classified into offender types through examination of their arrest records, with 87 percent of the offenders being placed in twelve of fifteen offender types. McKenna then sought to determine whether the combinations of characteristics said to differentiate role-career incumbents actually occurred among offenders. Only in one of the twelve types did the definitional dimension pattern emerge, while all the other types showed basic disagreements between the typological claims and the empirical observations. In other words, prisoners who had been assigned to one or another type in terms of offense patterns often exhibited a good deal of similarity to members of other offense types in terms of attitudes, self-concept patterns, and interactional setting. Accordingly, McKenna's findings indicated that many real-life offenders cannot be assigned with much precision to the categories of the role-career typology.

Role-Career Typologies: An Assessment

A good deal of skepticism about the ultimate payoff to be expected from typological ventures is in order. The research surveyed in this chapter indicates that no comprehensive offender typology yet exists. Furthermore, it is apparent that existing typologies of offenders are far from precise. The degree of patterning of offense behavior or other definitional configurations assumed in typologies appears not to exist in the real world of criminality.

These remarks come down to one central conclusion: The notion of identifiable careers in criminality is too clinical to be used as an hypothesis about behavior. The language of "types," "syndromes," "behavioral roles," and the like is inappropriate for many criminals. Instead, many lawbreakers exhibit relatively unique combinations of criminal conduct and attitudinal patterns, or at least they can only be grouped into some very general categories or types with considerable difficulty.

Criminological attention has been drawn in recent years to theorizing in the sociological field of deviance, particularly to the writings of labeling theorists. Labeling perspectives are examined in some detail in Chapter 6. Sociologists such as Edwin Lemert have argued that many deviants, including criminals and delinquents, drift into misbehavior or that their conduct is a risk-taking response to value conflicts in society.[37] The

[36] James J. McKenna, *An Empirical Testing of a Typology of Adult Criminal Behavior.* Doctoral dissertation, University of Notre Dame, 1972.
[37] Edwin M. Lenert, *Human Deviance, Social Problems, and Social Control,* 2nd ed. (Englewood Cliffs, N.J.: Prentice-Hall, 1972).

conventional image of the deviant which holds that his or her conduct is the consequence of internalized motives which differentiate him or her from non-lawbreakers is absent from the writings of labeling theorists. They have emphasized the importance of societal reactions, turning points, career contingencies, and the like, arguing that individual careers in deviance do not usually follow some kind of straight line progression of behavioral deviation. Instead, variability rather than regularity may be most characteristic of offenders; lawbreakers engage in flirtations with criminality; individuals get drawn into misconduct for a variety of reasons and many of them manage to withdraw from deviance. In all of this, labeling theorists have argued that deviant careers do not emerge from "within the skin" of actors, so to speak, so much as they develop in response to various contingent events that occur to them along the way, including experiences within correctional organizations.

Criminological arguments which have been informed by labeling perspectives and which stress the varied and twisting routes taken by lawbreakers as their careers in criminality unfold have been constructed in recent years. For example, one of these alternative views of etiology drew attention to "risk-taking" processes and situational pressures in criminality, involving persons who are not specifically motivated to engage in lawbreaking.[38] According to that view, many individuals become caught up in illegal activities due to situational influences which push them into nonconformity and exhibit no special criminal or antisocial motivational patterns that set them apart from nonoffenders. Other persons sometimes embark upon a line of conduct which involves some risk of turning into criminal activity, depending upon how that set of behavioral events unfolds. Assaults and homicides which arise out of interactional processes among a group of alcohol drinkers serve as relevant examples, as does naïve check forgery.[39]

In conclusion, the grand ambitions entertained for theoretically relevant typologies may be illusory, in that the regularity and patterning assumed to characterize lawbreaking may not exist. The real world may stubbornly resist efforts to simplify it by means of offender typologies.[40]

---

[38] Don C. Gibbons, "Observations on the Study of Crime Causation," *American Journal of Sociology,* 77 (September 1971):262–78.

[39] For some commentary on risk-taking elements in check forgery, see Lemert, *Human Deviance,* pp. 39–40.

[40] Generalizations might be sought which would describe the ways in which norm violators, social audiences, and agents of organizations such as prisons or probation agencies are all bound together in interactional patterns which result in various outcomes on the part of the deviant. John Irwin's account of the career of the felon is an example of this kind of analysis. See John Irwin, *The Felon* (Englewood Cliffs, N.J.: Prentice-Hall, 1970).

DELINQUENT SUBCULTURES AND CRIMINOLOGICAL THEORY

Although gang delinquency has been a subject of persistent interest to sociologists since the 1930s, relatively little theoretical or empirical work was carried out concerning gang misconduct in the period between the Chicago investigationsof Shaw and McKay and the 1950s.[41] Most sociologists remained content with the delinquency area studies and failed to raise new questions about gangs and their activities. Thus, the publication of Albert Cohen's *Delinquent Boys* in 1955 was a major criminological event, for it triggered an impressive resurgence of attention to delinquent gang behavior, in the form of both theoretical expositions and research endeavors.

Cohen and Delinquent Subcultures

An interesting indicator of continuity in the American criminological tradition is found in the fact that the major theoretical development in the 1950s was produced by a former student of Edwin Sutherland. In *Delinquent Boys,* Cohen indicated his interest in accounting for the emergence of delinquent subcultures in working-class neighborhoods of American cities.[42] He pointed out that earlier observers of delinquency in inner-city areas had taken the gang for granted. They had focused their attention on the processes through which individual boys came to take on delinquent values and the delinquent tradition, but did not study the gangs themselves.

According to Cohen, a delinquent subculture is "a way of life that has somehow become traditional among certain groups in American society. These groups are the boy's gangs that flourish most conspicuously in the 'delinquency neighborhoods' of our larger American cities" (p. 13). The delinquent subculture centers about nonutilitarian, malicious, and negativistic behavior. That is, Cohen argued that much of the stealing and other behavior of gang offenders is motivated by interest other than rational utilitarian gain, that gang delinquents, steal "for the hell of it." The malicious and negativistic nature of gang behavior is revealed most commonly in observations that gang members reap enjoyment from the discomfort they cause others and take pride in reputations they have acquired for meanness (pp. 25–30). Cohen also described subcultural de-

---

[41] Most of this section is an abridged version of Gibbons, *Delinquent Behavior,* pp. 114–39.

[42] On the issue of the social-class distribution of subcultural gang delinquency, Cohen argued: "It is our conclusion, by no means novel or startling, that juvenile delinquency and the delinquent subculture in particular are overwhelmingly concentrated in the male, working-class sector of the juvenile population" (p. 37).

93

viance in terms of *short-run hedonism,* as indicated by gang members' lack of long-term goals or planning. Finally, *group autonomy* is a hallmark of subcultural delinquency, and delinquent gangs were said to be socially integrated collectivities (pp. 30–32).

Why did the delinquent subculture develop among lower-class boys? Cohen concluded that working-class delinquency represented a social movement that arose as a solution to shared problems of low status among working-class youths. In Cohen's words, "the crucial condition for the emergence of new cultural forms is the existence, *in effective interaction with one another, of a number of actors with similar problems of adjustment"* (p. 59).

The shared problems of low status or esteem among gang boys stem from their placement in the social order. According to Cohen, working-class boys experienced status threats when they were evaluated by a middle-class measuring rod, by a set of social expectations regarding the characteristics of "good boys." These expectations center on such traits as ambition, individual responsibility, talent, asceticism, rationality, courtesy, and control of physical aggression (pp. 84–93). The exemplary youth, in the eyes of important members of the middle class such as school teachers, exhibits most or all of these social characteristics. But the working-class boy has been inadequately socialized, for he has acquired an attenuated understanding of the middle-class ethic and is deficient in the ability to conform to these notions of proper behavior. Hence, he finds himself at a disadvantage in classrooms and other social arenas as he competes with middle-class peers for recognition by adults. As Cohen has written,

> The delinquent subculture, we suggest, is a way of dealing with the problems of adjustment we have described. These problems are chiefly status problems: Certain children are denied status in the respectable society because they cannot meet the criteria of the respectable status system. The delinquent subculture deals with these problems by providing criteria of status which these children *can* meet (p. 121).

These boys who withdraw from situations of social hurt, such as the school, find their way into the subculture of the gang, which provides them with a social setting in which to become insulated against assaults on their self-esteem.

Cohen's portrayal of gang delinquency was based on a relatively sparse foundation of empirical evidence. Not surprisingly, a number of critics have drawn attention to alleged errors in his initial formulation. Gresham Sykes and David Matza, for example, have advanced some remarks about "techniques of neutralization," claiming that delinquents are at least partially committed to the dominant social order, experience guilt or shame when they engage in deviant acts, and contrive justifications in advance of their acts of lawbreaking in order to ward off guilt feelings.

These techniques of neutralization free potential delinquents from moral restraints, making it possible for them to flirt with delinquency.[43] Sykes and Matza enumerated some of these techniques of neutralization, which include denial of responsibility for one's behavior, denial of injury, and condemnation of one's condemners. However, a close reading of Cohen's theory indicates that he was not inattentive to the delinquent boy's sensitivity to middle-class ethical standards. The Sykes and Matza argument is thus compatible with Cohen's.

One of the most systematic evaluations of Cohen's theory was produced by John Kitsuse and David Dietrick.[44] They charged that Cohen failed to make a compelling case for the argument that working-class boys care about how the middle class views them. Kitsuse and Dietrick maintained that lower-class boys are not oriented to status in middle-class systems. Accordingly, in their view, Cohen's notion of the delinquent subculture as a reaction formation is seriously undermined. These critics also contended that Cohen's description of delinquent subcultures is faulty because real-life delinquents are more businesslike and less deliberately malicious toward respectable people than Cohen's theory suggests. Finally, they claimed that the theory is ambiguous on the issue of how subcultures are maintained once they come into existence. Kitsuse and Dietrick proposed an alternative formulation, and argued that the original motives of delinquent actors for participation in gangs are varied. Regardless of their original motive for joining a gang, once boys get involved in the subculture, hostile responses by respectable citizens, correctional agents, and others are directed at them. These negative reactions lead the offenders to reject their rejectors through further deviant conduct. "The delinquent subculture persists because, once established, it creates for those who participate in it, the very problems which were the bases for its emergence." [45]

David Bordua also raised questions about several theories of subcultural delinquency, including the one by Cohen.[46] Bordua noted that, in most of these theories, the image put forth of the delinquent is markedly

---

[43] Gresham M. Sykes and David Matza, "Techniques of Neutralization: A Theory of Delinquency," *American Sociological Review*, 22 (December 1957):664–70. A more detailed discussion of techniques of neutralization and processes of "drift," in which juveniles have become freed from moral bonds and available as recruits into delinquency, appears in David Matza, *Delinquency and Drift* (New York: Wiley, 1964).

[44] John I. Kitsuse and David C. Dietrick, "Delinquent Boys: A Critique," *American Sociological Review*, 24 (April 1959):208–15.

[45] *Ibid.*, p. 215.

[46] David J. Bordua, *Sociological Theories and Their Implications for Juvenile Delinquency*, Children's Bureau, Juvenile Delinquency, Facts and Facets, No. 2 (Washington, D.C.: U. S. Government Printing Office, 1960); "Delinquent Subcultures: Sociological Interpretations of Gang Delinquency," *Annals of the American Academy of Political and Social Science*, 338 (November 1961):119–36; "Some Comments on Theories of Group Delinquency," *Sociological Inquiry*, 32 (Spring 1962):245–60.

different from that advanced by Thrasher many years earlier.[47] Thrasher's boys found delinquency attractive because it was fun. The offenders described by contemporary theorists, on the other hand, are driven by stresses and anxieties emanating from a prejudicial and harsh social environment. In addition, Bordua contended that Cohen's theory placed undue emphasis on the nonutilitarian character of gang misconduct. Bordua also suggested that Cohen, as well as a number of other subcultural theorists, failed to give sufficient weight to family, ethnic, and certain other social variables in delinquency causation. He pointed out that class-linked family patterns may be the source of much of the stress experienced by delinquent boys. The relatively loosely structured parent-child relationships, absentee fathers, and other common characteristics of many working-class families may also have much to do with the development of problems and, subsequently, delinquency in lower-class boys.[48]

Delinquency and Opportunity Structures

Cohen's theory provoked some full-scale alternative formulations. One of the most important of these competing arguments was contained in Richard Cloward and Lloyd Ohlin's *Delinquency and Opportunity*.[49] For Cloward and Ohlin, the raw material for delinquent gangs consisted of boys concerned about economic injustice rather than with middle-class

---

[47] Frederick M. Thrasher, *The Gang,* abridged and with a new introduction by James F. Short, Jr. (Chicago: University of Chicago Press, 1963).

[48] Bordua, "Some Comments on Theories of Group Delinquency," pp. 249–56. See Cohen and Short, "Research on Delinquent Subcultures," for a response to a number of these criticisms. They agreed that there is more than one form of working-class gang delinquency and suggested that lower-class subcultures include the parent-male subculture, the conflict-oriented subculture, the drug addict subculture, and a subculture oriented around semiprofessional theft. The characteristics of the parent-male subculture were enumerated in *Delinquent Boys.* Cohen and Short employed the label of "parent subculture" in order to suggest that other gang forms are specialized offshoots from it, thus "it is probably the most common variety in this country—indeed, it might be called the 'garden variety' of delinquent subculture." (p. 24).

In endeavoring to account for the development of these different subcultural forms in individual neighborhoods, Cohen and Short laid much stress upon an earlier paper by Solomon Kobrin. See Solomon Kobrin, "The Conflict of Values in Delinquency Areas," *American Sociological Review,* 16 (October 1951):653–61. Kobrin pointed out that areas vary in the extent to which conventional and criminal value systems are mutually integrated, so that in some communities criminality is meshed with the local social structure; adult criminals are prestigious citizens and are active in local businesses, fraternal organizations, politics, and so on. They serve as local "heroes" or role models for juvenile apprentice criminals. In other neighborhoods, criminality is individualistic, uncontrolled, and alien to the conventional social organization.

[49] Richard A. Cloward and Lloyd E. Ohlin, *Delinquency and Opportunity* (New York: Free Press, 1960).

status. "It is our view that many discontented lower-class youth do not wish to adopt a middle-class way of life or to disrupt their present associations and negotiate passage into middle-class groups. The solution they seek entails the acquisition of higher position in terms of lower-class rather than middle-class criteria" (p. 92).

Cloward and Ohlin argued that working-class subcultures arose in the following way: Lower-class boys share a common American value commitment to success, measured largely in material terms. But these youths are at a competitive disadvantage compared to their middle-class counterparts. Either they do not have access to legitimate or conventional means to reach these success goals, or, if they do have objective opportunities for achievement, they perceive their chances of success as circumscribed. Accordingly, for many of them, a severe disjunction exists between aspiration levels and expectations, or between what they want out of life and what they anticipate they will receive. Pressures to engage in deviant behavior are generated by this goals-means discrepancy (pp. 77–143).

The particular adaptation assumed by working-class youths is heavily influenced by the opportunity structures for deviant behavior. Cloward and Ohlin argued that some lower-class areas are characterized by integration of criminalistic and conformist patterns of social organization, while others are lacking in stable criminalistic networks. In the well-organized neighborhoods, criminalistic gang subcultures develop in which boys are involved in instrumental acts of theft and in careers that often lead them into adult criminal behavior. In areas lacking in criminalistic traditions, gang delinquency takes the form of conflict subcultural behavior in which fighting predominates. Finally, some boys who are failures in both the legitimate and illegitimate opportunity structures disengage themselves from the competitive struggle and withdraw into the retreatist subculture of the drug addict.

Although initial reactions to Cloward and Ohlin's argument were extremely favorable, a series of critical comments were later advanced about their theory.[50] For one, the definition of subcultures employed by Cloward and Ohlin limits the applicability of their theory to a minority of all delinquents. Critics contended that much gang delinquency in working-class areas is more spontaneous and unstructured than acknowledged by Cloward and Ohlin. One critic termed many of these deviant collectives "near groups," in order to highlight their shifting membership, ambiguous

[50] Bordua, "Delinquent Subcultures," "Some Comments on Theories of Group Delinquency"; David Matza, review of *Delinquency and Opportunity, American Journal of Sociology,* 60 (May 1961):631–33; Clarence C. Schrag, *"Delinquency and Opportunity:* Analysis of a Theory," *Sociology and Social Research,* 46 (January 1962):167–75.

role definitions, lack of group identifications, and other characteristics.[51] Bordua and others who assessed the opportunity structure formulation also raised questions about its failure to deal systematically with variations in working-class family structures, racial factors, and other background variations among different working-class groups.[52] The major thrust of this commentary has been that real-life social structure in a society such as the United States is exceedingly complex, involving interwoven layers of social variables that are combined in varied ways and that produce behavioral outcomes such as delinquency. In short, theories of gang delinquency are not yet rich enough or elaborate enough to encompass the varieties of real-life experience.

Lower-Class Focal Concerns and Delinquency

Walter Miller advanced another explanation of gang behavior which is markedly at variance with that of Cohen.[53] For Miller, the structure of lower-class life plays the dominant role in gang misconduct. Delinquency is the product of long-established, durable traditions of lower-class life, rather than the result of responses to conflicts with middle-class values.

Miller contended that lower-class culture is most frequently located in the world of rural migrants to urban areas, for example, American Indians, Puerto Ricans, and urban blacks. These people are at the bottom of the social heap and have little prospect of ascending it. The culture of this segment of the population can be described by a series of structural elements peculiar to it and by a complex of "focal concerns."[54]

According to Miller, one of the major structural patterns in lower-class society is the female-based household, in which the stability of the family unit is provided by one or more adult females. The mother and older daughters play multiple roles, providing economic support for the family unit as well as discharging the domestic and affectional duties. This kind of family structure results from the practice of serial monogamy, in

---

[51] Lewis Yablonsky, "The Delinquent Gang as a Near-Group," *Social Problems,* 7 (Fall 1959):108–17.

[52] Bordua, "Some Comments on Theories of Group Delinquency," pp. 250–52.

[53] Walter B. Miller, "Lower Class Culture as a Generating Milieu of Gang Delinquency." *Journal of Social Issues,* 14, No. 8 (1958):5–19; "Implications of Lower Class Culture for Social Work," *Social Service Review,* 33 (September 1959):219–36; "Preventive Work with Street Corner Gangs: Boston Delinquency Project," *Annals of the American Academy of Political and Social Science,* 322 (March 1959):97–106; "The Impact of a Total-Community Delinquency Control Project," *Social Problems,* 10 (Fall 1962):168–91; William C. Kvaraceus and Miller, *Delinquent Behavior: Culture and the Individual* (Washington, D.C.: National Education Association, 1959).

[54] Miller, "Lower Class Culture as a Generating Milieu of Gang Delinquency."

which women find themselves involved in repetitive sequences of mate-finding, legal or common-law marriage, and divorce or desertion by the male. Thus, the household may be made up of a number of children, each of whom has the same mother but a different father.

For the boy who grows up in the female-dominated family, life is fraught with anxieties about sex-role identification. The young male is bombarded from all sides by verbal assertions that "men are no damn good" and feels he must become a "real man" as quickly as possible. The male adolescent peer group, territorially located on city streets, provides the training ground and milieu in which lower-class males seek a sense of maleness, status, and belonging.

These elements, along with the pervasive sense of material and social deprivation common to lower-class members, result in life patterns and experiences organized around focal concerns. Focal concerns or values represent a series of broad themes that condition the specific acts of lower-class people. The focal concerns of lower-class society include trouble, toughness, smartness, excitement, fate, and autonomy. "Trouble" refers to an interest in avoiding entanglements with the police, social welfare agencies, and similar bodies, while "toughness" denotes a concern for continued demonstrations of bravery, daring, and other traits that show that one is not feminine or "soft." "Smartness" is a label for the ability to dupe or outwit others, live by one's wits, and earn a livelihood through a "hustle." Miller identified "excitement" as a generic concern for seeking out weekend activities to disrupt the monotony of weekday routine jobs, and "fate" has to do with the feeling that lower-class citizens have that their lives are ruled by forces over which they have little control, that luck plays a major part in their life chances. Finally, "autonomy" refers to avoidance of control or domination by others.

These structural elements and focal concerns combine in several ways to produce criminality. Those who respond to some of these focal concerns automatically violate the law through their behavior. When faced with a choice of lines of conduct, they select a deviant form of activity as the most attractive. Miller's core argument was that to be lower-class in contemporary American society is to be in a social situation that contains a variety of direct influences toward deviant conduct, one form of which is juvenile delinquency.

Critics of Miller's notions have noted that he failed to account for the varieties of gang delinquency posited by other observers.[55] A second quarrel is over Miller's failure to spell out the detailed variations that can be observed in patterns of lower-class culture. Specifically, the picture of serial monogamy and female-based households may be most accurate for

[55] Bordua, "Some Comments on Theories of Group Delinquency" and "Delinquent Subcultures."

blacks, but may be less so for other low-income, disadvantaged groups. A third dispute centers about the danger of tautology in the focal concerns used to account for delinquent conduct. Miller was not always careful to distinguish between observations about these interests and evidence of the behavior they are designed to explain. Finally, Bordua observed that Miller did not effectively refute Cohen's contention that working-class boys are sensitive to middle-class standards.[56] In Bordua's view, it is possible that Cohen and Miller are both partially correct. Perhaps many lower-class boys do not initially internalize middle-class values as a part of their socialization, but when they get into schools and other competitive situations, these status-measuring standards are forced upon them. These experiences may then alienate lower-class boys, driving them into involvement in delinquent subcultures.[57]

Some Other Perspectives

The three subcultural formulations by Cohen, Cloward and Ohlin, and Miller are the best-known and most influential theories regarding working-class delinquency. But other arguments were also constructed during this period. Herbert Bloch and Arthur Niederhoffer claimed that a cross-cultural perspective on youth behavior would correct the ethnocentric bias in Cohen's theory.[58] Bloch and Niederhoffer contended that adolescent crises about the transition from childhood to adulthood occur in all societies and that ganging is the universal response to these problems. In this sense, lower-class delinquent gangs have much in common with middle-class ones, and they, in turn, share many ingredients with peer collectivities in other lands.

Bloch and Niederhoffer made a good deal of sense when commenting on structural similarities among adolescent groups in various locales. However, their thesis was flawed by anthropological observations of questionable accuracy, as well as by highly suspect assertions regarding American society, such as the claim that class or status differentials are

---

[56] Bordua, "Delinquent Subcultures," pp. 129–30.

[57] Another effort to reconcile these discrepant views on lower-class values can be found in Hyman Rodman, "The Lower-Class Value Stretch," *Social Forces,* 42 (December 1963):205–15. Rodman argued that lower-class people have a wider range of values than others within the society. They share general societal values with members of other classes, but, additionally, they stretch these values or develop alternative ones that help them to adjust to their deprived circumstances. See also Herbert H. Hyman, "The Value Systems of Different Classes: A Social Psychological Contribution to the Analysis of Stratification," in Reinhard Bendix and Seymour M. Lipset, eds., *Class, Status and Power* (New York: Free Press, 1953), pp. 426-42.

[58] Herbert A. Bloch and Arthur Niederhoffer, *The Gang* (New York: Philosophical Library, 1958).

disappearing in this country.[59] Most important, while they raised some challenges to parts of Cohen's description of gang behavior, the cornerstone of his argument remains unchallenged: that serious, repetitive, organized, subcultural delinquency is a working-class phenomenon in the United States, qualitatively different from peer behavior in other strata or in most other cultures.

Lewis Yablonsky's account of gang delinquency held that the central figures in these gangs were sociopaths, socially deficient boys who could not manage the social struggle as adequately as other lower-class youths, but who found in the gang a social structure in which they could survive.[60] Yablonsky's critics charged that he offered little evidence for the sociopathy hypothesis independent of the aggressive delinquency it is supposed to explain.[61]

One final contribution was that of Matza and Sykes, which stressed the role of "subterranean values" in delinquency.[62] Matza and Sykes noted that the view of middle-class culture that emphasizes ascetic devotion to thrift, hard labor at a work task defined as a calling, and so on, is one-sided. There are other respectable but subterranean or unpublicized values to which large numbers of conventional citizens respond, such as pursuit of hedonistic fun or tolerance for certain kinds of aggression and violence. Thus the delinquent's search for "kicks," his disdain for work, desire for the "big score," and posture of aggressive toughness make him an exaggerated and immature version of many middle-class people. These ideas serve as a reminder that delinquency may have considerable positive appeal to youngsters at all class levels, including those in the working class, who for one reason or another are indifferent to or alienated from schools, adult role preparation, and so forth.

Delinquency Theories and Research Evidence

The half-dozen or so years following the publication of Cohen's book were characterized by an explosion of theoretical speculation, supported by only thin strands of empirical evidence. However, research activity eventually overtook this theorizing, so that by 1970 a rather massive, but also confusing, body of research findings on gang delinquency had

---

[59] *Ibid.*, p. 175. One study that reported evidence counter to Bloch and Niederhoffer's argument is Nicholas A. Reuterman, Mary J. Love, and Fred Fiedler, "A Partial Evaluation of Bloch and Niederhoffer's Theory," *Criminology*, 10 (February 1973):415–26.

[60] Lewis Yablonsky, *The Violent Gang* (New York: Macmillan, 1962).

[61] Solomon Kobrin, Review of *The Violent Gang, American Sociological Review*, 28 (April 1963):316–17.

[62] David Matza and Gresham M. Sykes, "Juvenile Delinquency and Subterranean Values," *American Sociological Review*, 26 (October 1961):712–19; Matza, *Delinquency and Drift.*

been produced. Much of this evidence seemed to indicate that none of the theoretical perspectives we have looked at were entirely accurate. These findings demonstrated that the real world of gang activity is richer and more diverse than the views captured in sociological theories. Although this book is not the appropriate place for an examination and evaluation of all this research material, some attention needs to be given to a sample of it before passing on to other theoretical issues.[63]

DIMENSIONS OF GANG BEHAVIOR. An initial question for research is: What do delinquent gang members do in the way of lawbreaking? Is subcultural deviance patterned in the ways suggested by Cohen and Short and by Cloward and Ohlin? Gerald Robin, conducting an investigation in Philadelphia, studied the official and unofficial police records of over 700 black male members of 27 gangs.[64] Most of these youths showed progressive movement toward deviant acts of increasing seriousness, and, in many cases, these culminated in adult criminal careers. One-fourth of all these delinquencies were property oriented, 37 percent were general disorderly conduct, and 17 percent were violent acts directed at other people. About two thirds of the boys had engaged in at least one offense involving physical violence. Robin interpreted this finding as support for Cloward and Ohlin's claims concerning the existence of a conflict subculture in delinquency.[65]

---

[63] This research evidence is reviewed in greater detail in Gibbons, *Delinquent Behavior*, pp. 125–40. Several collections of research on delinquent subcultures are available, including James F. Short, Jr., ed., *Gang Delinquency and Delinquent Subcultures* (New York: Harper & Row, 1968); *Delinquency, Crime and Society;* Malcolm W. Klein, ed., *Juvenile Gangs in Context: Theory, Research and Action* (Englewood Cliffs, N.J.: Prentice-Hall, 1967). See Klein's introduction, pp. 1–12, for a good brief critique of subcultural research. Also see Klein, *Street Gangs and Street Workers* (Englewood Cliffs, N.J.: Prentice-Hall, 1971), pp. 26–43.

[64] Gerald D. Robin, "Gang Member Delinquency: Its Extent, Sequence and Typology," *Journal of Criminal Law, Criminology and Police Science,* 55 (March 1964): 59–69.

[65] Irving Spergel also provided evidence in several separate studies which seemed to confirm the Cloward and Ohlin description of different delinquent subcultures. See Irving Spergel, "Male Young Adult Criminality, Deviant Values, and Differential Opportunities in Two Lower Class Negro Neighborhoods," *Social Problems,* 10 (Winter 1963):237–50; "An Exploratory Research in Delinquent Subcultures," *Social Service Review,* 35 (March 1961):33–47; Spergel, "Deviant Patterns and Opportunities of Pre-Adolescent Negro Boys in Three Chicago Neighborhoods," in Klein, *Juvenile Gangs in Context,* pp. 38–54; Spergel, *Racketville, Slumtown, Haulburg* (Chicago: University of Chicago Press, 1964). Spergel's research in Chicago ("Male Young Adult Criminality") indicated that delinquency and crime tended toward a criminalistic form in a relatively stable black slum area, while in a more unstable neighborhood, criminality was untrammeled and violent in character. However, in another study in these areas ("Deviant Patterns and Opportunities"), Spergel discovered that black preadolescents eight to twelve years of age most frequently admitted assaultive acts, rather than theft, in interviews. The deviants in both areas were involved in assaultive conduct to the same extent, so that the Cloward and Ohlin claim that social milieu influences the form of deviance regardless of age

Another report on the unlawful behavior of gang offenders was done by Walter Miller, who uncovered a body of national data pointing to the predominance of theft behavior among juvenile lawbreakers.[66] He also noted that theft was the dominant form of criminal behavior among the Boston gangs he studied. Acts of theft were two or three times more frequent than assaults. Furthermore, the gang members were involved in an average of four theft-oriented behaviors per month, and about 60 percent of the thefts involved more than one participant.

The richest body of empirical evidence on gang delinquency and gang behavior is found in the Chicago studies of Short and others.[67] One investigation examined the delinquent and nondelinquent conduct of about 600 members of Chicago gangs. Street workers maintained detailed records of the day-to-day activities of these boys, and their findings showed that most of the offenders were involved in a wide range of deviant and non-

---

was *not* confirmed. In his New York investigation (*Racketville*), Spergel indicated that conflict behavior was most common in Slumtown, a disorganized area, while criminalistic delinquency was oriented around theft activities in one relatively integrated neighborhood and around racketeering in another community area which was heavily populated by Italian-Americans. Spergel described Slumtown, the locale of conflict behavior, as an area with a Puerto Rican and black population suffering from extremely low socioeconomic status and the highest index of social breakdown as shown by public assistance caseloads, venereal disease rates, and other indicators of social liabilities. Haulburg, the community area in which theft behavior predominated, was populated by second generation Americans of European stock and stood highest of the three in measures of socioeconomic status, occupational structure, and absence of social breakdown. Racketville was intermediate between the other two on most of these measures of community structure.

Spergel's material provided a footnote to the Cloward and Ohlin framework by suggesting that criminalistic delinquency comes in several varieties. However, it ought to be noted that this study was based upon very small samples of delinquents and nondelinquents. In addition, some of the procedures utilized by Spergel were not entirely clear, so that the results of the investigation must be treated gingerly. Also see Erdman B. Palmore and Phillip E. Hammond, "Interacting Factors in Juvenile Delinquency," *American Sociological Review,* 29 (December 1964): 848–54. This investigation involved youngsters in the Aid to Dependent Children welfare program in Greater New Haven, Connecticut. The records of these youths followed from age 6 to 19, showed that 34 percent had become known to the police or juvenile court. Palmore and Hammond argued that the Cloward and Ohlin theory implies that legitimate and illegitimate opportunities have a multiplicative effect upon youths. Deviance should be particularly frequent among persons who are cut off from legitimate opportunities and who live in circumstances in which illegal activities are numerous. The results agreed with this hypothesis; delinquency was most common among black youngsters who were school failures and who lived in situations of high family and neighborhood deviation. Delinquency rates were markedly lower among white youths who were school successes and who were from stable families and neighborhoods relatively free of criminalistic influences.

[66] Walter B. Miller, "Theft Behavior in City Gangs," in Klein, *Juvenile Gangs in Context,* pp. 25–38.

[67] James F. Short, Jr., "Gang Delinquency and Anomie," in Marshall B. Clinard, ed., *Anomie and Deviant Behavior* (New York: Free Press, 1964), pp. 98–127; Short and Fred L. Strodtbeck, *Group Process and Gang Delinquency* (Chicago: University of Chicago Press, 1965).

deviant acts, rather than in the narrowly focused patterns suggested by Cloward and Ohlin. Short and his colleagues argued that an undifferentiated "parent delinquent subculture" exists from which more specialized deviant groups emerge. In other words, the generic form of gang behavior involves behavioral versatility, and that, from this broad form, cliques and subgroups branch off into more specialized careers in deviant conduct.[68]

In a relatively recent study by Walter Miller, behavioral versatility again emerged as the most appropriate adjective describing delinquent gangs in Philadelphia and Boston.[69] In Philadelphia, most gangs exhibit "a 'versatile' repertoire of activities including the conventional forms of slum youth crime—theft, vandalism, drinking, and drugs—along with less violent kinds of assault." While in Boston, "the most common form of offense is 'creating a disturbance'—a variety of activities such as noisy roughhousing, obscene conversation, impeding public passage, and the like. Next most common are relatively mild forms of the 'violent crimes'— assault and property damage—also in a variety of manifestations, such as stoning passing vehicles, small-scale set-to's, breaking school windows, and so on." [70]

The claim that there are distinct forms of delinquent subcultures in American cities has suffered the fate of many other plausible sociological contentions, namely, it has failed to pass the test of evidence. The studies reviewed briefly here suggest that this portion of the Cloward and Ohlin formulation requires a good deal of qualification.

SOCIAL PROCESSES IN GANG DELINQUENCY. What does the research evidence show regarding the causal arguments on gang delinquency? In one investigation, which involved a large number of juvenile males in the Nashville metropolitan area, Albert Reiss and Albert Rhodes found no simple or uniform linkage between social class position and delinquency.[71] While those boys most frequently encountered in the population of officially designated offenders were from the lower class, delinquency life chances or risks were not the same for all working-class youths. Juvenile misconduct was most common in homogeneous lower-class neighborhoods. Accordingly, Reiss and Rhodes held that the behavior of working-class boys is conditioned by the social class structure and cultural traditions of the community areas in which they live. Youths whose parents are work-

[68] Short, "Gang Delinquency and Anomie," pp. 103–5; Short, Ray A. Tennyson, and Kenneth I. Howard, "Behavior Dimensions of Gang Delinquency," in Short and Strodtbeck, *Group Process and Gang Delinquency*, pp. 77–101.

[69] Walter B. Miller, "Youth Crime in the Urban Crisis Era," in Short, *Delinquency, Crime, and Society*, pp. 91–128.

[70] *Ibid.*, pp. 100, 103.

[71] Albert J. Reiss, Jr., and Albert Lewis Rhodes, "The Distribution of Juvenile Delinquency in the Social Class Structure," *American Sociological Review*, 26 (October 1961):720–32; see also Reiss and Rhodes, "Status Deprivation and Delinquency," *Sociological Quarterly*, 4 (Spring 1963):135–49.

ing-class individuals have a high risk of delinquent involvement if they live in areas populated largely by other lower-class persons, but they are not as likely to become offenders if they live in neighborhoods of mixed or predominantly middle-class socioeconomic status. This state of affairs is implied in the theories of Cohen, Cloward and Ohlin, and Miller, all of whom claimed that one requirement for the emergence of delinquent sub-cultures is the existence of similarly disadvantaged lower-class boys who are in sustained interaction with one another.

The most detailed and comprehensive data regarding position discontent, delinquent norms and values, and related matters are found in the Chicago material of Short and others.[72] These findings showed that delinquents exhibited greater discrepancies between occupational aspirations and expectations than did nondelinquents. More delinquent boys viewed educational opportunities as closed to them than did nonoffenders. But these relationships were far from clear. For example, black youths who showed the greatest divergence between their aspirations and expectations, compared to the achievements of their fathers, were at the same time the least delinquent. Also, contrary to the hypotheses in the Cloward and Ohlin theory, those boys who had high educational aspirations but poor school adjustment or who perceived educational opportunities as relatively closed to them were less delinquent than youths with low educational aspirations.[73] Short interpreted these results in the following way: "A possible explanation of findings reported in this paper lies in the hypothesis that for our boys, high aspirations are indicative of identification with conventional values and institutions. The stake in conformity thus indexed serves to protect the boys from delinquency involvement." [74]

Short and his colleagues also examined the question of value commitments of delinquent boys. They found that, contrary to theories that contend that subcultural delinquents are in rebellion against middle-class ideals, individual offenders verbalized allegiance to such middle-class values as cohesive family life, stable jobs, and conformist behavior.[75] However, the structure of gang life inhibited youngsters from expressing

[72] Short, "Gang Delinquency and Anomie"; Short and Strodtbeck, *Group Process and Gang Delinquency*. Also see Ramon Rivera and James F. Short, Jr., "Occupational Goals: A Comparative Analysis," in Klein, *Juvenile Gangs in Context,* pp. 70–90. Another test of the Cloward and Ohlin formulation regarding the hypothesized disjunction between what boys want and what they expect to get out of life, is found in Spergel, *Racketville, Slumtown, and Haulburg*. Delbert Elliott has also reported on the question of perceptions of legitimate opportunities on the part of delinquent boys. See "Delinquency and Perceived Opportunity," *Sociological Inquiry,* 32 (Spring 1962):216–27.
[73] Short, "Gang Delinquency and Anomie," pp. 105–15.
[74] *Ibid.,* p. 115.
[75] Short, "Gang Delinquency and Anomie," pp. 115–21. For some parallel findings, see Edward Rothstein, "Attributes Related to High School Status: A Comparison of Perceptions of Delinquent and Non-delinquent Boys," *Social Problems,* 10 (Summer 1962):75–83.

these sentiments openly, so that a state of "pluralistic ignorance" prevailed in which gang members saw each other in distorted terms.

Finally, and most important, Short argued that, although gang behavior is not a direct revolt against middle-class values or a protest against generalized invidious rankings of the boys by the wider society, status considerations are nevertheless of major importance in comprehending lower-class delinquency. He contended that delinquent activities are often a response to a host of real or imagined status threats experienced by boys, and that most of these status threats emanate from the more immediate social world, including threats to the boys' status as males, gang members, and so on.[76]

The status-threat reactions of delinquent boys are related to the social liabilities they exhibit in the form of defective role-playing skills and related characteristics. Short and Strodtbeck described gang delinquents as markedly lacking in social assurance and dependent on gang relationships for security and nurturance, a portrayal that stands in marked contrast to the description of gang offenders provided by Cloward and Ohlin.[77]

Subcultural Theory: An Evaluation

What can be concluded from all of this material? Subcultural theories do not fare equally well when confronted with relevant evidence.[78] Most of Cohen's arguments are seriously undermined by data that seem to show that lower-class boys do not reject middle-class values. The one part

[76] Short, "Gang Delinquency and Anomie," pp. 117–27.
[77] Short and Strodtbeck, *Group Process and Gang Delinquency*, pp. 217–47. Also see Robert A. Gordon, "Social Level, Disability, and Gang Interaction," *American Journal of Sociology*, 73 (July 1967):42–62; Scott Briar and Irving Piliavin, "Delinquency, Situational Inducements, and Commitment to Conformity," *Social Problems*, 13 (Summer 1965):35–45. Briar and Piliavin somewhat paralleling Short and Strodtbeck, have argued that delinquents exhibit lack of commitment to conformity, rather than positive motivation to lawbreaking. The relatively attenuated stake in conformity shown by delinquents was traced to certain social class factors and class-related family experiences. Somewhat later, Short again reported that social liability continues to be a hallmark of gang delinquency, standing in the way of efforts to divert gang youths into cooperative, lawabiding pathways. See James F. Short, Jr., "Youth, Gangs, and Society: Micro- and Macrosociological Processes," *Sociological Quarterly*, 15 (Winter 1974):3–19. Finally, Horowitz and Schwartz reported some observations on an inner-city Chicago gang, claiming that these youths are characterized by social marginality but that they don't exhibit the social disability reported by Short. See Ruth Horowitz and Gary Schwartz, "Honor, Normative Ambiguity and Gang Violence," *American Sociological Review*, 39 (April 1974):238:51.
[78] A number of critics of subcultural theories have noted that these formulations are relatively silent on the issue of *within-class* variations in family structure, which may operate as contingencies or intervening variables in delinquency and nondelinquency. Some of the evidence on working-class family patterns and delinquency is reviewed in Gibbons, *Delinquent Behavior*, pp. 132–35.

of his theory that does survive the test of evidence is that of a parent-delinquent subculture. Much of the data on behavioral dimensions of gang delinquency indicates that versatility, rather than specialization, most accurately characterizes gang misconduct. The highly differentiated forms of gang subcultures hypothesized by Cloward and Ohlin are apparently relatively uncommon.

Miller's claims also receive little support from the available evidence. His arguments about female-dominated households and lower-class focal concerns are not buttressed by research findings. The opportunity structure theory of Cloward and Ohlin receives some support from the empirical evidence, which bears out their arguments concerning the role of illegitimate opportunity structures in delinquency. Some findings also lend support to the contentions regarding perceived discrepancies between expectations and aspirations. However, many instances have also been observed of youth whose aspirations and expectations were out of agreement, but who were not involved in delinquency. These data suggest that the operation of intervening variables, such as particular family patterns, must be taken into account if gang delinquency is to be adequately comprehended.

One final set of comments regarding subcultural delinquency theories and research activities has to do with the waxing and waning of interest in this phenomenon. Walter Miller has shown that mass media interest in gang delinquency, particularly in New York City, was intense during the 1950s, but then waned away in the 1960s as the delinquency problem seemed to have vanished.[79] In the 1970s, the mass media rediscovered gangs, and newspapers and other media sources became filled with statements decrying their existence. Miller demonstrated that these fluctuations in attention directed at gangs were largely unrelated to the actual prevalence of youth subcultures. Gangs continued to exist during this entire period, whether or not anyone was noticing them. Miller argued that, in the 1960s, "gangs and their activities were, in effect, driven from media coverage by the advent of far more serious and spectacular forms of domestic violence—massive urban riots, dramatic student demonstrations, armed conflict between police and black militants." [80]

Sociological interest in gang delinquency has taken a somewhat different course. The publication of Cohen's slim volume provoked the development of an extremely prominent concentration of scholarly interest in sociology which persisted through the 1960s. However, there has been a marked attenuation of work on this question in the 1970s, even though there is little reason to argue that delinquent subcultures have ceased to

[79] Miller, "Youth Gangs in the Urban Crisis Era," pp. 95–99.
[80] Ibid., p. 99.

exist. Criminologists have turned to other questions such as deterrence, leaving subcultural delinquency as a played-out theoretical vein.

CONCLUDING COMMENTS

This chapter is the first of two dealing with the development of mainstream criminology from about 1955 to 1970. The themes discussed here were designated as parts of mainstream criminology because they are criminological ideas that are shared by the majority of American criminologists.

What can be said about the reciprocal relationships between sociology and mainstream criminology? How much interplay was there between criminology and sociology, in the way of core concepts that have been borrowed from general sociology and utilized in criminological theories, and contributions from criminological inquiry that have been incorporated into general sociology?

There is little doubt that the numerous studies of unreported or hidden delinquency have played an important role in the development of the labeling or social interaction perspective on deviance, to be discussed in Chapter 6. One of the central themes of that framework is that being labeled or officially tagged as a deviant of one kind or another is often a function of one's biography, rather than of behavior. A frequently encountered hypothesis of labeling theorists is that an individual's chances of being identified publicly as a deviant or of escaping that fate hinge upon such contingencies as social class background, race, sex, and other social characteristics.[81] Sociologists who are enamored of this contention have frequently invoked the research on hidden delinquency in support for it, arguing that delinquents and nondelinquents are equally involved in misbehavior, that delinquent behavior is exceedingly commonplace at all social class levels, and that the juvenile justice system operates in a discriminatory manner, picking out only those youths from socially disadvantaged groups to be dealt with as delinquents. This general argument rests on shaky ground insofar as it depends for support on the hidden delinquency investigations, because as this chapter has indicated, those

[81] Labeling theory is discussed in Don C. Gibbons and Joseph F. Jones, *The Study of Deviance* (Englewood Cliffs, N.J.: Prentice-Hall, 1975), pp. 124–81. Labeling theorists have also voiced a corollary argument, holding that those individuals who have been unfortunate enough to fall into the hands of official social control agents are frequently driven further into deviance by that stigmatizing experience. This claim is one of the plausible hypotheses that has become widely accepted, even though there is little firm evidence supporting it. For a review of the data on the effects of labeling or social reaction experiences upon a variety of kinds of deviants, see *ibid.*, pp. 144–81.

studies do not contain convincing evidence that juveniles from all social class levels are equally involved in lawbreaking.

The typological ventures pursued by criminologists were idiosyncratic activities that held little interest for other sociologists. This is not to say that sociologists have been disinterested in typification processes and the construction of typologies; to the contrary, typological methods of theoretical exploration have been advocated by many of them. Indeed, a number of the giants of the field, including Weber, Durkheim, and Tönnies centered much of their sociological analysis around ideal types and constructed types. These approaches have continued to hold much appeal for a number of sociologists.[82] The principal explanation for the neglect by other sociologists of criminological efforts in the typological genre is probably that most of these have been conceptually and methodologically flawed products that are hardly more sophisticated or useful than the types developed by laymen.[83]

Considerably more mutual enrichment took place between criminology and general sociology in the case of theorizing about subcultural delinquency. On the one hand, Cohen's *Delinquent Boys* was a theoretical collage assembled from a variety of bits and pieces of sociological evidence. It joined the delinquency research of Shaw and McKay and a number of other investigators with some of the classics on social stratification and the sociology of educational institutions such as August Hollingshead's *Elmtown's Youth,* placing them together in a provocative and stimulating pattern of argument.[84] It is probably this aspect of Cohen's book that was most responsible for the widespread applause that it garnered from sociologists. Cohen's argument quickly found its way into the pages of most introductory sociology textbooks that were published in the late 1950s, and it continues to occupy an important place in the sociological literature.

---

[82] A detailed examination of typological methods, including their use by the major figures in European and American sociology, problems of typology construction, and related issues can be found in John C. McKinney, "Sociological Theory and the Process of Typification," in McKinney and Edward A. Tiryakian, eds., *Theoretical Sociology* (Englewood Cliffs, N.J.: Prentice-Hall, 1970), pp. 236–69.

[83] McKinney employed the existential label to designate typifications or behavioral concepts that have grown out of the interactional experiences of humans as they have gone about their daily lives. Existential types are differentiated from constructed types, in that the latter have been developed explicitly by social scientists to aid them in theoretical and empirical inquiry. Lay notions of "crazies," "weirdos," and "kooks" can be offered as cases of existential types, while "residual rulebreaking" stands as a constructed type that is intended to embrace the same phenomena. The notion of residual rule-breaking comes from Thomas J. Scheff, *Being Mentally Ill: A Sociological Theory* (Chicago: Aldine Publishing Co., 1966), pp. 31–54. Concerning the disinterest of other sociologists in the typological ventures of criminologists, it is worth noting that no mention was made in McKinney, *op. cit.* of criminological typologies.

[84] August B. Hollingshead, *Elmtown's Youth* (New York: Wiley, 1949).

Cohen's book contained a chapter outlining a general theory of subcultures that was subsequently employed in his explanation of gang delinquency.[85] That general statement argued that subcultures arise when a number of individuals who are in physical and social proximity and who share common problems of adjustment become engaged in exploratory social gestures that lead to a social invention such as the gang or a religious cult that holds the promise of alleviating their shared discomfort.

These relatively brief observations by Cohen regarding the processes of subculture formation played a significant role in the development of widespread interest in contracultures, countercultures, and subcultures in American society in the years since those remarks first appeared. For example, Cohen's insights can be detected in Milton Yinger's influential paper on contracultures and subcultures that appeared in 1960.[86] In that essay, Yinger indicated that the term "counterculture" is appropriately used "whenever the normative system of a group contains, as a primary element, a theme of conflict with the values of the total society, where personality variables are directly involved in the development and maintenance of the group's values, and whenever its norms can be understood only by reference to the relationship of the group to a surrounding dominant culture."

What accounts for the growing popularity of the counterculture theme in sociology? [87] Much of it is due to the fact that the real world of delinquent gangs, Black Panthers, Hare Krishna followers, Sexual Freedom League members, "rolfing" cultists, and other so-called deviant groups has impinged on sociology and has required the development of concepts that capture some of the major ingredients of these groups and social movements. John Irwin's analysis of emerging "scenes" represents another attempt to get a sociological grasp on some newly emerging alternative life styles in the United States.[88] Counterculture hypotheses also seem called for so that some sociological understanding can be gained concerning the Weatherman faction of SDS (Students for a Democratic Society), the Symbionese Liberation Army, the Red Guerilla Army, the George Jackson Brigade, and a host of other militant, revolutionary groups that have emerged in American society during the past decade or so. In short, the counterculture concept has gained broad support among American sociologists in considerable part because it focuses on a major social trend in this country toward the fracturing of society into myriad component groups,

[85] Cohen, *Delinquent Boys,* pp. 49–72.

[86] J. Milton Yinger, "Contraculture and Subculture," *American Sociological Review,* 25 (October 1960):629.

[87] For a progress review regarding the counterculture concept, see J. Milton Yinger, "Presidential Address: Countercultures and Social Change," *American Sociological Review,* 42 (December 1977):833–53.

[88] John Irwin, *Scenes* (Beverly Hills, Calif.: Sage, 1977).

in which many of the members show attenuated loyalties to societal values.

The thesis that societal fracturing, value pluralism, and growing estrangement between social class groups are emerging as central features of modern American society is one that will reappear in some other recent criminological formulations to be discussed in the remaining pages of this book.

CRIMINOLOGY: 1955–1970, Continued

5

INTRODUCTION

Five criminological issues or theoretical problems consumed much of the interest of criminologists during the 1955–1970 period: hidden delinquency, offender typologies, theories and research on delinquent gangs or subcultures, social control formulations and investigations, and the study of correctional organizations. The first three of these topics were dealt with in the previous chapter, while this one takes up the latter two matters.

But, before embarking on a review of work on social control and correctional organizations, it would be well to reiterate a point made earlier. This book is a survey of the major efforts and accomplishments that have taken place in the criminological enterprise in America since about 1900. In this sense, the book is similar to historical accounts of other social enterprises: It is selective in emphasis rather than encyclopedic in coverage. There are a good many criminological endeavors of some significance that are mentioned only in passing, if at all, in these pages.

Perhaps it would be well to acknowledge some of the mainstream criminological work that is *not* singled out for special mention in this account. For one, the typological formulations of criminologists received some support from a large number of important, independent studies of particular forms of crime and offender patterns. Some of these have already been noted, such as the investigations of white-collar crime and check forgery. Some additional examples would include Marvin Wolfgang's research on criminal homicide, Menachem Amir's study of forcible rape, and Donald Cressey's report on organized crime.[1] A very impressive

---

[1] Marvin E. Wolfgang, *Patterns of Criminal Homicide* (Philadelphia: University of Pennsylvania Press, 1958); Menachem Amir, "Forcible Rape," *Federal Probation,* 31 (March 1967):51–58; and Donald R. Cressey, *Theft of the Nation* (New York: Harper & Row, 1969).

collection of empirical research of this kind has accumulated, providing much of the hard evidence on which contemporary sociological criminology rests.[2]

Although the hidden delinquency investigations and subcultural delinquency endeavors qualify as two of the most notable achievements of criminologists who centered their attention upon juvenile lawbreaking, there were other important contributions that are slighted in this volume. For example, the theories of middle-class delinquency developed by Ralph England and Joseph Scott and Edmund Vaz come quickly to mind, as does Lois DeFleur's comparative study of juvenile offenders in Argentina and the United States.[3] Again, criminologists produced a very impressive supply of empirical evidence on juvenile delinquency during this period.[4]

SOCIAL CONTROL

Social control is a term without which most sociologists would feel conceptually naked, but which, like many other sociological labels, has no standardized meaning or definition. The field of social control was at one time a relatively prominent area of sociological writing and inquiry, as indicated by the once-numerous textbooks and courses dealing with that topic. In more recent decades, however, texts on social control and sociology courses bearing that title have all but disappeared. Although this field of specialization has withered away, the concept of social control has remained alive and is currently one of the major ingredients in the study of deviance and criminality.[5]

Alexander Clark and Jack Gibbs, in their summary of the study of social control, have pointed out that two divergent conceptions of this phenomenon existed side by side.[6] The broad definition of social control

[2] A large sampling of these studies can be found in Don C. Gibbons, *Society, Crime, and Criminal Careers,* 3rd ed. (Englewood Cliffs, N.J.: Prentice-Hall, 1977), pp. 273–463.

[3] Ralph W. England, Jr., "A Theory of Middle Class Juvenile Delinquency," in Edmund W. Vaz, ed., *Middle-Class Juvenile Delinquency* (New York: Harper & Row, 1967), pp. 242–51; Joseph W. Scott and Edmund W. Vaz, "A Perspective on Middle Class Delinquency," in Vaz, *Middle-Class Juvenile Delinquency,* pp. 207–22; and Lois DeFleur, *Delinquency in Argentina—A Study of Cordoba's Youth* (Pullman, Wash.: Washington State University Press, 1970).

[4] Much of this evidence is summarized in Don C. Gibbons, *Delinquent Behavior,* 2nd ed. (Englewood Cliffs, N.J.: Prentice-Hall, 1976), pp. 104–220.

[5] For example, see Nanette J. Davis, *Sociological Constructions of Deviance* (Dubuque, Ia.: Brown, 1975), pp. 192–224; and Edwin M. Lemert, *Human Deviance, Social Problems, and Social Control,* 2nd ed. (Englewood Cliffs, N.J.: Prentice-Hall, 1972), pp. 26–101.

[6] Alexander L. Clark and Jack P. Gibbs, "Social Control: A Reformulation," *Social Problems,* 13 (Spring 1965):399–415. Also see Gibbs, "Social Control, Deterrence, and Perspectives on Social Order," *Social Forces,* 56 (December 1977): 408–23.

included the processes of socialization through which individuals come to internalize norms or "inner controls," as well as myriad influences from the individual's environment which were viewed as "external" or "outer" controls. One example of this broad definition of social control can be found in Kingsley Davis's classic textbook, *Human Society,* in which he specified that internalized norms, including folkways, mores, and law, and the various enforcement mechanisms that have been developed for dealing with norm violators, are all elements of social control.[7] As Clark and Gibbs indicated, the central problem with this broad view is that it is so comprehensive. Virtually everything can be considered to be a form of social control, and thus the study of control becomes coterminous with the study of social behavior.

The narrow version of social control, as identified by Clark and Gibbs, specified that social control involves the means employed by authorized agents of the state, such as police, judges, prison guards, and the like, to secure conformity to formal norms. This definition thus deals exclusively with formalized agents of control and the relatively formalized sanctions employed by those individuals.

Clark and Gibbs did not opt for either of these perspectives. They defined social control as *"social reactions to behavior defined as deviant, including over-conformity to, as well as violations of, norms."* [8] They included informal and nonlegal reactions to deviance as well as formalized responses in their definition, which also encompassed reactions to deviance in small collectivities as well as at the societal level. If one were to follow Clark and Gibb's suggestions, the study of social control would focus on five matters.

1. The norms specifying the appropriate reactions to norm violations.
2. The rules identifying the appropriate people to react to violations, such as laymen, policemen, or psychiatrists.
3. The patterns of reaction that actually take place.
4. The characteristics of those who actually do the reacting.
5. The degree of correspondence between the normative and actual dimensions of control activities.

Although not mentioned by Clark and Gibbs, this list could be expanded to include both the intended and actual effects of reactions on norm violators.

These recommendations did not lead to the resurgence of social control as a specialization within sociology. However, many of the themes that are found in social control arguments have been included in some

[7] Kingsley Davis, *Human Society* (New York: Macmillan, 1948), pp. 52–82.
[8] Clark and Gibbs, "Social Control," p. 401.

relatively recent lines of criminological theorizing. Containment theory, which is a case of old wine in a new bottle, is considered first. Containment theory is an updated version of the old, broad conception of social control which spoke of inner and outer controls. A different brand of social control theory, advocated by Travis Hirschi, emphasizes the psychological and social ties that link individuals to conformity. Finally, another modern variant of social control interests centers on deterrence, that is, the impact of punishment on potential and/or actual lawbreakers.

Containment Theory

Causal theorizing in criminology has tended to be truncated and compartmentalized, rather than holistic in form. Relatively few efforts can be identified in which theorists have tried to deal in a sophisticated and systematic way with the social-structural factors, the situational and interactional forces, and the psychological and biological characteristics of individuals that may combine in particular ways to push people along lawabiding or lawbreaking pathways.[9] However, some of the writings of Walter Reckless represent an effort, albeit unsuccessful, to develop a formulation that includes most of these factors.

Walter Reckless was one of the pioneers of mainstream American criminology, although he ranked a distant second to Sutherland in importance in the development of the field. Like Sutherland, Reckless was a product of the University of Chicago department of sociology and was one of Robert Park's students. His doctoral dissertation, *Vice in Chicago,* was published in 1933.

Reckless's first venture into textbook writing was in 1940, followed by *The Crime Problem* in 1950.[10] The most striking feature of the 1950 work was his frank lack of interest in causation. In the Preface to that text, Reckless indicated that "the discussion of the very dubious causative factors is kept at a minimum. The accent has been placed on how behavior becomes criminal, how it gets officially reported, how liabilities for arrest and imprisonment operate, how regional and area variations happen, how crime gets shaped into careers and business." His preference in that book was for the study of *categoric risks*. At one point, he noted that "crime risks are essentially categoric risks which indicate the differential chances of persons in various sub-categories for getting arrested or

---

[9] Two exceptions to this claim are Juan B. Cortés and Florence M. Gatti, *Delinquency and Crime: A Biopsychosocial Approach* (New York: Seminar Press, 1972); and John M. Martin and Joseph P. Fitzpatrick, *Delinquent Behavior: A Redefinition of the Problem* (New York: Random House, 1964).

[10] Walter C. Reckless, *Vice in Chicago* (Chicago: University of Chicago Press, 1933); *Criminal Behavior* (New York: McGraw-Hill, 1940); and *The Crime Problem* (Englewood Cliffs, N.J.: Prentice-Hall, 1950).

getting admitted to prison" (p. 57). In that same discussion, he conceded that the study of categoric risks or criminal liabilities does assume the operation of causes, but also insisted that the former is not the same as the study of etiology.

In later editions of *The Crime Problem,* Reckless began to modify his stance against causal analysis. Doubtless a major influence in this direction came from the series of studies which he and his associates became involved in. In these studies, samples of boys in Columbus, Ohio, nominated by teachers as "good" boys, unlikely to get into trouble with the law, and "bad" boys, thought to be headed for trouble, were followed over a four-year period in order to see which ones became caught up in juvenile lawbreaking.[11] According to Reckless et al., the findings indicated that the youngsters selected by teachers as "good" boys were well regarded by their mothers and showed positive self-concepts, while the "bad" boys were on poorer terms with their parents and had less positive self-images. Also, a much higher proportion of "bad" boys acquired official records with the police or juvenile court than did the "good" boys. Reckless and Dinitz concluded that a positive self-image can work to insulate boys against involvement in lawbreaking. At one point, they argued that "a good self concept, undoubtedly a product of favorable socialization, veers slum boys away from delinquency, while a poor self concept, a product of unfavorable socialization, gives the slum boy no resistance to deviancy, delinquent companions, or delinquent sub-culture."[12]

Reckless ultimately expanded these notions about insulating factors in delinquency into what he termed "containment theory."[13] This argument bears more than a slight similarity to a formulation offered considerably earlier by Lowell Julliard Carr, who argued that criminality and

[11] Walter C. Reckless, Simon Dinitz, and Ellen Murray, "Self-Concept as an Insulator against Delinquency," *American Sociological Review,* 21 (December 1956): 744–56; Reckless, Dinitz, and Murray, "The 'Good Boy' in a High Delinquency Area," *Journal of Criminal Law, Criminology and Police Science,* 48 (May-June 1957):18–25; Reckless, Dinitz, and Barbara Kay, "The Self-Component in Potential Delinquency and Potential Nondelinquency," *American Sociological Review,* 22 (October 1957):566–70; Dinitz, Kay, and Reckless, "Group Gradients in Delinquency Potential and Achievement Scores of Sixth Graders," *American Journal of Orthopsychiatry,* 28 (July 1958):598–605; Jon Simpson, Dinitz, Kay, and Reckless, "Delinquency Potential of Pre-Adolescents in a High Delinquency Area," *British Journal of Delinquency,* 10 (January 1960):211–15; Frank R. Scarpitti, Murray, Dinitz, and Reckless, "The 'Good Boy' in a High Delinquency Area: Four Years Later," *American Sociological Review,* 25 (August 1960):555–58; Dinitz, Scarpitti, and Reckless, "Delinquency Vulnerability: A Cross Group and Longitudinal Analysis," *American Sociological Review,* 27 (August 1962):515–17; Reckless and Dinitz, "Pioneering with Self-Concept as a Vulnerability Factor in Delinquency," *Journal of Criminal Law, Criminology and Police Science,* 58 (December 1967):515–23.

[12] Reckless and Dinitz, "Pioneering with Self-Concept," p. 517.

[13] Walter C. Reckless, "A New Theory of Delinquency and Crime," *Federal Probation,* 25 (December 1961):42–46; *The Crime Problem,* 5th ed. (Englewood Cliffs, N.J.: Prentice-Hall, 1973).

conformity result from the workings of a variety of internal and social environmental pressures toward lawbreaking, which are either counteracted or encouraged by a number of internal and external control influences.[14]

Containment theory is based on the broad contention that nearly all individuals encounter, in varying degrees of intensity, a variety of environmental pressures and pulls in the direction of lawbreaking and that nearly all individuals have biological and psychological pushes toward deviance in their makeup. Individual behavior, whether deviant or conforming, is heavily influenced by these external pressures and pulls and by the pushes emanating from within the person. However, much of the time these criminalistic influences are controlled or contained by inner and outer containment factors. Reckless's description of these processes indicated that

> containment theory is an explanation of conforming behavior as well as deviancy. It has two reinforcing aspects: an inner control system and an outer control system. . . . Inner containment consists mainly of self-components, such as self-control, good self-concept, ego strength, well-developed superego, high frustration tolerance, high resistance to diversions, high sense of responsibility, goal orientation, ability to find substitute satisfactions, tension-reducing rationalizations, and so on. These are the inner regulators.
>
> Outer containment represents the structural buffer in the person's immediate social world which is able to hold him within bounds. It consists of such items as a presentation of a consistent moral front to the person, institutional reinforcement of his norms, goals, and expectations, the existence of a reasonable set of social expectations, effective supervision and discipline (social controls), provision for reasonable scope of activity (including limits or responsibilities), as well as for alternatives and safety-valves, opportunities for acceptance, identity, and belongingness. Such structural ingredients help the family and other supportive groups contain the individual.[15]

Schrag has pointed out that containment theory contains very few explicit and interconnected propositions from which testable hypotheses might be deduced.[16] The theory exhibits many of the defects that mar many of the other written expositions that pass for theory in sociology. Most of its key terms are vague, and the empirical indicators of these

---

[14] Lowell Julliard Carr, *Delinquency Control*, rev. ed. (New York: Harper & Row, 1950).

[15] Reckless, *The Crime Problem*, 5th ed., pp. 55–56.

[16] Clarence Schrag, *Crime and Justice: American Style* (Rockville, Md.: National Institute of Mental Health, 1971), pp. 82–89.

concepts remain unspecified. Instead of offering specific statements setting out those observable items of information that constitute the component phenomena making up the concepts, Reckless either defined key terms by examples and illustrations or by assertions about how they function to control conduct. Because of these conceptual problems, it would be extremely difficult, if not impossible, to test claims such as the contention that weak inner containment is more likely to result in criminality than is attenuated outer containment.

The research studies of self-concept as an insulator against delinquency, out of which containment theory was generated, have also been subjected to much criticism. As the critics have identified a large number of methodological inadequacies in this research, a presentation of this critical literature would be too lengthy for this book. The general thrust of these evaluations is that these inquiries have not yet demonstrated that a positive self-concept does in fact insulate youngsters against the deleterious influence of bad companions and other criminogenic influences.[17]

Michael Schwartz and Sandra Tangri have presented evidence indicating only moderate correlations between self-conceptions held by youths and their perceptions of the opinions of them held by others. They drew attention to a number of methodological problems in these research studies by Reckless and others, including the use of court records as the sole measure of delinquent involvement. They also argued that many of the questionnaire and test items used as self-concept measures were questionable indicators of self-evaluations. Instead, these items probably tapped perceptions of objective reality on the part of juveniles. For example, questions that ask boys whether they regard the police as corrupt or whether they think they are likely to become involved in delinquency or be taken to juvenile court concern factual matters rather than self-evaluations. Self-concept is useless in explanations of delinquency and nondelinquency if no limits are placed on the scope of the term and if ad hoc decisions are made to designate any attitudinal difference between delinquents and nondelinquents as a self-concept variation.[18]

James Orcutt has offered some of these same criticisms, as well as others that compromise the results reported by Reckless and associates. For example, he commented that their sampling procedures were faulty.

[17] Ibid.; Michael Schwartz and Sandra S. Tangri, "A Note on Self-Concept as an Insulator against Delinquency," American Sociological Review, 30 (December 1965): 922–26; Tangri and Schwartz, "Delinquency Research and the Self-Concept Variable," Journal of Criminal Law, Criminology and Police Science, 58 (June 1967):182–90; James D. Orcutt, "Self-Concept and Insulation against Delinquency: Some Critical Notes," Sociological Quarterly, 2 (Summer 1970):381–90.

[18] Schwartz and Tangri, "A Note on Self-Concept as an Insulator against Delinquency."

Many of the boys presumed to reside in high delinquency risk areas may actually have been from neighborhoods where delinquency was uncommon and hence had little for their self-concept to insulate them against.[19]

Clarence Schrag has provided a succinct summary of many of the logical and methodological problems that are found in these studies by Reckless and his associates. Speaking first of the self-concept items, Schrag remarked that

> such items were initially selected on the basis of their ability to differentiate between students who were nominated by their teachers as "good" boys and "bad" boys. Teacher nominations, it seems, would reflect a boy's status, reputation, and school performance more than his responsiveness to criminogenic pulls and pressures. Indeed, many teachers may not be sufficiently informed about variations in the pressures confronting their pupils to take such things into account in making their nominations. If so, the self concept, as operationalized in these studies, does not necessarily demonstrate any inner containment or insulation against the influence of evil companions and the like. Instead, it reveals the attitudes of boys who have bad companions or have themselves been in trouble as compared with boys who have not.
>
> To argue that boys who have no delinquent companions are insulated against delinquent companions by inner containment is pure tautology, of course. So is the argument that boys who have never been labeled "bad" are insulated against harmful influences. If insulation means resistance against harmful influences, then we need to study boys who have bad companions but have resisted their impact, as compared with boys who have succumbed to such influence, in order to discover what it is that provides the insulation. We cannot get the answer by comparing boys having good companions with those having bad companions.[20]

It would be difficult to deny that containment theory has a ring of plausibility, for it is couched in terms that are familiar to most sociologists and criminologists. Indeed, while Schrag offered the judgment that Reckless's argument had considerable promise and potential, he also contended that it would need a major overhaul if it were to become more than a relatively vague heuristic device for making some sense out of various facts on criminality.[21] This is an evaluation with which it is difficult to disagree.

---

[19] Orcutt, "Self-Concept and Insulation against Delinquency."
[20] Schrag, *Crime and Justice*, p. 88.
[21] *Ibid.*, pp. 88–89.

Hirschi's Social Control Theory

Another version of social control theory, offered by Travis Hirschi, is considerably more detailed and formalized than containment theory.[22] The central thesis of this argument is that juveniles become free to commit delinquent acts when their ties to the conventional social order are severed. Many delinquent acts are intrinsically attractive to youths or represent the most expedient route to some desirable goal. Consequently, most youths would engage in these acts if they were not constrained from doing so by their social links to others. Thus, no special motivation to engage in law-breaking is required once these social ties are broken.

In his explication of social control theory, Hirschi identified several dimensions along which the bond of the individual to society varies, including attachment, commitment, involvement, and belief. *Attachment* has to do with the strength of ties to others such as parents or peers, while *commitment* designates the person's devotion to conformist lines of conduct. Individuals also vary in *involvement,* that is, in the degree to which they are engaged in activities that restrict the time they have available for deviant activities. They also differ in *belief,* that is, the strength of their attitudes toward conformity. Regarding belief, Hirschi contended that "there is *variation* in the extent to which people believe they should obey the rules of society, and, furthermore ... the less a person believes he should obey the rules, the more likely he is to violate them." [23]

This argument about social control provided the framework for Hirschi's study in Richmond, California, in which he obtained self-report data on delinquent activities and on social control variables through questionnaires administered to a large sample of juveniles in that community. The delinquency index consisted for the most part of relatively petty acts of misbehavior. Using that measure of juvenile lawbreaking, Hirschi found that boys from all social class levels reported about the same degree of involvement in such acts.

The major findings of this research were consistent with the basic theory. Delinquent youths showed less attachment to parents, school and school teachers, peers, and conventional activities. The offenders also exhibited less positive attitudes toward conformity.

Hirschi's research findings have been substantially confirmed in some other investigations, including one by Michael Hindelang.[24] Also, John Hepburn has examined three competing theories of delinquency causation that involve differing claims about the relationships between lack

---

[22] Travis Hirschi, *Causes of Delinquency* (Berkeley: University of California Press, 1969).

[23] *Ibid.,* p. 26.

[24] Michael J. Hindelang, "Causes of Delinquency: A Partial Replication and Extension," *Social Problems,* 20 (Spring 1973):471–87.

of family support, development of delinquent attitudes or definitions, involvement with delinquent peers, and delinquent conduct.[25] Differential association theory implies that lack of family support leads youths into delinquent associations. These two experiences, in turn, should produce delinquent definitions, resulting in delinquent conduct. An opposing formulation by Glueck and Glueck contends that poor family relationships produce delinquent attitudes, followed by delinquent activities, which then lead delinquent "birds of a feather" to flock together in delinquent peer groups.[26] By contrast, Hirschi's theory argues that inadequate family relationships lead to attenuated ties to conformity, with those youths having less allegiance to societal rules being more likely to interact with delinquent companions. Boys who exhibit delinquent definitions and who have delinquent friends are quite prone to engage in acts of lawbreaking, while youngsters who have a high stake in conformity are unlikely to have either delinquent norms or delinquent friends. Hepburn's research among a group of 14- to 17-year-old males in a medium-sized Midwestern city found the greatest degree of empirical support for Hirschi's formulation.

Hirschi's version of social control theory has generated considerable interest on the part of a number of criminologists, and research studies that have been guided by his argument are being carried on at the present time. Some delinquency investigations that were conducted prior to Hirschi's study turned up evidence that anticipated his findings, at least in a general way.[27] In summary, there are several signs that suggest that Hirschi's theory is likely to be one of the more enduring contributions to criminology.

Deterrence

Punishment is one major form of social control that is directed at criminals and potential offenders. According to Webster's dictionary, punishment, or the deliberate infliction of physical or psychological pain, is designed to deter, that is, "to turn aside, discourage, or prevent from acting (as by fear)." Punishment is supposed to stop people from breaking the law through threats ranging from fines, probation, and other relatively mild punishments up to life imprisonment or execution. Punishment that is inflicted on apprehended offenders in order to deflect them away from further lawbreaking is usually designated as *individual* or *specific*

[25] John R. Hepburn, "Testing Alternative Models of Delinquency Causation," *Journal of Criminal Law and Criminology,* 67 (December 1976):450–60.
[26] Sheldon Glueck and Eleanor Glueck, *Unraveling Juvenile Delinquency* (Cambridge, Mass.: Harvard University Press, 1950).
[27] James F. Short, Jr., and Fred L. Strodtbeck, *Group Process and Gang Delinquency* (Chicago: University of Chicago Press, 1965), pp. 217–47; Scott Briar and Irving Piliavin, "Delinquency, Situational Inducements, and Commitment to Conformity," *Social Problems,* 13 (Summer 1965):33–45.

deterrence. In contrast, *general* deterrence, which refers to the prevention of criminal acts on the part of potential lawbreakers, is brought about through the example of punishments carried out against apprehended wrongdoers.

The subject of deterrence is an extraordinarily important, markedly complex, and, until recently, virtually ignored topic for criminological inquiry.[28] The prevailing posture of criminologists toward punishment and deterrence was established quite early. This stance, which minimized the significance of punishment as a crime control measure or which dismissed deterrence entirely, is contained in these remarks from the first edition of Sutherland's *Criminology*.

> Punishment has evident values, but its values are limited and are off-set by effects not designed, so that it is a relatively inefficient method of dealing with criminals. And because of this inefficiency, regardless of the right of the state to punish or the fact that the criminal may deserve to suffer, it is desirable to substitute the scientific procedure for the emotional procedure.[29]

Barnes and Teeters, who were less cautious in denouncing punishment and deterrence, argued that apologists for punishment are entirely wrong-headed: "In this concept of *deterrence* there is a childlike faith in punishment." [30] Similarly, while Walter Reckless conceded that punishment might be effective in certain unusual circumstances, he also offered the pronouncement that "for the great mass of infractions of the law, however, the fear of consequences or the fear of punishment probably enters very little into causation." [31]

Until very recently, little or no evidence could be marshalled that punishment deters criminals (and delinquents), or that it is ineffectual as a deterrent. The utterances of criminologists on this subject were forceful and unequivocal pronouncements, but they were not derived from research findings. The idea of punishment went against the grain, so that criminologists either expressed great hostility toward it or were uninterested in research on deterrence, opting instead for "scientific" efforts to treat and rehabilitate offenders.

However, a remarkable change has occurred recently. The study of deterrence has become a criminological "growth industry." A large and

---

[28] The complex nature of the deterrence question is indicated in detail in Jack P. Gibbs, *Crime, Punishment, and Deterrence* (New York: Elsevier, 1975).
[29] Edwin H. Sutherland, *Criminology* (Philadelphia: Lippincott, 1924), p. 360.
[30] Harry Elmer Barnes and Negley K. Teeters, *New Horizons in Criminology*, 3rd ed. (Englewood Cliffs, N.J.: Prentice-Hall, 1959), p. 286.
[31] Walter C. Reckless, *The Crime Problem*, 4th ed. (Englewood Cliffs, N.J.: Prentice-Hall, 1967), p. 504. For a contrary view, see Paul W. Tappan, *Crime, Justice and Correction* (New York: McGraw-Hill, 1960), pp. 241–61.

extremely complicated theoretical literature on deterrence, along with a rapidly growing number of empirical studies on the deterrent impact of criminal sanctions, has appeared. No attempt is made here to provide any more than a brief overview of some of the major questions and answers that have arisen to date regarding this phenomenon.

Franklin Zimring has provided some idea of the range of considerations that must be kept in mind in the study of deterrence.[32] He articulated a number of important distinctions, such as that between partial and marginal deterrence. *Partial deterrence* has to do with threats or punishment that reduce the magnitude of the threatened or punished activity, but do not curtail it entirely. *Marginal deterrence* designates that amount by which some specific penalty reduces the rate of illegal behavior below that produced by some other, lesser form of punishment.

Those who have speculated about deterrence have often pointed out that a comprehensive and adequate examination of the deterrent effects of punishment would have to seek to discover the impact of different kinds of punishment on the diverse forms of crime, as well as on the various kinds of people who may be potential lawbreakers. Clearly, some offenders or potential wrongdoers may be more deterrable than others. Specific penalties may deter some kinds of criminality and potential law violators, while punishment may have little influence upon other kinds of illegality.

Deterrence theorists have also had much to say about the relative importance of the celerity, certainty, and severity of punishments. *Celerity* refers to the swiftness with which punishment follows the commission of an offense, while *certainty* and *severity* need no definition. A good deal of criminological opinion has it that punishment is probably most effective when it is relatively certain and that certainty is more important or effective than severity of punishment.

Research studies on deterrence have produced results that are difficult to interpret, in considerable part because of their inadequate methodology. Most of the investigations have examined the relationships between crime patterns, as indexed by official statistics and crime rates, and various relatively crude measures of the certainty or severity of inflicted punishments.[33] Whatever the results that turn up in these studies, questions quickly arise about the adequacy of the measures of crime and punishment that have been employed. Additionally, even if the results are

[32] Franklin E. Zimring, *Perspectives on Deterrence* (Washington, D.C.: National Institute of Mental Health, 1971). Also see Gibbs, *Crime, Punishment, and Deterrence.*

[33] An early and somewhat different kind of deterrence study, dealing with parking violations on a Midwestern university campus was William J. Chambliss, "The Deterrent Influence of Punishment," *Crime and Delinquency,* 12 (January 1966): 70–75. This study found that violations were apparently reduced after certain and relatively severe penalties were introduced.

accepted as accurate, a number of alternative interpretations of them are possible. For example, low crime rates in states where large numbers of individuals are committed to prison might be a consequence of the incapacitative effects of imprisonment, rather an effect of deterrence.[34]

In one of the early investigations of deterrence, Jack Gibbs devised indexes of the certainty and severity of punishment for homicide in the United States and found evidence to indicate that homicide was least frequent where apprehension was relatively certain and where prison sentences were severe. Charles Tittle's study was similar to that of Gibbs, but involved a number of criminal offenses. Tittle found that certainty of punishment, as measured by commitment rates to state prisons, was related to these offenses, but that severity of punishment was not. In other words, Tittle found that crime rates were lowest in those states in which proportionately large numbers of offenders were sentenced to prison.[35]

Relatively few research studies of deterrence have endeavored to get inside people's heads, so to speak, in order to gather evidence on perceptions of punishment held by actual and potential offenders. Nonetheless, this is the key problem for study, for in the last analysis, punitive sanctions are only likely to operate as deterrents insofar as individuals are aware of these penalties and believe that they run some risk of being punished if they engage in lawbreaking.[36]

[34] For summaries of this research see Gibbs, *Crime, Punishment, and Deterrence;* Charles W. Thomas and J. Sherwood Williams, eds., *The Deterrent Effect of Sanctions: A Selected Bibliography,* Metropolitan Criminal Justice Center, College of William and Mary, 1975; Charles R. Tittle and Charles H. Logan, "Sanctions and Deviance: Evidence and Remaining Questions," *Law and Society Review,* 7 (Spring 1973):371–92; Tittle, "Punishment and Deterrence of Deviance," in Simon Rottenberg, ed., *The Economics of Crime and Punishment* (Washington, D.C.: American Enterprise Institute for Public Policy Research, 1973), pp. 85–102; Franklin Zimring and Gordon J. Hawkins, *Deterrence: The Legal Threat in Crime Control* (Chicago: University of Chicago Press, 1973).

[35] Jack P. Gibbs, "Crime, Punishment, and Deterrence," *Southwestern Social Science Quarterly,* 28 (March 1968):515–30; and Charles R. Tittle, "Crime Rates and Legal Sanctions," *Social Problems,* 16 (Spring 1969):409–23. Another study that turned up results generally parallel to those of Gibbs and Tittle was Theodore G. Chiricos and Gordon P. Waldo, "Punishment and Crime: An Examination of Some Empirical Evidence," *Social Problems,* 18 (Fall 1970):200–17.

[36] The perceptual dimensions of deterrence are discussed in Michael R. Geerken and Walter R. Gove, "Deterrence: Some Theoretical Considerations," *Law and Society Review,* 9 (Spring 1975):497–513. For some survey evidence on citizen perceptions of punishment and the criminal justice system, see Don C. Gibbons, "Who Knows What about Correction?" *Crime and Delinquency,* 9 (April 1963): 137–44; Assembly Committee on Criminal Procedure, *Deterrent Effects of Criminal Sanctions* (Sacramento: California State Legislature, 1968). For some findings on perceptions of criminal sanctions held by offenders, see Leonard H. Goodman, Trudy Miller, and Paul DeForest, *A Study of the Deterrent Value of Crime Prevention Measures as Perceived by Criminal Offenders* (Washington, D.C.: Bureau of Social Research, 1966); One study of this kind was Gordon P. Waldo and Theodore G. Chiricos, "Perceived Penal Sanction and Self-Reported Criminality: A Neglected

Some evidence can be brought to bear on the question of perceptions of punishment, including findings from two investigations using self-reported measures of involvement in delinquency or crime. Matthew Silberman conducted a study among a sample of college students and found that self-reported criminality was related not only to perceived certainty and severity of punishment, but also to moral commitment to legal norms and to the associational ties exhibited by individuals.[37] In other words, the individuals in that study were apparently influenced by a variety of factors that played on them. Somewhat similarly, Maynard Erickson, Jack Gibbs, and Gary Jensen carried out a study involving high school students, in which they reported an inverse relationship between self-reported involvement in various offenses and perceived certainty of punishment.[38] However, they also found that involvement in misbehavior was related to the perceived seriousness of the particular criminal acts. They concluded that, in addition to perceptions of the certainty of punishment, perceptions of the level of social condemnation of specific criminal acts may be an important factor in deterrence.

The study of deterrence is likely to continue for some time, particularly as a result of the apparent failure of our correctional system to rehabilitate offenders.[39] Because of the myriad theoretical issues that are bound up in deterrence and the difficulties of research on this subject, firm

---

Approach to Deterrence Research," *Social Problems,* 19 (Spring 1972): 522–40. These researchers asked a sample of college students about their involvement in theft behavior and marijuana use. They found evidence that perceived certainty of punishment had some impact as a deterrent influence upon these activities.

[37] Matthew Silberman, "Toward a Theory of Criminal Deterrence," *American Sociological Review,* 41 (June 1976):442–61.

[38] Maynard L. Erickson, Jack P. Gibbs, and Gary F. Jensen, "The Deterrence Doctrine and the Perceived Certainty of Legal Punishments," *American Sociological Review,* 42 (April 1977):305–17.

[39] One of the factors that will probably contribute to continued interest in deterrence is the decline of "the rehabilitative ideal" in the face of much evidence that treatment of offenders is relatively ineffective. Until recently, most American criminologists have been vigorous advocates of correctional treatment directed at juvenile and adult offenders. But, correctional treatment and rehabilitative efforts have been called into question by a number of surveys of evaluative studies, all indicating that treatment programs have failed to produce lower recidivism rates than are produced by strictly punitive and custodial efforts. See Walter C. Bailey, "An Evaluation of 100 Studies of Correctional Outcome," *Journal of Criminal Law, Criminology and Police Science,* 57 (June 1966):153–60; James Robison and Gerald Smith, "The Effectiveness of Correctional Programs," *Crime and Delinquency,* 17 (January 1971):67–80; Douglas Lipton, Robert Martinson, and Judith Wilks, *The Effectiveness of Correctional Treatment—A Survey of Treatment Evaluation Studies* (Springfield, Mass.: Praeger, 1975); David F. Greenberg, "The Correctional Effects of Corrections," in Greenberg, ed., *Corrections and Punishment* (Beverly Hills, Calif.: Sage Publications, 1977), pp. 111–48. For a broader discussion of correctional treatment and related matters, see Don C. Gibbons, "Punish the Criminal or Rehabilitate the Offender? The Current Debate," in Abraham S. Blumberg, ed., *Current Perspectives on Criminal Behavior,* 2nd ed. (New York: Random House, in press).

conclusions about the deterrent effects of punishment are not yet warranted, although these brief paragraphs have identified some of the tentative conclusions that have resulted from the existing studies.

THE SOCIOLOGY OF CORRECTIONAL ORGANIZATIONS

In an often quoted definition of criminology, Sutherland and Cressey indicated that "criminology is the body of knowledge regarding delinquency and crime as social phenomena. It includes within its scope the processes of making laws, of breaking laws, and of reacting toward the breaking of laws. These processes are three aspects of a somewhat unified sequence of interactions." [40] A cursory examination of criminology textbooks would quickly turn up evidence indicating that, until recently, criminologists tended to treat causal and correctional topics as quite separate matters. Etiological issues were dealt with as analytically separate from responses to lawbreaking. For example, the Sutherland and Cressey volume is divided into two parts: "The Study of Delinquency and Crime," involving thirteen chapters, and "The Processing of Delinquency and Crime," consisting of fourteen chapters.

Criminology textbooks have traditionally been filled with descriptive details of police administrative practices, correctional routines, and statistics of one kind or another, but sociological analyses of the workings of correctional organizations and structures have been infrequent. Additionally, the separation of criminological subject matter has meant that criminologists have rarely entertained the hypothesis that the steps taken by official agents of the state in their reactions to lawbreaking may play a causal role in criminal careers by pushing offenders further into lawbreaking rather than driving them out of it.

However, during the 1950s and 1960s, a flurry of criminological activity developed around organizational analyses of parts of the crime control machinery, and, in particular, around examinations of various facets of "the prison community." Beginning in the 1960s and continuing up to the present, a number of criminologists and other sociologists began to probe the question of the possible criminogenic influences of correctional intervention. That line of thought is taken up in detail in Chapter 6.

This book would stray too far afield if it attempted to present a detailed summary and analysis of all of the specific instances of theorizing and research that have been carried on in the sociological examination of the crime control apparatus. Inquiry into the law enforcement and correctional machinery is tangential to the central thrust of this volume, which is the development of sociological formulations concerning crime causation.

[40] Edwin H. Sutherland and Donald R. Cressey, *Criminology,* 9th ed. (Philadelphia: Lippincott, 1974), p. 3.

Accordingly, only a cursory and incomplete sampling of this material is presented.[41]

Sociological inquiries into police operations in American and other societies have taken a variety of specific directions, but it is possible to identify a relatively small number of major interests that run through these works.[42] For one, a number of commentators who have examined the social conditions that gave rise to modern, full-time police agencies in Western societies have indicated that organized police agencies represented a response to changing political-economic conditions in emerging urban-industrial societies. A closely related matter centers around inquiry into police-society relationships, with particular emphasis on identifying the sources of hostility and social distance between the police and the citizenry.

Other investigators have drawn attention to the multiple tasks that police agencies are called upon to carry out and the varied roles that police agents are required to fill. This focus of interest has also led a number of police theorists and researchers to examine variations in enforcement patterns and practices that arise out of the differing organizational goal definitions that characterize particular police agencies. For example, some departments stress peace keeping and thus produce fewer arrests than departments that emphasize strict enforcement of the law. Students of police systems have also exhibited a good deal of interest in the patterns of police discretion and differential enforcement that can be observed in individual departments.

Other investigators have zeroed in on the internal organization of specific police agencies, examining the effect of ethnicity and other factors on occupational mobility within departments. Some observers have paid particular attention to police socialization and police careers and have uncovered a sizable quantity of evidence regarding the development of "the policeman's working personality," that is, the attitudes of suspicion and hostility toward citizens and police views of themselves as craftsmen, which are acquired by policemen as they become enmeshed in the day-to-day requirements of modern police work. Finally, considerable interest has been shown by some other investigators in such facets of police work as police corruption, illegal violence employed by police, and other abuses of police powers.

Although this review is too brief to do justice to the richness of the literature that has grown up in the past two decades, it can fairly be

[41] A generous portion of the sociological literature on correctional social organization is summarized in Gibbons, *Society, Crime and Criminal Careers*. Police studies are discussed on pp. 49–77, investigations of court operations are examined on pp. 79–99, while studies of prisons and other correctional organizations and agencies are summarized on pp. 485–521.

[42] A few of the more important studies are Jerome Skolnick, *Justice without Trial* (New York: Wiley, 1966); James Q. Wilson, *Varieties of Police Behavior* (Cambridge, Mass.: Harvard University Press, 1968); and David J. Bordua, ed., *The Police: Six Sociological Essays* (New York: Wiley, 1967).

said that this material has gone far to remedy a long-standing situation in which criminologists were often abysmally ignorant about the police in modern society, in which criminology textbooks included only a few descriptive comments and gratuitous attacks on the police, and in which the complex role of the police in modern society went largely unrecognized.

Sociological interest in the workings of the court systems in American society has also flourished in the past dozen or so years.[43] Although the specific interests manifested by investigators of court functioning have been varied, a central theme does run throughout much of this work. Observers have stressed the ways in which the ostensibly independent actors in the judicial machinery—prosecutors, defense attorneys and public defenders, judges, and other workers—in fact congeal to form a people-processing system in which organizational interests take precedence over the interests of accused individuals who represent the raw material for the justice machinery. There is a large gap between idealized descriptions of how this apparatus is supposed to function to ensure the accused person's rights of due process and the social reality that has been uncovered in studies of prosecutorial and court operations.

By far the most voluminous body of literature on social control organizations has accumulated around the topic of prisons and other correctional institutions. Although some investigators have explored the relationships between penal institutions and the surrounding environment, much more attention has been paid to description and analysis of the internal workings of prisons.[44] For example, one classic ethnography of prison life commented on the limits of total power in prisons, the pains of imprisonment experienced by convicts, and the social roles that are exhibited by different congeries of prisoners.[45] Other researchers have

[43] Some representative works on court operations are David W. Neubauer, *Criminal Justice in Middle America* (Morristown, N.J.: General Learning Press, 1974); Abraham S. Blumberg, *Criminal Justice* (Chicago: Quadrangle Books, 1967); Arthur Lewis Wood, *Criminal Lawyer* (New Haven, Conn.: College and University Press, 1967); David Sudnow, "Normal Crimes: Sociological Features of the Penal Code in a Public Defender Office," *Social Problems,* 12 (Winter 1965):255–76; George F. Cole, "The Decision to Prosecute," *Law and Society Review,* 4 (February 1970): 331–43; Harry Kalven, Jr., and Hans Zeisel, *The American Jury* (Boston: Little, Brown, 1966); Robert M. Emerson, *Judging Delinquents* (Chicago: Aldine, 1969); Anthony M. Platt, *The Child Savers* (Chicago: University of Chicago Press, 1969).

[44] For two exceptions, see James B. Jacobs, "The Politics of Corrections: Town/Prison Relations as a Determinant of Reform," *Social Service Review,* 50 (December 1976):623–31; and Erich Steele and James B. Jacobs, "A Theory of Prison Systems," *Crime and Delinquency,* 21 (April 1975):149–62.

[45] Gresham M. Sykes, *The Society of Captives* (Princeton, N.J.: Princeton University Press, 1958). Also see Clarence Schrag, "Some Foundations for a Theory of Correction," in Donald R. Cressey, ed., *The Prison* (New York: Holt, Rinehart and Winston, 1961), pp. 309–57; Peter G. Garabedian, "Social Roles in a Correctional Community," *Journal of Criminal Law, Criminology and Police Science,* 55 (September 1964):338–47; and John Irwin and Donald R. Cressey, "Thieves, Convicts and the Inmate Culture," *Social Problems,* 10 (Fall 1962):142–55.

explored some of the organizational problems that differentiate institutions oriented toward custodial care from those oriented toward treatment.[46]

A number of investigations have demonstrated that inmates exhibit a variety of different social roles or adjustment patterns in prison. Some prisoners are socially isolated and dangerous "outlaws," some are naïve "square Johns," others are "right guys," and others exhibited still other behavior patterns. Some theorists have gone beyond these observations to offer a functional argument that the inmate code or normative system and these social roles arise to reduce the pains of imprisonment experienced by prisoners. In this view of things, the oppositional prisoner code and prisoner roles are indigenous products that are nurtured by factors inside the prison.[47] However, most of the available evidence indicates that a diffusion interpretation of inmate norms and behavior is required in order to account for the prisoner normative system and behavioral roles. A number of studies have demonstrated that many of the values and behavior patterns exhibited by American prisoners are imported into the penitentiary from the surrounding society. For example, investigations of prisons in other countries indicate that the endemic violence and hostility toward the prison authorities that characterize American institutions are almost entirely absent from European penal institutions.[48] On this same point, several studies of women's prisons have demonstrated that the patterns of adjustment that arise among female convicts cannot be understood without taking into account a number of aspects of women's roles and social position in the surrounding society.[49]

During the 1950s and 1960s, a wave of prison disturbances and riots swept through American penal institutions, apparently as an inmate response to administrative changes introduced into these places in the effort to convert them into treatment-oriented prisons. Prison uprisings diminished in the latter half of the 1960s, but in the 1970s, riots, dis-

---

[46] Donald R. Cressey, "Contradictory Directives in Complex Organizations: The Case of the Prison," *Administrative Science Quarterly,* 4 (June 1959):1–19. Also see Cressey, "Prison Organizations," in James G. March, ed., *Handbook of Organizations* (Chicago: Rand McNally, 1965), pp. 1033–54.

[47] Gresham M. Sykes and Sheldon L. Messinger, "The Inmate Social System," in Richard A. Cloward, Donald R. Cressey, George H. Grosser, Richard McCleery, Lloyd E. Ohlin, Gresham M. Sykes, and Sheldon L. Messinger, *Theoretical Studies in Social Organization of the Prison* (New York: Social Science Research Council, 1960), pp. 5–19.

[48] Stanton Wheeler, "The Comparative Analysis of Prison Social Structure." Paper presented at the meeting of the American Sociological Association, September 1962; Terence Morris and Pauline Morris, *Pentonville* (London: Routledge and Kegan Paul, 1963); Hugh J. Klare, *Anatomy of Prison* (Baltimore: Penguin Books, 1962); Thomas Mathieson, *The Defenses of the Weak—A Sociological Study of a Norwegian Correctional Institution* (London: Tavistock, 1965).

[49] Rose Giallombardo, *Society of Women* (New York: Wiley, 1966); David A. Ward and Gene G. Kassebaum, *Women's Prison* (Chicago: Aldine, 1965); Esther Heffernan, *Making It in Prison: The Square, the Cool, and the Life* (New York: Wiley, 1972).

turbances, and turmoil sprang up again. The single most violent of these disorders took place in 1971 at Attica State Prison in New York, in which 43 inmates and hostages were killed during efforts by police and the National Guard to regain control of the institution following a prisoner strike and revolt. However, sociological commentaries on these most recent episodes, many of which appear to involve growing racial tensions in prison, along with a new form of militancy on the part of prisoners, have been relatively infrequent.[50]

Sociological investigators have also contributed a number of research reports on juvenile training schools to the criminological literature. These studies indicate that training schools share a number of attributes in common with adult penal institutions.[51] For example, a social system exists among training school wards as well as among prison inmates, involving victimization of some wards by older, stronger inmate leaders or "dukes." Furthermore, this status order among training school youths is tacitly supported by many staff members, who manipulate the ward social system as a means of maintaining control over their charges.

Contemporary criminology has witnessed the ebbing and flowing of interest in some of the topics to which criminologists have attended, including the study of hidden or self-reported crime and delinquency. Inquiry into the social structure and operations of correctional organizations is another area of investigation that has shown some dimunition of activity in recent years. Studies of prison social structure in particular have been fewer in the 1970s, even though there are a number of important sociological questions about penal institutions that remain unanswered.

The sociological analysis of legal and correctional organizations is a topic that merges into other areas of sociological interest and is not distinctively criminological in focus. Rather than being narrow criminological

[50] However, see Maurice Floch and Frank E. Hartung, "A Social-Psychological Analysis of Prison Riots: An Hypothesis," *Journal of Criminal Law, Criminology and Police Science,* 47 (May–June 1956):51–57; Lloyd E. Ohlin, *Sociology and the Field of Corrections* (New York: Russell Sage Foundation, 1956), pp. 23–24; John Pallas and Bob Barber, "From Riot to Revolution," in Richard Quinney, ed., *Criminal Justice in America* (Boston: Little, Brown, 1974), pp. 340–55; James B. Jacobs, "Street Gangs behind Bars," *Social Problems,* 21, No. 3 (1974):395–409; Jacobs, "Stratification and Conflict among Prison Inmates," *Journal of Criminal Law and Criminology,* 66 (December 1975):476–82; Leo Carroll, *Hacks, Blacks, and Cons— Race Relations in a Maximum Security Prison* (Lexington, Mass.: Lexington Books, 1974); Theodore R. Davidson, *Chicano Prisoners: The Key to San Quentin* (New York: Holt, Rinehart and Winston, 1974): John Irwin, "The Changing Social Structure of the Men's Prison," in Greenberg, *Corrections and Punishment,* pp. 21–40.

[51] For example, see Sethard Fisher, "Social Organization in a Correctional Residence," *Pacific Sociological Review,* 4 (Fall 1961):87–93; Gordon H. Barker and W. Thomas Adams, "The Social Structure of a Correctional Institution," *Journal of Criminal Law, Criminology and Police Science,* 49 (January–February 1959):417–22; Howard W. Polsky, *Cottage Six* (New York: Russell Sage Foundation, 1962).

queries, many of the questions that have been raised regarding these social organizations come from the study of formal organizations and bureaucracies in general. Many of the sociologists who have studied correctional organizations have proceeded on the assumption that these structures probably share many elements in common with other complex organizations, so that similarities between the conflicting roles assigned to prison guards and industrial foremen have been uncovered, communication problems that plague many kinds of formal organizations have been examined within prison settings, and informal social structures within penal institutions have been likened to informal organizational patterns that arise in a variety of other complex social systems. For these reasons, a number of research studies on correctional organizations have been published or reprinted in volumes on organizational analysis and have been incorporated into the literature of that area of sociological interest.[52] A number of the researchers who have studied legal and correctional organizations define themselves as organizational sociologists rather than criminologists.

THE HISTORICAL ROOTS OF MAINSTREAM CRIMINOLOGY

Reprise

Why has mainstream criminological inquiry taken the form it has, rather than some other? Examination of this question should perhaps begin with a backward look at the account of criminological development presented so far.

As we have seen, the parent discipline, sociology, was eclectic, reform oriented, and lacking in coherence and sophistication during its early years. The nascent discipline was in considerable part a progeny of the Progressive Era, representing a new field of study that responded to widespread social reform interests in the nation. For the most part, pioneering criminological essays written by Henderson, Parmelee, Parsons, Gillin, and Sutherland mirrored the characteristics of sociology.

The two decades from 1930 to 1955 might be regarded as the period during which criminology reached early adulthood. The seminal works of Shaw and McKay, centering around ecological correlates of delinquency and social learning processes in juvenile delinquency, constituted part of the product of this period. Even more important, Sutherland developed his theory of differential association and carried out his studies of professional theft and white-collar crime between 1930 and 1950.

---

[52] For example, see Cressey, "Prison Organizations"; Richard H. McCleery, "Policy Change in Prison Management," in Amitai Etzioni, ed., *A Sociological Reader on Complex Organizations,* 2nd ed. (New York: Holt, Rinehart and Winston, 1969), pp. 200–222.

Sellin's commentary on culture conflict and crime and Merton's theory of anomie and deviant behavior were also articulated during these years. Contemporary criminologists continue to draw heavily on these materials, which are major themes that continue to inform the theoretical expositions found in textbooks and elsewhere.

A number of contributions to sociological criminology were made between 1955 and 1970. These newer works embroidered on the central themes contained in the 1930–1955 brand of criminology, enriching criminological thought in its details, but they did not offer any fundamental challenge to the central tenets of mainstream criminology. Inquiries into hidden or self-reported crime and delinquency were produced in abundance, and a number of criminologists were drawn to typological approaches to criminal behavior. A great deal of sophisticated theorizing and research activity was generated on the subject of subcultural or gang delinquency. Finally, some important advances were made on social control and containment formulations, and an impressive collection of studies on the social workings of agencies within the crime control machinery was produced.

Mainstream criminology has had much to say about the behavior of criminals, but has given scant attention to questions having to do with the criminality of behavior. American criminologists have exhibited a great deal of theoretical curiosity concerning queries such as "Why do they do it?" but have tended to slight the question of why whatever "it" might be got singled out by the lawmakers as a crime in the first place.

It also ought to be apparent from these accounts of major criminological interests and theories that, while mainstream criminology has emphasized a viewpoint that points toward a host of pervasive criminogenic characteristics of modern society as the root causes of criminality, the societal order as a whole has been viewed as viable and relatively healthy. American criminologists have authored criticisms of American society, drawing attention to its structural deficiencies that engender crime, but these negative comments have almost without exception been relatively mild ones. Until very recently, few criminologists could be found uttering calls for social or economic revolution in America in the name of crime prevention or control. Consider, as a case in point, Sutherland's disavowal of radical sentiments in his book on white-collar crime, in which he announced: "This book is a study in the theory of criminal behavior. It is an attempt to reform the theory of criminal behavior, not to reform anything else." [53] This disclaimer did not entirely ring true, for his writings on white-collar crime betrayed a reformer's indignation regarding the costly depre-

---

[53] Edwin H. Sutherland, *White Collar Crime* (New York: Dryden Press, 1949), p. *v.*

dations of corporations and American businesses. Even so, there was little in Sutherland's work to suggest that he advocated anything more drastic than closer regulation of corporate activities or heavier penalties for commercial misconduct. There was no hint in Sutherland's essays that he felt that corporations ought to be disbanded in favor of state socialism, for example.

Sociology, Criminology, and American Society

Although the central concern in this section revolves around an explanation of why mainstream criminology has taken a liberal, reformist direction rather than exhibiting a more radical posture, there is a larger query that also must be addressed: Why has American sociology in general shown those same characteristics? [54]

The answer to this question is apparent, at least in gross outline. Stated boldly, the *American* Boy Scouts, the *American* Catholic church, the *American* Communist Party, the *American* class structure, *American* sociology and criminology, and all other things American in derivation are cultural products that bear the stamp of the society that nurtured them. However much sociologists go about insisting that sociology is an objective and value-free science, the fact of the matter is that American sociology

[54] In the discussion to follow, contemporary sociology and criminology are described as liberal in character. Neither this term nor the conservative label fit comfortably, for sociology and criminology contain elements of both postures. On the one hand, sociologists and criminologists in the United States have generally supported programs directed at poverty, racism, and other social ills, while criminologists have also favored treatment of offenders, rather than harshly punitive approaches. In these ways, sociology and criminology seem aptly described as liberal in tone. On the other hand, some critics of modern sociology have argued that most sociologists are quite restrained in their liberalism, so that they are actually conservative in their proposals. For example, Alvin Gouldner has contended that Howard Becker and other students of deviance are critical of the police, prison guards, psychiatrists, and other figures who are involved in social control efforts directed at criminals and other deviants. But, according to Gouldner, a more vigorous liberalism would attack the repressive social control machinery and the power structure lying behind it. For Becker's views, see Howard S. Becker, "Whose Side Are We On?" *Social Problems,* 14 (Winter 1967):239–47. Gouldner's remarks appeared in: Alvin W. Gouldner, "The Sociologist as Partisan: Sociology and the Welfare State," *The American Sociologist,* 3 (May 1968):103–16. In the commentary in this chapter, sociology and criminology will be described as liberal in form, by which is meant that sociologists and criminologists have often favored various kinds of "tinkering" and "fine tuning" of the social and economic structure, rather than more radical approaches to amelioration of social problems.

The liberal thrust of American sociology is revealed in detail in the 1959 compendium, *Sociology Today.* See Robert K. Merton, Leonard Broom, and Leonard S. Cottrell, Jr., eds., *Sociology Today* (New York: Basic Books, Inc., 1959). The liberal character of American criminology is illustrated in that volume in Marshall B. Clinard's chapter, "Criminological Research," pp. 509–36. His discussion includes, remarks on differential association theory, anomie and subcultural delinquency arguments, typological approaches, and the sociology of correctional organizations.

and criminology have flourished in a nominally democratic and equalitarian society that has been driven by an economic motor of corporate capitalism that has produced great wealth for some and relatively marked affluence for many others. That political-economic system has made the United States the most powerful nation in the world. No wonder, then, that American sociologists have often constructed theories and accounts on a foundation of ethnocentric assumptions that reflect a sanguine view of their own society. American society contains a variety of stresses and imperfections, including criminogenic influences of various kinds, but these have all been seen as relatively short-run imperfections that can be remedied through social intervention and tinkering with the social order.

This characterization of sociology and criminology, with their hidden biases favoring the status quo, is one with which many people would now agree, but that has not always been the case. Only in recent years has a sociology of sociology begun to focus a probing light on the hidden and implicit thoughtways of sociology and criminology.

Mainstream Criminology and the Status Quo

Richard Quinney has recently provided a strong condemnation of mainstream criminology.

> Contemporary criminology is closely tied to the state's interests. In the name of developing knowledge about crime, some criminologists support the institutions at the expense of human freedoms. The needs of the people are identified with the social policies of the American state. And instead of understanding crime as created by the political authority that defines behavior as criminal, it has been understood in terms of the offender's behavior. Seeking a critical understanding and questioning the legal system have traditionally fallen outside the dominant ideological and scientific interests of most criminologists.
>
> The liberal ideology underlies most research and theory in contemporary criminology. Although it is by no means monolithic or consistent, ... most of its assumptions are shared by criminologists today. Following this ideology, criminologists (1) follow a legalistic definition of crime, accepting the state's definitions, (2) support reformist measures in rehabilitating "criminals" and amelioristic reforms of society, (3) reject general theory and macroscopic historical analysis, favoring pragmatism and social behaviorism, and (4) are susceptible to cynicism and a lack of passion, ignoring the possibility of far-ranging changes in society. These liberal values are translated into the kinds of research criminologists conduct, the theories they construct, and the way in which they are ideologically tied to the state.
>
> Criminologists are the ancillary agents of political power. They provide the kinds of information that governing elites use to manipulate

and control those who threaten the system. As "experts," criminologists inform the managers of the state. This alliance between criminology and the state, however, is far from being an explicit conspiracy; rather, the relationship is much more natural and subtle. That is, criminologists automatically serve the interests of the state by following their own unexamined assumptions about the world and their understanding of it. By pursuing a narrow scientific model, supported by a liberal ideology, criminologists find their interests tied to those of the state.[55]

These paragraphs provide a reasonable description of mainstream criminology. However, comments of this kind sometimes slip over into assertions implying that criminologists have entered into some kind of direct conspiracy with the powerful elements in society, becoming amoral lackeys who do the dirty work of the ruling class. Chapter 7 will take up that more contentious line of argument.

Jon Snodgrass has commented on the character of American criminology, through an examination of the social backgrounds and scholarly products of six major figures in this field of inquiry: William Healy, Clifford Shaw and Henry McKay, Edwin Sutherland, and Sheldon Glueck and Eleanor Glueck.[56] His volume was filled with little-known facts about these starring actors in the criminological drama. For example, both Shaw and McKay were graduate students in sociology at the University of Chicago at one time, but neither received Ph.D. degrees, principally because they both stumbled on the language requirement. Snodgrass also filled in many of the details regarding the history of the Institute for Juvenile Research, indicating that it was inaugurated in 1909 as the Chicago Juvenile Psychopathic Institute, with Healy as its first director. The institute was taken over by the state of Illinois in 1920 and renamed the Institute for Juvenile Research. Shaw and McKay became affiliated with it a few years later. Snodgrass also revealed that, although Sutherland held a research professorship at the University of Chicago from 1930 to 1935, he did not receive a permanent appointment there, apparently because he was not considered to be "University of Chicago calibre." Finally, Snodgrass indicated that Sutherland was capable of earthier criticisms of criminological endeavors than is sometimes supposed, as, for example, when he described the research of William Sheldon as "crap."[57]

[55] Richard Quinney, *Criminology* (Boston: Little, Brown, 1975), p. 13. Also see Barry Krisberg, *Crime and Privilege: Toward a New Criminology* (Englewood Cliffs, N.J.: Prentice-Hall, 1975), pp. 1–19.

[56] Jon D. Snodgrass, *The American Criminological Tradition: Portraits of the Men and Ideology in a Discipline.* Doctoral dissertation, University of Pennsylvania, 1972. The arguments of Healy and the Gluecks lie outside the sociological tradition being considered here, because these theorists were psychiatrically oriented and eclectic in their views.

[57] William H. Sheldon, Emil M. Hartl, and Eugene McDermott, *Varieties of Delinquent Youth* (New York: Harper & Row, 1949).

Snodgrass's central thesis, particularly regarding Shaw, McKay, and Sutherland, was that all three of these architects of sociological criminology were from rural, middle-class, Protestant backgrounds, which provided much of the coloring for their theories on criminality. According to Snodgrass, Shaw and McKay were imbued with the view that delinquency was wrong and that delinquency areas must be remade into communities resembling the small towns in which they had been reared. He argued that Shaw and McKay did not attend to the inequities of power and the political economy, nor did they examine these political-economic factors as dimensions of delinquency causation.[58] Snodgrass claimed that all these criminological theorists were attuned to liberal assumptions that failed to raise critical questions about pervasive defects in the American social order. According to Snodgrass, "the unacceptability of class and material conditions arose primarily from the fact that the social world the criminologists perceived and understood was not laden with material domination and class struggle." [59]

Sociology and Criminology

Although Shaw, McKay, and Sutherland have deservedly large reputations as key figures in the rise of sociological criminology, they are at the same time representatives of the larger group of sociological criminologists. Most of the distinguishing features of their works, which have been identified by Snodgrass and others, are characteristic of the entire criminological cohort within sociology. Moreover, the liberal biases of criminological theory do not stand alone. Most of them are implicit presuppositions that have permeated the entire discipline of sociology.

Roscoe Hinkle and Gisela Hinkle's brief volume provided some illustration of the liberal character of modern American sociology, as did *Sociology Today,* and the more recent *American Sociology.* All three of these volumes were self-congratulatory in tone and celebrated the attainment of scientific status by American sociology. Few strident complaints about flaws and fissures in American social structure were voiced in the pages of these three books.[60]

[58] For a contrary view, see Harold Finestone, "The Delinquent and Society: The Shaw and McKay Tradition," in James F. Short, Jr., ed., *Delinquency, Crime, and Society* (Chicago: University of Chicago Press, 1976), pp. 31–36.

[59] Snodgrass, *The American Criminological Tradition,* p. 38.

[60] Roscoe C. Hinkle and Gisela J. Hinkle, *The Development of Modern Sociology* (New York: Random House, 1954); Robert K. Merton, Leonard Broom, and Leonard S. Cottrell, Jr., eds., *Sociology Today* (New York: Basic Books, 1959); and Talcott Parsons, *American Sociology: Perspectives, Problems, Methods* (New York: Basic Books, 1968). The observation about *American Sociology* was also made by Alvin Gouldner, who commented that "the dominant mood of this volume, published in the midst of the ongoing war in Vietnam and written during a period when hostili-

Hinkle and Hinkle described three stages in the development of American sociology: the Progressive years from 1905 to the end of World War I; the 1918 to 1935 period, which centered around the attempt to make sociology scientific; and the years from 1935 to 1954, in which earlier gains were consolidated and in which sociology is said to have come of age as a science.

In their account of the developments between 1935 and 1954, Hinkle and Hinkle identified those European theorists who allegedly had the greatest impact on American sociology: Vilfredo Pareto, Emile Durkheim, Sigmund Freud, and Max Weber. They gave only scant and passing attention to Karl Marx and declared that his writings were influential only to some small extent. According to Hinkle and Hinkle, "the basic reason for the nonacceptance of Marxist theories appears to derive from his economic determinism, which is often interpreted as a fundamental denial of American individualism and which is inconsistent with the multicausational position of most American sociologists." [61]

Hinkle and Hinkle's interpretation of the unpopularity of Marxist theory is only part of the story. The main reason why Marxist theory has been uncongenial to most American sociologists is not principally because it is deterministic, nor because it has either been inaccessible to American sociologists or because it is dense and turgid in form. Marxist theory has great difficulty in taking root in American soil because it seems to emphasize alien values that clash markedly with the view that the American system of corporate capitalism, married to a nominally democratic political structure, is a pattern without fundamental flaws that other societies ought to emulate.

Some of the most trenchant observations on the development and character of American sociology have been provided by Alvin Gouldner in his massive volume, *The Coming Crisis of Western Sociology*. Critics have taken issue with many particulars of this work, including Gouldner's description of academic American sociology, which many feel is overdrawn.[62] There is considerable merit to this complaint, for it is difficult to agree with Gouldner that American sociology since 1930 has been almost exclusively dominated by structural-functional analysis and the social systems theorizing of Talcott Parsons. Gouldner's analysis slighted large areas of sociological work, including the symbolic interactionism of social

---

ties between the black and white communities in American cities had reached the point of recurrent summer violence and rioting, was, despite this, one of self-congratulatory celebration." See Alvin W. Gouldner, *The Coming Crisis in Western Sociology* (New York: Basic Books, 1970), p. 48.

[61] Hinkle and Hinkle, *Development of Modern Sociology*, p. 54.

[62] For example, see the Review Symposium of Gouldner's book by Guy E. Swanson, Steven E. Deutsch, and Richard A. Peterson, *American Sociological Review*, 36 (April 1971):317–28.

psychology, ecological and demographic analysis, and much of the inquiry in subfields of sociology such as criminology.

However, after the distortions and exaggerations in Gouldner's analysis are taken into account, much that remains is penetrating and valid. His book constituted a critical examination of the rise of American sociology, and more particularly, the evolution of structural-functionalism as the major theoretical system to which American sociologists have held allegiance. A substantial portion of his book was given over to an exegesis of the systems theorizing of Parsons, for Gouldner quite correctly contended that Parsons's views are central to an understanding of the directions taken by American sociology from the 1920s to the present. Although there have been other brands of sociology besides structural-functionalism, and other major contributors to American sociology besides Parsons, many of the generalizations about this perspective and this theoretician can be extended to the entire discipline. Most varieties of American sociology have shared the noncritical posture that Gouldner attributed to Parsonian sociology: American sociologists have tended to support and praise their own society through their sociological writings, rather than raising critical questions about it.

Gouldner's central purpose was to provide a critique of contemporary society and mainstream sociology, in order that the latter might be utilized in the search for a better society. Thus, at one point, he noted that "the extrication of the liberative potential of modern academic sociology from its encompassing conservative structure is a major task of contemporary cultural criticism." [63] Somewhat later, Gouldner laid out a more detailed description of a critique of modern society and sociology.

> The critique of contemporary society cannot be deepened except insofar as the intellectual instruments of this critique, including sociology and other social sciences, are themselves critically sharpened. Correspondingly, a critique of sociology will be superficial unless the discipline is seen as the flawed product of a flawed society and unless we begin to specify the details of this interconnection. What is required therefore is an analysis on different levels, in which sociology is seen in its relation to larger historical trends, to the macro-institutional level, and especially to the state; it also means seeing sociology in the setting of its most immediate locale, the university; it means seeing it as a way in which men work as teachers and researchers,

[63] Gouldner, *The Coming Crisis in Western Sociology*, p. 12. Footnote 54 commented on the liberal character of mainstream sociology, while Gouldner has characterized it as conservative. This differing interpretation of the thrust of contemporary sociology arises because the liberal proposals of sociologists have not usually been far-reaching, while the sociological critique of American society has been timid and has not attacked any fundamental flaws in the operation of that society. Seen in that light, American sociology can be described as conservative in form.

and operate within an intellectual community with a received occupational culture, where they pursue careers, livelihoods, material ambitions, as well as intellectual aspirations.

Finally, and centrally, a critique of sociology also requires detailed and specific analysis of the dominant theoretical and intellectual products that sociology has created. It is these intellectual products that distinguish sociology from other activities, that justify its existence, and that produce its distinctive impact on the larger surrounding society. There can be no serious critique of sociology without a fine-grained, close analysis of its theories and its theorists.[64]

Gouldner's volume was a richly textured and complex book and cannot be summarized adequately in a paragraph or two. But, it is useful to consider some portions of his analysis.

One major point around which much of Gouldner's explication of the character of Western sociology turned had to do with the role of background and domain assumptions, sentiments, and the infrastructure of sociological theory. *Background assumptions* are the implicit cultural values and beliefs that are the unspoken postulates on which social theories are constructed by sociologists and laymen alike. The operating premise that human behavior is volitional and not determined by biological or cultural forces would be an example of a background assumption. *Domain assumptions* are background assumptions that apply more narrowly to some behavioral domain, as, for example, the unstated premises held by criminologists that criminality arises out of social factors rather than from accidents of biology. Gouldner contended that sociological theories are rarely if ever evaluated solely in terms of scientific standards of hard evidence. Instead, "background assumptions also influence the *social* career of a theory, influencing the responses of those to whom it is communicated." [65]

Sentiments such as optimism or pessimism arise from the viscera, rather than being matters of belief and hard evidence. Gouldner pointed out that, although theories about the social order are often undergirded by domain assumptions and supportive affective states or sentiments, this is not always the case. Particularly in periods of rapid and marked social change, many people may come to hold sentiments toward prevailing world views that are dissonant with those perspectives. Gouldner employed the term *infrastructure* to refer to these subtheoretical domain assumptions and sentiments. Theoretical statements represent much more than bundles of words resembling a verbal photograph of social reality, for they include these cultural and individual elements as well. Others have also observed

[64] *Ibid.*, p. 14.
[65] *Ibid.*, p. 29.

that sociologists are not some special breed of people that can stand apart from the influences of the society in which they live, or who can somehow slice off a portion of themselves, the detached and objective scientist, from the rest of their body and mind. But, Gouldner's discussion of these matters was particularly incisive.

Gouldner's account traced modern sociology back to the early 1800s in Europe, arguing that it was a response to people's estrangement from the societal structure that had emerged out of industrialization. In particular, industrialization and the concomitant breakdown of the feudal social order generated widespread impersonalization, individualism, and utilitarianism. Utilitarianism provoked anomie or normlessness. As a result, people abandoned older moral codes because "in all spheres of life their concern with the 'useful' leads them to a prior and focal concern with the consequences of their actions, and thereby makes moral judgment auxiliary to factual questions concerning consequences." [66]

Gouldner identified four stages in the development of sociology: sociological positivism in the first quarter of the nineteenth century; Marxism, which developed in the middle of the nineteenth century; the period of classical sociology from about 1900 to 1918; and the modern period of structural-functionalism. Vestiges of early positivism that can be detected in contemporary sociology include the viewpoint that it is a "master science" that encompasses society as a whole and the gross neglect of economic forces in social behavior.

Gouldner claimed that early sociology in Western Europe underwent a process of "binary fission" prior to 1900, in which Marxism became centered in the Soviet Union and virtually ignored elsewhere, while "academic sociology," based on the writings of the classical theorists, Pareto, Weber, and Durkheim, came to fruition in America. That brand of sociology that ultimately culminated in structural-functionalism and mainstream American sociological analysis has been obdurately hostile to Marxist diagnoses, which find fundamental flaws in the new social order of industrialism and, more recently, corporate capitalism. Thus, although Durkheim and Weber felt that there was something deeply wrong with modern industrial societies, they did not denounce the capitalist economic structure and claim that the industrial order must be overturned. Liberal optimism and faith in the viability of the capitalistic system has persisted in the writings of Parsons and most other American sociologists, at least until the most recent decade.

What is the nature of the coming crisis in Western sociology? Traditional structural-functional theories, which are supportive of laissez-faire capitalistic economy and which allow sociologists to seek solutions to

[66] *Ibid.,* p. 67.

remedies for social ills without challenging the underlying societal premises or economic structure, have come under increasing attack. The rise of the welfare state—increased governmental regulation of the economy and accelerated governmental involvement in the handling and processing of various economically superfluous or dependent groups within the population—has created the demand for revised sociological theories. However, structural-functionalism has been able to accommodate to many of these pressures.

> Functional sociology corresponds to the standpoint of a society, or of those groups within it, that does not conceive of its social problems as rooted in its basic property institutions, but which must regulate the disruptive impact of its market institutions and adjust its allocative arrangements, lest these result in threats to the property institutions. Insofar as functional sociology conceives itself as a science of purely "social" relationships, which premises that social order can be maintained regardless of the level and distribution of economic gratifications, and thus treats economic arrangements as "givens," it is somewhat remote from the income-reallocating strategies of the Welfare State. Yet its social utilitarianism may induce functionalism to accept various kinds of social rearrangements, including the welfare state, that promise to control or remedy the socially disruptive impact of individualistic market competition.[67]

However, the developing crisis of Western sociology extends beyond the pressures on structural-functionalists to evolve theories and professional practices supportive of the welfare state. Gouldner argued that the emergence of the New Left and the radicalization of many of the young, including graduate students in sociology, the turbulence in the streets and on the campuses, the immoral war waged by the United States against the Vietnamese, and a host of other, interrelated developments have undermined many people's faith in mainstream sociology. New forms of sociological imagery, based on markedly different domain assumptions than those contained in Parsonian theory, have emerged, at the same time that the distinctiveness of functional analysis has been blurred, as it has converged with some of these other perspectives. Although Gouldner's forecasts regarding the ultimate form that American sociology will take are not entirely clear and unequivocal, he predicted a resurgence of interest in Marxism and political-economic theories on the part of those sociologists whose sentiments and assumptions are out of tune with more traditional lines of liberal, status quo sociology.

Gouldner's book was published in 1970, the last year of the criminological period under consideration in this chapter. During the decade of

[67] *Ibid.,* p. 343.

the 1970s, a relatively small but highly vocal group of criminological dissidents began to hurl challenges at mainstream criminology in the form of new viewpoints variously identified as "conflict criminology," "the new criminology," "radical criminology," "critical criminology," or "Marxist criminology." Much of this commentary has been exceedingly shallow, bombastic, and otherwise flawed, and has exhibited many of the worst features of vulgar Marxism. Some have sought to dismiss out of hand these challenges to establishment criminology. This is a grave mistake. These voices of an advance guard signal the appearance of some formidable challenges to the criminological perspectives that have been examined so far.

NEW DIRECTIONS
IN CRIMINOLOGICAL
THEORY

6

INTRODUCTION

Mainstream criminology in American society continues to have many adherents in this last quarter of the Twentieth Century. However, two challenges to that criminological tradition have arisen in recent years. The first contends that some major revisions are in order in that perspective, and the second argues that mainstream criminology must be abandoned in favor of entirely new theories. The revisionist challenge has grown out of a loosely formed collection of themes that are often identified as labeling theory, while the all-out attacks on mainstream criminology are represented by some lines of theorizing that have been designated variously as the new criminology, or as radical, conflict, critical, or Marxist criminology. These two developments are the center of attention in Chapters 6 and 7.

LABELING THEORY

The Labeling Perspective

Sociological theorizing about nonconforming behavior of various kinds has been a part of American sociology from its earliest beginnings.[1] In the early history of the discipline, deviants were regarded as people apart from the majority of upright, conformist citizens. Deviants were seen as carriers of social pathology and were thought to be the products of various individual pecularities, biological forces, or temporary social

---

[1] Various sociological viewpoints on deviance, including social pathology, social disorganization, and social problems arguments are reviewed in Don C. Gibbons and Joseph F. Jones, *The Study of Deviance* (Englewood Cliffs, N.J.: Prentice-Hall, 1975), pp. 14–27.

aberrations. Somewhat later, norm-violating conduct was interpreted within a social disorganization framework, in which deviance was attributed to various rents and tears in the social fabric caused by urbanization, industrialization, rapid social change, and kindred developments in modern society. In both of these perspectives, little attention was paid to questions about the nature or origins of the norms that deviants were alleged to be violating. Also, early theorists who directed their attention at deviant behavior followed an implicit assumption that apprehended or publicly identified norm violators were a representative sample of all nonconformists. Thus, little or no concern was voiced about the role of social audiences in the identification or processing of deviants. Finally, early students of deviant behavior emphasized a correctional stance toward deviants, urging that intervention efforts be undertaken to draw those who had strayed from the straight and narrow back to conformist pathways.[2]

Labeling arguments grew up in response to the shortcomings that were perceived in these older viewpoints. What are the central arguments of the labeling view? [3]

To begin with, labeling arguments stress that deviance is problematic and the result of social definitions, because the standards or norms that are transgressed are not universal or unchanging in character. Deviance comes about through social judgments imposed on individuals by a social audience. On this point, it has become almost obligatory to cite the remarks of Howard Becker.

> Social groups create deviance by making the rules whose infractions constitute deviance, and by applying those rules to particular people and labeling them as outsiders. From this point of view, deviance is *not* a quality of the act the person commits, but rather a consequence of the application by others of rules and sanctions to an "offender." The deviant is one to whom that label has been applied; deviant behavior is behavior that people so label.[4]

Such statements are sometimes taken to mean that only those individuals who have engaged in nonconformity *and* who have been subjected to specific labeling experiences are deviants. But labeling theorists often speak of secret deviants, who have not been publicly identified, or of primary deviance, which has not been publicly identified through a societal response. Either way, nearly all theorists agree that those nonconformists

---

[2] The core elements of different sociological perspectives on deviance are examined in David Matza, *Becoming Deviant* (Englewood Cliffs, N.J.: Prentice-Hall, 1969).

[3] The commentary here on the labeling perspective closely parallels remarks in Gibbons and Jones, *Study of Deviance*, pp. 124–26. See pp. 124–81 of that book for relatively detailed discussion of labeling theory.

[4] Howard S. Becker, *Outsiders* (New York: Free Press, 1963), p. 9.

who are apprehended by the police, who fall into the hands of mental health workers, or who encounter other social audiences face adjustment problems concerning spoiled identity that undetected violators of norms do not encounter. Indeed, this is the core proposition of the labeling orientation.

Another theme in these writings is that deviance arises out of diverse sources or circumstances. Labeling theorists do not assume that some small body of cultural values accounts for the myriad forms of deviance in complex societies. Instead, they emphasize value pluralism and underscore the importance of subcultural normative patterns in nonconformity. Deviant acts often occur when people find themselves pulled and tugged by competing interests and values. Thus, the factors producing norm violation cannot be subsumed by some all-embracing theory such as anomie.

Some labeling theorists have given minimal attention to the question of the causes of primary deviance, which refers to initial acts of norm violation, apparently because they assume that it is not possible to specify the varied circumstances out of which such acts flow. Others have suggested that value pluralism and risk-taking hypotheses apply to many kinds of deviant acts and that it is possible to identify the origins of deviant acts. In either case, labeling perspectives have paid relatively little attention to rates of deviance and social-structural factors accounting for them. In short, the labeling viewpoint and social-structural arguments have developed as divergent alternative interpretations of deviance, rather than as complementary formulations. Sociologists have made relatively few attempts to develop detailed theoretical statements that speak to both rates of deviance and the processes operating in individual deviant career pathways. Nanette Davis has commented that labeling theory "as practiced, has been largely astructural, ahistorical, and noncomparative, and tends to promote a sociology of the segmental, the exotic, and the bizarre." [5]

Labeling theorists contend that deviant behavior ought to be examined as a social process that involves both the acts of nonconformists and the reactions of others to these violations. They draw attention to "careers," in which individuals who become enmeshed in deviance exhibit changes in behavior and attitudinal patterns over time. Many of these changes are thought to be closely related to social reactions that are directed toward deviant individuals.

Those who have emphasized social labeling have often pointed to examples in which initial acts of deviance have been "normalized" because the actors denied or disavowed them. The person, the social audience, or

[5] Nanette J. Davis, "Labeling Theory in Deviance Research: A Critique and Reconsideration," *Sociological Quarterly,* 13 (Autumn 1972):453.

both are thus initially able to define the nonconforming behavior as un-important or peripheral to the individual's real self. But, repeated social reactions directed at the individual ultimately undermine his or her claim to normality, driving the person toward an altered identity as a deviant or, less frequently, away from norm violation.

Labeling formulations also frequently contend that the organiza-tions and agencies that are designed to bring the deviant back into con-formity often produce quite different results. They stigmatize individuals, seal them off from opportunities to withdraw from deviance, and create other social impediments to rehabilitation. Training schools, prisons, mental hospitals, and other people-changing institutions are suspected of exacer-bating, rather than reducing, the adjustment problems of their charges.

This description of the basic ingredients of labeling theory re-sembles rather closely a number of other descriptions that have appeared in the sociological literature. But there is something out of joint with these characterizations. On closer examination, labeling theory is revealed to be an extremely loose set of themes rather than an explicit and coherent theory. To some extent, it turns out to be a phantom theory. Critics of this perspective often allude to some unnamed group of people who are said to be labeling theorists, but it is difficult if not impossible to divine the identity of those individuals. One rarely encounters a sociologist who de-clares himself or herself to be a labeling theorist, unlike the case of the self-defined criminologist.

There are a half-dozen or so individuals who are often cited as architects of labeling theory, but these people do not show allegiance to any single theoretical argument. On this point, Edwin Lemert, a key figure in the development of these themes, has indicated that

> I have observed to some of my colleagues that labeling theory seems to be largely an invention of its critics. By this I mean that with a few commendable exceptions critics tend to impute common ideas to a number of authors, including myself, whose writings in reality are quite diverse. Critics even derive hypotheses for us or enumerate our underlying assumptions, most recently reaching an impressive total of nine. Having done this, they proceed to demonstrate the logical, methodological, and empirical insufficiencies of the theory. When confronted, those who have been identified with the theory or "school," so-called, must deny or refute that which they haven't said or defend ideas they don't necessarily share, or accept only with qualifications.[6]

---

[6] Edwin M. Lemert, "Response to Critics: Feedback and Choice," in Lewis A. Coser and Otto N. Larsen, eds., *The Uses of Controversy in Sociology* (New York: Free Press, 1976), p. 244.

For these reasons, which will be discussed in more detail, it seems reasonable to speak of a labeling perspective or orientation, rather than to talk of a theory or paradigm shared by an identifiable cadre of like-minded theorists.

The Development of the Labeling Perspective

Some students of deviance have indicated that they detect the seeds of the labeling orientation in the writings of historian Frank Tannenbaum, who over forty years ago drew attention to "dramatization of evil," which was his term for the societal reaction experiences that allegedly drove the deviant further into misconduct.[7] One can also find hints in the direction of labeling views in the writings of Maurice Parmelee over a half-century ago (see Chapter 2).

A much more convincing case can be made for locating the origins of labeling viewpoints in Edwin Lemert's 1951 volume, which carried the misleading title, *Social Pathology.*[8] Lemert's book centered on the analysis of sociopathic behavior, which he defined as "behavior which is effectively disapproved of in social interaction" (p. 449). Clearly, that definition and the substantive problems of political radicalism, prostitution, crime, alcoholism, and mental disorders are the stuff of modern deviance analysis, although it ought to be noted that Lemert also included commentary on blindness and speech defects, which are generally given short shrift in current discussions of deviance.

The central thrust of Lemert's views is captured in a series of seven postulates (pp. 22–23).

1. There are modalities in human behavior and clusters of deviations from these modalities which can be identified and described for situations specified in time and space.
2. Behavioral deviations are a function of culture conflict which is expressed through social organization.
3. There are societal reactions to deviations ranging from strong approval through indifference to strong disapproval.
4. Sociopathic behavior is deviation which is *effectively* disapproved.
5. The deviant person is one whose role, status, function, and self-definition are importantly shaped by how much deviation he engages in, by the degree of its social visibility, by the *particular* exposure he has to the societal reaction, and by the nature and strength of the societal reaction.
6. There are patterns of restriction and freedom in the social participation of deviants which are related directly to their status, role, and self-definitions.

[7] Frank Tannenbaum, *Crime and the Community* (New York: Ginn, 1938), pp. 19–21.

[8] Edwin M. Lemert, *Social Pathology* (New York: McGraw-Hill, 1951).

The biological strictures upon social participation of deviants are directly significant in comparatively few cases.

7. Deviants are individuated with respect to their vulnerability to the societal reaction because: (a) the person is a dynamic agent, (b) there is a structuring to each personality which acts as a set of limits within which the societal reaction operates.

Lemert devoted considerable attention to the contexts in which deviance takes place and introduced the distinctions between individual, situational, and systematic deviation. *Individual deviation* designates nonconformity that arises out of internal psychic pressures, while *situational deviation* is the result of situational stresses or pressures. By *systematic deviation,* Lemert meant patterns of deviant behavior that become organized into subcultures or behavior systems.

Another major conceptual distinction was between primary and secondary deviation. *Primary deviation* was Lemert's term for initial acts of norm violation that arise out of myriad sources and that are not regarded as personally significant by the deviant actor. *Secondary deviation,* on the other hand, occurs when the actor reorganizes his or her social-psychological characteristics around the deviant role. According to Lemert, secondary deviation most commonly develops out of a feedback process in which repeated misconduct or deviance triggers societal reactions that in turn call forth additional instances of deviance, ultimately culminating in the acceptance of a deviant social status and efforts at adjustment on the basis of the associated role.

These arguments regarding the social-interactional processes in deviance were further elaborated by Lemert who applied his insights to research studies of alcoholics, the development of paranoid social patterns, and the genesis of certain forms of criminality.[9] Lemert's book was a dozen years ahead of its time when it first appeared because it represented almost the sole challenge to the anomie and social disorganization [10] perspectives, which dominated the field of sociology at that time.

Beginning in the early 1960s, the social reaction views first articulated by Lemert began to be voiced by a large number of other sociologists. For example, Howard Becker presented a number of claims in his book, *Outsiders,* that closely paralleled those of Lemert. Becker's volume quickly became one of the critical works to which many others paid homage when

[9] Edwin M. Lemert, *Human Deviance, Social Problems, and Social Control,* 2nd ed. (Englewood Cliffs, N.J.: Prentice-Hall, 1972), pp. 102–22; 207–45; 137–82; and 246–64.

[10] Robert E. L. Faris, *Social Disorganization* (New York: Ronald Press, 1955). Social disorganization and anomie arguments are discussed in Gibbons and Jones, *Study of Deviance,* pp. 18–22, 84–93.

presenting labeling themes.[11] It is fair to say that this broad point of view rapidly became one of the most popular sociological formulations of the day.

Lemert and Becker loom large among the putative founders of the labeling perspective, but they and others who contributed to this viewpoint did not create it in some entirely spontaneous fashion. Nor is labeling a wholly new set of ideas having little or no connection with an earlier theoretical tradition among sociologists. While the connecting links between labeling views and earlier endeavors in sociology are somewhat indistinct, these links do exist. David Matza has pointed out that the central themes of the labeling argument are closely related to symbolic interactionist theory in social psychology, particularly as articulated by George Herbert Mead. Matza observed that "a theme that has more or less unified the neo-Chicagoans [Lemert, Becker, and Erving Goffman] has been the emphasis on the *process of becoming deviant* and the part played by the official registrars of deviation in that process." [12]

Nanette Davis has also called attention to the theoretical ties between labeling theory and symbolic interactionism. She asserted that, "claiming direct descent from G. H. Mead and Herbert Blumer, labeling practitioners have identified with the symbolic interactionist perspective." [13] Davis's argument was that both symbolic interactionists and labeling theo-

---

[11] Some of the major works that are usually included in catalogues of labeling viewpoints are Jack D. Douglas, "Deviance and Order in a Pluralistic Society," in John C. McKinney and Edward T. Tiryakian, eds., *Theoretical Sociology* (Englewood Cliffs, N.J.: Prentice-Hall, 1970), pp. 367–401; Douglas, *American Social Order* (New York: Free Press, 1970); Douglas, ed., *Deviance and Respectability* (New York: Basic Books, 1970); Kai T. Erikson, "Notes on the Sociology of Deviance," *Social Problems,* 9 (Spring 1962):307–14; John I. Kitsuse, "Societal Reaction to Deviant Behavior: Problems of Theory and Method," in Howard S. Becker, ed., *The Other Side* (New York: Free Press, 1964), pp. 87–102; John Lofland, *Deviance and Identity* (Englewood Cliffs, N.J.: Prentice-Hall, 1969); Matza, *Becoming Deviant;* Thomas J. Scheff, *Being Mentally Ill* (Chicago: Aldine, 1966); Edwin M. Schur, *Labeling Deviant Behavior* (New York: Harper & Row, 1971); John DeLameter, "On the Nature of Deviance," *Social Forces,* 46 (June 1968):445–55; Eliot Freidson, "Disability as Social Deviance," in Marvin B. Sussman, ed., *Sociology and Rehabilitation* (Washington, D.C.: American Sociological Association, 1965), pp. 71–99; Robert A. Scott and Jack D. Douglas, eds., *Theoretical Perspectives on Deviance* (New York: Basic Books, 1972); Earl Rubington and Martin S. Weinberg, *Deviance: The Interactionist Perspective,* 2nd ed. (New York: Macmillan, 1973); Edwin M. Lemert, "Beyond Mead: The Societal Reaction to Deviance," *Social Problems,* 21 (April 1974):457–68; Patrick W. Conover, "A Reassessment of Labeling Theory: A Constructive Response to Criticism," in Coser and Larsen, *Uses of Controversy,* pp. 228–43; and Erich Goode, "On Behalf of Labeling Theory," *Social Problems,* 22 (June 1975):570–83.

[12] Matza, *Becoming Deviant,* p. 37. For a detailed discussion of symbolic interaction theory, see Herbert Blumer, *Symbolic Interactionism* (Englewood Cliffs, N.J.: Prentice-Hall, 1969).

[13] Nanette J. Davis, *Sociological Constructions of Deviance* (Dubuque, Ia.: Brown, 1975), p. 170.

rists view the self as a *process,* rather than as a fixed structure inside the head of the individual, so to speak. The self is an ever-emerging social product that arises out of socialization experiences and that continues to develop as the individual moves from one interactional setting to another. Also, labeling theorists and symbolic interactionists regard self and society as reciprocal processes. Socialization experiences link individuals to the ongoing structure of norms and values in the community, while the continuing interactions of groups and individuals are the stuff of which society is composed.

One of the most thorough attempts to identify the theoretical sources of labeling arguments has been made by Edwin Schur. He, too, contended that the major theoretical strand from which labeling theory has borrowed is the symbolic interactionist tradition represented in the writings of Charles Horton Cooley, G. H. Mead, and W. I. Thomas. At one juncture, he argued that, "indeed, the central notion that societal reaction 'produces' deviance is, in a way, simply a reworking of Thomas's well-known dictum that 'if men define situations as real, they are real in their consequences.' " [14]

Schur also asserted that a "microsociological-phenomenological" strand derived particularly from the arguments of Erving Goffman and Harold Garfinkel is woven throughout labeling theory. Schur quite correctly pointed out that, although Goffman's writings on social interaction, asylums, and stigma are in the Chicago tradition of symbolic interactionism, they have a somewhat distinctive cast that sets them off from the views of Lemert and Becker.[15] Garfinkel has been a source of insights for labeling theorists in that his ethnomethodological propositions and methodological procedures place much emphasis on comprehending behavior as it is understood by the individuals themselves.[16]

Finally, Schur claimed to see elements of functionalism and conflict perspectives embedded in labeling theory. Functional themes can be detected in particular in essays by Kai Erikson and Lewis Coser that endeavored to identify the positive social consequences that stem from the social identification of deviant persons, while conflict notions emerge in labeling assertions about rule making as a political process.[17]

---

[14] Edwin M. Schur, "Reactions to Deviance: A Critical Assessment," *American Journal of Sociology,* 75 (November 1969):318. Also see Schur, *Labeling Deviant Behavior.*

[15] Erving Goffman, *The Presentation of Self in Everyday Life* (Garden City, N.Y.: Doubleday Anchor Books, 1959); *Asylums* (Garden City, N.Y.: Doubleday Anchor Books, 1961); and *Stigma* (Englewood Cliffs, N.J.: Prentice-Hall, 1963).

[16] Harold Garfinkel, *Studies in Ethnomethodology* (Englewood Cliffs, N.J.: Prentice-Hall, 1967).

[17] Erikson, "Notes on the Sociology of Deviance"; and Lewis A. Coser, "Some Functions of Deviant Behavior and Normative Flexibility," *American Journal of Sociology,* 68 (September 1962):171–81.

Criticisms of Labeling Views

Labeling arguments struck a responsive chord with many sociologists for a variety of reasons, a major one being that they provided a set of contentions that sociologists could counterpose to the claims of psychiatrists and psychologists that hold that deviants are pathological people. However, the labeling view comprises a very loosely articulated argument drawn from a variety of sociological sources rather than a rigorous theoretical statement constructed of precise definitions and explicit propositions. Those who have urged support for this viewpoint have done so largely on the basis of impressionistic and anecdotal kinds of evidence rather than on research data that confirm the accuracy of the argument. The situation could hardly be otherwise, given the looseness of the labeling viewpoint. However, it is also the case that few attempts have been made to derive specific hypotheses from the broad perspective and to submit these to research scrutiny.

The large number of critiques and commentaries on the alleged inadequacies of the labeling orientation bear testimony to its ambiguous character.[18] The sociological literature contains a large number of evaluations and commentary designed to sharpen and clarify this perspective.

Some of these negative comments have been meritricious ones, in which straw men have been set up and then attacked. For example, some have argued that certain unidentified labeling theorists have suggested that publicly identified deviants differ from nondeviants only by virtue of having been labeled. According to this criticism, those theorists aver that labeling

---

[18] These include David J. Bordua, "Recent Trends: Deviant Behavior and Social Control," *Annals of the American Academy of Political and Social Science,* 369 (January 1969):149–63; Ronald L. Akers, "Problems in the Sociology of Deviance: Social Definitions and Behavior," *Social Forces,* 46 (June 1968):455–65; Jack P. Gibbs, "Conceptions of Deviant Behavior: The Old and the New," *Pacific Sociological Review,* 9 (Spring 1966):9–14; Gibbs, "Issues in Defining Deviance," in Scott and Douglas, *Theoretical Perspectives on Deviance,* pp. 39–68; Gibbs and Maynard L. Erickson, "Major Developments in the Sociological Study of Deviance," in Alex Inkeles, James Coleman, and Neil Smelser, eds., *Annual Review of Sociology* (Palo Alto: Annual Reviews, 1975), pp. 21–42; Schur, "Reactions to Deviance"; Davis, "Labeling Theory in Deviance Research"; Peter K. Manning, "Survey Essay: On Deviance," *Contemporary Sociology,* 2 (March 1973):123–28; Manning, "Deviance and Dogma," *British Journal of Criminology,* 15 (January 1975):1–20; Milton Mankoff, "Societal Reaction and Career Deviance: A Critical Analysis," *Sociological Quarterly,* 12 (Spring 1971):204–18; Ian Taylor, Paul Walton, and Jock Young, *The New Criminology* (London: Routledge & Kegan Paul, 1973), pp. 139–71; Paul G. Schervish, "The Labeling Perspective: Its Bias and Potential in the Study of Political Deviance," *The American Sociologist,* 8 (May 1973):47–57; John I. Kitsuse, "Deviance, Deviant Behavior, and Deviants: Some Conceptual Problems," in William J. Filstead, ed., *An Introduction to Deviance* (Chicago: Markham Publishing Co., 1972), pp. 233–43; Paul Rock, "The Sociology of Deviancy and Conceptions of Moral Order," *British Journal of Criminology,* 14 (April 1974):139–49. These critiques are discussed in detail in Gibbons and Jones, *Study of Deviance,* pp. 130–33.

of deviants is a capricious event or one based almost entirely on the social background characteristics of those who are unfortunate enough to get labeled and that it in no way hinges on the commission of nonconforming acts. It is difficult to identify any sociologist who actually has advanced such a patently questionable claim.

A more telling criticism of labeling arguments is that these viewpoints are overly deterministic, in that they often attribute too much significance to societal reactions to deviance and too little importance to the varied social backgrounds of deviant actors as determinants of their deviant career pathways.[19] However, the most marked deficiency has already been noted: These claims have not congealed into a body of testable theory. As Nanette Davis has indicated,

> labeling theory, characteristically oriented within a symbolic interaction framework, has suffered from a "methodological inhibition" often associated with this social psychological approach. Conceptual impoverishment is facilitated by an absorption with general imagery, with unsystematic, elusive, and suggestive empirical presentations, rather than definitive tests of interaction framework.[20]

Labeling Arguments and Criminology

The labeling perspective deals with deviance of many kinds and is not restricted to criminality. Nonetheless, many of the illustrative cases used to support its arguments have been drawn from the area of criminality. Also, its supporters have often applied it to crime and delinquency, particularly in the form of arguments contending that labeling experiences drive apprehended lawbreakers further into careers as deviants, rather than drawing them away from criminal pathways.[21]

What can be said about this ironic view of reactions to criminality? What does the available evidence show regarding the proposition that correctional intervention actually impels offenders further into lawbreaking? Clarence Schrag's explication of the basic assumptions of labeling theory provides a starting point.

1. No act is intrinsically criminal . . .
2. Criminal definitions are enforced in the interest of powerful groups by their official representatives, including the police, courts, correctional institutions, and other administrative bodies . . .
3. A person does not become a criminal by violating the law. Instead, he is designated a criminal by the reactions of authorities who confer upon him

---

[19] For example, see Bordua, "Recent Trends," p. 53.
[20] Davis, "Labeling Theory in Deviance Research," pp. 457–60.
[21] For example, see Edwin M. Schur, *Radical Non-Intervention: Rethinking the Delinquency Problem* (Englewood Cliffs, N.J.: Prentice-Hall, 1973).

the status of an outcast and divest him of some of his social and political privileges . . .

4. The practice of dichotomizing people into criminal and noncriminal categories is contrary to common sense and empirical evidence . . .

5. Only a few persons are caught in violation of the law though many may be equally guilty . . .

6. While the sanctions used in law enforcement are directed against the total person and not only the criminal act, the penalties vary according to the characteristics of the offender . . .

7. Criminal sanctions also vary according to other characteristics of the offender, and for any given offense they tend to be most frequent and most severe among males, the youth (excepting juveniles handled in civil courts), the unemployed or underemployed, the poorly educated, members of the lower classes, members of minority groups, transients, and residents of deteriorated urban areas . . .

8. Criminal justice is founded on a stereotyped conception of the criminal as a pariah—a willful wrongdoer who is normally bad and deserving of the community's condemnation.

9. Confronted by public condemnation and the label of an evil man, it may be difficult for an offender to maintain a favorable image of himself.[22]

The confusion surrounding the labeling perspective is illustrated by the fact that not everyone would agree that these assumptions are central to the viewpoint. For one thing, the claims that laws represent the interests of powerful groups appear in more explicit form in emerging conflict or radical versions of criminology. On this same point, Schrag attributed these assumptions to Turk and Quinney, even though these two sociologists would not be identified as labeling theorists by many others.[23]

Charles Wellford has reviewed the theoretical and research literature bearing on these assumptions or propositions of the labeling argument. He contended that the initial claim that no acts are intrinsically criminal is in error, because murder, rape, assault, robbery, and a number of other garden-variety crimes are consistently prohibited across different societies.[24] Wellford also argued that contentions that the social char-

---

[22] Clarence Schrag, *Crime and Justice: American Style* (Rockville, Md.: National Institute of Mental Health, 1971), pp. 89–91.

[23] Austin T. Turk, *Criminality and Legal Order* (Chicago: Rand McNally, 1969); Richard Quinney, *The Social Reality of Crime* (Boston: Little, Brown, 1970).

[24] Charles Wellford, "Labelling Theory and Criminology: An Assessment," *Social Problems*, 22 (February 1975):332–45. On this point, see also Robert B. Edgerton, *Deviance: A Cross-Cultural Perspective* (Menlo Park, Calif.: Cummings, 1976). Wellford concluded that (p. 336): "Similar behaviors are proscribed cross-culturally and are assessed in terms of seriousness by different national samples. On those criminal behaviors that have been the focus of criminology, there is social consensus." However, there are a number of kinds of crime that were not included in the group discussed by Wellford, such as anti-trust violations, misrepresentation in advertising, automobile theft, etc., that are *not* found everywhere in all societies. If

acteristics of labeled deviants are the major bases on which differential decisions are made regarding their fates in the correctional machinery lack empirical support. Instead, he argued that most officially identified offenders get into the hands of the authorities because of actual lawbreaking in which they have engaged, and that the major determinant of subsequent decisions about them centers about offense seriousness.

Wellford reported that the claim that nearly all citizens are equally involved in criminality (assumption 4) also lacks evidential support (see the discussion of hidden or self-reported lawbreaking in Chapter 4). Finally, Wellford argued that the contention that labeling experiences drive individuals further into repetitive criminality is, at the very least, overly simple in character. For one thing, it has not been established that labeling processes do commonly lead to self-concept and attitudinal changes on the part of stigmatized offenders. Additionally, even if these societal re-actions do sometimes have such consequences, the varying social circumstances in which labeled deviants find themselves are probably implicated heavily in the lines of conduct that they subsequently pursue.[25]

Others have also found labeling viewpoints unconvincing. For example, Walter Gove contended that labeling theory revolves around two pivotal questions: Why do some people and not others become labeled as deviants, and what are the consequences to the individual of being labeled? He asserted that the available evidence indicates that labeling follows from the commission of deviant acts and that it is not the cause of stabilized deviant behavior.[26] Although he did not deal directly with empirical evidence on labeling processes, Solomon Kobrin has echoed the judgment of

---

nothing else, this observation illustrates a major point in this discussion, namely that *some* evidence can be marshalled to support a variety of interpretations of labeling views or their counterarguments. Further evidence in support of Wellford's conclusion can be found in Graeme Newman, *Comparative Deviance: Perception and Law in Six Cultures* (New York: Elsevier, 1967). Newman questioned samples of residents in six countries: India, Indonesia, Italy, Yugoslavia, Iran, and the United States. These persons were quizzed about nine acts: robbery, incest, failing to render aid to a person in danger, abortion, factory pollution, homosexuality, non-violent political protest, embezzlement of government funds, and drug use. The respondents were asked whether they thought the act in question should be prohibited by criminal law, their view of the seriousness of the act, and several other questions. Newman found a high degree of consensus concerning disapproval of certain crimes and acts of deviance across these six cultures. For an American study of citizen views on the seriousness of crimes, see Peter Rossi, Emily Waite, Christine Bose, and Richard Berk, "The Seriousness of Crimes: Normative Structure and Individual Differences," *American Sociological Review,* 39 (April 1974):224–37. For a more general discussion of the issue of social support for criminal laws, see Gwynn Nettler, *Explaining Crime,* 2nd ed. (New York: McGraw-Hill, 1978), pp. 214–19.

[25] For one analysis that endeavored to examine these forces operating in the career lines pursued by offenders, see John Irwin, *The Felon* (Englewood Cliffs, N.J.: Prentice-Hall, 1970).

[26] Walter R. Gove, "Deviant Behavior, Social Intervention, and Labeling Theory," in Coser and Larsen, *Uses of Controversy,* pp. 219–227.

others that labeling arguments offer an overly simplified conceptualization of reactions to offenders and of their subsequent responses to those social labeling experiences.[27]

On the whole, the existing evidence lends relatively little support to sweeping claims that have sometimes been advanced about the allegedly deleterious effects of correctional intervention efforts on offenders.[28]

Labeling Views and Criminology: An Assessment

What can be concluded about the labeling perspective and the analysis of criminality? Wellford's judgment was that criminal labels are not assigned to individuals capriciously and that labeling does not affect subsequent behavior in the ways postulated by adherents of these views. He suggested that criminological theories need to more fully explore the impact of a number of situational determinants of the behavior patterns and career lines pursued by offenders, which are probably more important than stigmatizing labels, lowered self-images, and negative attitudes that are produced by social reactions to offenders.[29] Finally, he asserted that labeling processes may be significant for forms of deviance other than lawbreaking, and that these themes may have an important place in some kind of more comprehensive theory.

Certain key insights in labeling perspectives are likely to survive in the criminological formulations of the future. Although the current versions of this orientation are entirely too gross or simplistic, it may ultimately be possible to articulate a more reasonable and more sophisticated line of argument that speaks to such matters as differences among the individuals who are labeled, variations in the reaction experiences, and other contingencies that must be taken into account in uncovering the relationships between norm-violating acts, societal reactions to those acts, and subsequent careers in deviance or conformity.[30]

---

[27] Solomon Kobrin, "The Labeling Approach: Problems and Limits," in James F. Short, Jr., ed., *Delinquency, Crime, and Society* (Chicago: University of Chicago Press, 1976), pp. 239–53.

[28] An extensive body of evidence on the impact of training schools is summarized in Don C. Gibbons, *Delinquent Behavior* 2nd ed. (Englewood Cliffs, N.J.: Prentice-Hall, 1976), pp. 244–56. Also see Jack Donald Foster, Simon Dinitz, and Walter C. Reckless, "Perceptions of Stigma Following Public Intervention for Delinquent Behavior," *Social Problems*, 20 (Fall 1972):202–9. The most thorough review of the evidence on juvenile justice system responses and their effects on youths is Ann Rankin Mahoney, "The Effect of Labeling Upon Youths in the Juvenile Justice System: A Review of the Evidence," *Law and Society Review*, 8 (Summer 1974): 583–614.

[29] Some of these arguments are examined in Don C. Gibbons, "Observations on the Study of Crime Causation," *American Journal of Sociology*, 77 (September 1971): 262–78.

[30] For one attempt along these lines, see Bernard A. Thorsell and Lloyd W. Klemke, "The Labeling Process: Reinforcement or Deterrent?" *Law and Society Review*, 6 (February 1972):393–403.

THE DEVELOPMENT OF CONFLICT AND RADICAL CRIMINOLOGY

Chapter 5 concluded by noting that some strident and full-blown challenges to the perspectives of mainstream criminology are now being voiced, in the form of arguments that have been identified variously as conflict, radical, Marxist, or critical criminology.[31] The dividing points between social conflict arguments and radical or Marxist criminological theories are not always clear-cut. These contentions often blend into each other. Moreover, some of those who have commented on these new directions have tended to merge them, further blurring whatever lines of separation that might otherwise be discerned between them. Finally, some of the advocates of these new versions of criminological thought have themselves become more radicalized. Even so, pluralistic conflict viewpoints ought to be distinguished from more recent, Marxist propositions about criminality.

Contrary to some of the claims made by contemporary radicals, the pioneers of American criminology were not totally oblivious to the role of social conflict in the creation of laws and lawbreakers. For example, some hints in this direction appeared in Maurice Parmelee's 1918 book, in Sellin's extended discussion of culture conflict and crime, and in some of Sutherland's writings. A relatively well-developed version of conflict theory was contained in Vold's 1958 volume.[32]

CONFLICT AND INTEREST GROUP THEORIES IN CRIMINOLOGY [33]

The distinguishing feature of interest-group or conflict arguments is that they attribute law making and criminality to a relatively diffuse and pluralistic pattern of conflicting interest-group actions and phenomena

[31] This development has been reviewed in Don C. Gibbons and Peter G. Garabedian, "Conservative, Liberal, and Radical Criminology: Some Trends and Observations," in Charles E. Reasons, ed., *The Criminologist: Crime and the Criminal* (Pacific Palisades, Calif.: Goodyear, 1974), pp. 51–65; Gresham M. Sykes, "The Rise of Critical Criminology," *Journal of Criminal Law and Criminology,* 65 (June 1974): 206–13; Eugene Doleschal and Nora Klapmuts, "Toward a New Criminology," *Crime and Delinquency Literature,* 5 (December 1973):607–26; Tony Platt, "Prospects for a Radical Criminology in the United States," *Crime and Social Justice,* 1 (Spring–Summer 1974):2–10; Raymond J. Michalowski and Edward W. Bohlander, "Repression and Criminal Justice in Capitalist America," *Sociological Inquiry,* 46, No. 2 (1976):95–106.

[32] Maurice F. Parmelee, *Criminology* (New York: Macmillan, 1918), pp. 32–36; Thorsten Sellin, *Culture Conflict and Crime* (New York: Social Science Research Council, 1938); Albert K. Cohen, Alfred Lindesmith, and Karl Schuessler, eds., *The Sutherland Papers* (Bloomington, Ind.: Indiana University Press, 1956), pp. 103–104; and George B. Vold, *Theoretical Criminology* (New York: Oxford University Press, 1958), pp. 203–61.

[33] Conflict theories have been reviewed in Taylor, Walton, and Young, *The New Criminology,* pp. 237–67. It also ought to be noted that the rise of conflict theories

in American society, rather than to some monolithic force such as political-economic structure. Stuart Hills's assertions on social conflict and criminality are representative.

> In a rapidly changing pluralistic society such as the United States, however—with its racial, religious, ethnic, and class diversity; its sharply competing economic and political interest groups; its conflicting life styles and value orientations among different subcultures; and its frequent recourse to the criminal law to regulate and prohibit a wide variety of behavior—the interest-group perspective would seem more useful in understanding the enactment and selective enforcement of law involving marijuana use, organized crime, and white-collar crime.[34]

Austin Turk is one well-known conflict theorist who has turned away from "the behavior question" centered on criminal etiology and toward an examination of criminality as status. Turk regarded the search for answers to the question "Why do they do it?" as a relatively futile one and has argued that "nothing and no one is intrinsically criminal; criminality is a definition applied by individuals with the power to do so, according to illegal and extra-legal, as well as legal criteria." [35] Lawbreaking cannot be distinguished from conformity, except for the reactions of authorities who have applied criminal status to some people. The implications of this perspective are far-reaching.

> Unless one assumes that legal processes somehow operate in a vacuum, entirely apart from the conflicts intrinsic to social relations—an assumption now rather thoroughly discredited—it is unreasonable to suppose that differences in criminality rates among different categories of

---

in criminology was part of a larger development, in which sociologists rediscovered social conflict in the 1950s. T. B. Bottomore has pointed out that mainstream sociologists in the 1930s and 1940s most frequently embraced social systems theories and equilibrium models of society, which treated social conflict as temporary and aberrant in nature. See Bottomore, "Sociological Theory and the Study of Social Conflict," in John C. McKinney and Edward A. Tiryakian, eds., *Theoretical Sociology* (New York: Appleton-Century-Crofts, 1970), pp. 137–53. Bottomore contended that Simmel, Cooley, Small, and many other early figures in sociology had much to say about social conflict. Also, according to Bottomore, the revival of interest in social conflict came about in large measure as a result of World War II and the international tensions that have continued since then, racial conflict in the United States, and other real world events that have impinged upon sociological perspectives. For another useful discussion of the general background within which conflict theories in criminology are located, see William J. Chambliss, ed., *Sociological Readings in the Conflict Perspective* (Reading, Mass.: Addison-Wesley, 1973), pp. 1–38.

[34] Stuart L. Hills, *Crime, Power, and Morality* (Scranton, Pa.: Chandler, 1971), p. 6; also see John F. Galliher and James L. McCartney, *Criminology: Power, Crime, and Criminal Law* (Homewood, Ill.: Dorsey Press, 1977).

[35] Turk, *Criminality and Legal Order*, p. 10.

people are solely due to corresponding variations in their behavior patterns. Therefore, instead of assuming the criminality of some of the behavior patterns of persons in certain social categories, and proceeding to look for the sources of the behavior patterns presumably to explain their criminality (a neat circle) one is lead to investigate the tendency of laws to penalize persons whose behavior is more characteristic of the less powerful than of the more powerful and the extent to which some persons and groups can and do use legal processes and agencies to maintain and enhance their power position vis-à-vis other persons and groups.[36]

In his analysis, Turk had much to say about social order, arguing that, in modern societies, the prevailing situation is one of conflict among different groups who all seek to gain social and material advantages over other collectivities. These conflicts are kept under control in part through legal norms and patterns of norm enforcement which the *authorities* (those in dominant social positions) impose on the *subjects* (those relatively powerless groups). Successful authority-subject relationships are based on the submission of the relatively powerless to the authorities, rather than being maintained by coercion. Indeed, "lawbreaking is taken to be an indicator of the failure or lack of authority; it is a measure of the extent to which rules and ruled, decision-makers and decision-acceptors, are not bound together in a perfectly stable relationship." [37]

Turk dealt at considerable length with the conditions under which cultural and social differences between authorities and subjects are likely to result in conflict and the conditions under which criminalization will probably occur. Criminalization is the assignment of criminal status to people through the norm-enforcement mechanisms of arrest and trial.

There are many important insights embedded in Turk's book. At the same time, his essay is abstract in character and is relatively silent on a number of important points. For example, at one juncture he indicated that

how authorities come to be authorities is irrelevant. It is sufficient that a social structure built out of authority relations exists which is to say that authority and subject status categories are implicit in actual behavior patterns, whether or not people more or less accurately perceive and symbolize the patterns.[38]

Turk's comment was logically correct, in that the issue of who the authorities are was irrelevant to the formal structure of his argument. But

---

[36] *Ibid.*, p. 18.
[37] *Ibid.*, p. 48.
[38] *Ibid.*, p. 51.

this question remains a fundamental one and lies at the center of disagreements between mainstream and radical criminologists. Radical criminologists claim that effective power in American society is wielded by the members of a corporate ruling class, which is a very different view from that espoused by mainstream criminologists, including conflict theorists such as Turk who opt for a pluralistic conception of interest groups and power relationships in modern society.

A detailed and sophisticated exposition of a conflict perspective on crime, law, and social control has been put forth by William Chambliss and Robert Seidman.[39] They rejected the views that criminal laws are buttressed by a high degree of normative consensus throughout society and that the state, as represented by the police and the courts, enforces laws in an even-handed and value-neutral fashion. Instead, they contended that criminal laws in complex societies reflect value antagonisms and value pluralism, in which the interests of the socially powerful are most likely to become embodied in criminal statutes. Also, they argued that criminal laws and other legal norms are most frequently applied to those who lack social power.

> It is our contention that, far from being primarily a value-neutral framework within which conflict can be peacefully resolved, the power of the state is itself the principal prize in the perpetual conflict that is society. The legal order—the rules which the various law-making institutions in the bureaucracy that is the state lay down for the governance of officials and citizens, the tribunals, official and unofficial, formal and informal, which determine whether the rules have been breached, and the bureaucratic agencies which enforce the law—is in fact a self-serving system to maintain power and privilege. In a society sharply divided into haves and have-nots, poor and rich, blacks and whites, powerful and weak, shot with a myriad of special interest groups, not only is the myth false because of imperfections in the normative system: It is *inevitable* that it be so.[40]

Chambliss and Seidman provided a generous body of commentary on the role of value conflicts in work of legislatures, arguing that legisla-

---

[39] William B. Chambliss and Robert B. Seidman, *Law, Order, and Power* (Reading, Mass.: Addison-Wesley, 1971).

[40] *Ibid.*, p. 4. Hopkins charged that Chambliss and Seidman equated business interests with powerful interest groups and failed to see that other collectivities may also be influential in law-creation. See Andrew Hopkins, "On the Sociology of Criminal Law," *Social Problems*, 22 (1975):608–19. As a result, they were compelled to try to explain away certain statutes such as the antitrust laws, which seem inimical to business interests. They did so by contending that these statutes were actually pro-business in design, intended to drive marginal companies out of business and to dampen public hostility aroused by the rapacious activities of certain captains of industry. Hopkins commented (p. 617): "But there is something curiously artificial about this argument. The fact is that from time to time big business is forced to give ground. Yet Chambliss and Seidman interpret this retreat as a victory."

tion is most often a response to the demands of socially powerful groups, thus, "deviancy is not a moral question; it is a political question." [41] These theorists also had much to say about the ways in which social conflicts and differences in social power enter into the enforcement activities of the police and the decision making of the courts. They stressed the point that others have also made: The police and courts engage in goal substitution and goal displacement, in which they come to orient their activities around their own organizational needs and interests, rather than around pursuit of the official goals that have been enunciated for them. Some of the studies that point to the perversion of organizational goals in various law-enforcement, judicial, and people-processing structures were noted in Chapter 5.

The final example of conflict theory is Richard Quinney's *The Social Reality of Crime,* in which he enunciated a set of six propositions regarding crime and social reactions to it.

1. *Crime is a definition of human conduct that is created by authorized agents in a politically organized society.*
2. *Criminal definitions describe behaviors that conflict with the interests of the segments of society that have the power to shape public policy.*
3. *Criminal definitions are applied by the segments of society that have the power to shape the enforcement and administration of criminal law.*
4. *Behavior patterns are structured in segmentally organized society in relation to criminal definitions, and within this context persons engage in actions that have relative probabilities of being defined as criminal.*
5. *Conceptions of crime are constructed and diffused in the segments of society by various means of communication.*
6. *The social reality of crime is constructed by the formulation and application of criminal definitions, the development of behavior patterns related to criminal definitions, and the construction of criminal conceptions.*[42]

Although Quinney regarded these six statements as propositions that, taken together, form a theory, the propositional status of at least some of the assertions is questionable. For example, Gibbs and Erickson have remarked that

> by his own admission (1970:18) one of the propositions is a definition, and the analytical character of the other propositions is ignored. Consider his third proposition (1970:18): "Criminal definitions are applied by the segments of society that have the power to shape the enforcement and administration of criminal law." How is the "application of criminal definitions" logically distinct from "enforcement and admin-

41 Chambliss and Seidman, *Law, Order, and Power,* p. 4.
42 Richard Quinney, *The Social Reality of Crime* (Boston: Little, Brown, 1970), pp. 15–23.

istration of criminal law"? One may as well proclaim that taxidermists stuff animals.[43]

The definition masquerading as a proposition, to which Gibbs and Erickson referred, is the first one, specifying that crime is a societally created definition of conduct. However, Quinney's sixth assertion is also a definition, for it is difficult to assign any meaning to "the social reality of crime" apart from the ingredients listed by Quinney.

The most fundamental criticism that has been directed at Quinney's views on the social reality of crime is the one that has also been leveled at other conflict theorists, namely, that their model favors diffuse, pluralistic conceptions of social conflicts, interest groups, and social structure.[44] Consider Quinney's comments on the institutional orders within which interests operate:

> For our use, these may be called: (1) *the political*, which regulates the distribution of power and authority in a society; (2) *the economic*, which regulates the production and distribution of goods and services; (3) *the religious*, which regulates the relationship of man to a conception of the supernatural; (4) *the kinship*, which regulates sexual relations, family patterns, and the procreation and rearing of children; (5) *the educational*, which regulates the formal training of the society's members; and (6) *the public*, which regulates the protection and maintenance of the community and its citizens. Each segment of society has its own orientation to these orders. Some, because of their authority position in the interest structure, are able to have their interests represented in public policy.[45]

According to the critics, such arguments fail to acknowledge the overpowering significance of class relationships growing out of productive arrangements in societies, which lead to monopolization of effective power by a ruling class rather than myriad interest groups.

Some of those who have espoused conflict views of this kind have been unwavering in support of these themes, but Chambliss and Quinney have modified their perspectives markedly in recent years, rejecting pluralistic views of social order in favor of Marxist arguments stressing class

---

[43] Jack P. Gibbs and Maynard L. Erickson, "Major Developments in the Sociological Study of Deviance," in Inkeles, Coleman, and Smelser, *Annual Review of Sociology*, p. 38. Also see Manning, "Deviance and Dogma" (p. 12), who commented: "The overall impression the reader takes away is one of enormous simplification, reification, and an almost appalling absence of sensitivity to the complexity of human social interaction."

[44] Taylor, Walton, and Young, *The New Criminology*, pp. 237–67.

[45] Quinney, *The Social Reality of Crime*, p. 38.

relations and ruling-class domination. Their revised perspectives are considered in Chapter 7.

RESPONSES TO LABELING ARGUMENTS AND CONFLICT THEORY

Large numbers of mainstream criminologists have been influenced by labeling and conflict contentions and have incorporated some of these notions into their theoretical positions. At least two separate assessments of changes in the theoretical structure of criminology have appeared, drawing attention to the developments discussed here. In one of these, Eugene Doleschal and Nora Klapmuts have commented on the rise of a "new criminology." Their review of the chronology of developments in criminology indicated that earlier conservative and mainstream thoughtways are being challenged by this new criminology.

> The new criminology concentrates not on the officially designated criminal but on (1) the definition of crime—the decision to make, for instance, intoxication by marijuana or other drugs criminal while intoxication by alcohol (the drug of those who make the laws) is noncriminal; and (2) the selection of certain lawbreakers for identification as criminals—for example, the decision to arrest, prosecute, and imprison the lower-class man who steals a hundred dollars and to deal informally with the upper-class embezzler of thousands of dollars by quiet settlement to avoid damaging his reputation.
>
> The new criminology views crime as an integral part of society—a normal, not a pathological, kind of human behavior. It assumes that crime cannot be eliminated—although its structure and form might be affected by changes in crime control policy, and that crime in some form serves useful purposes by integrating what is known as law-abiding society and in defining its boundaries. Most of all, it points out that deviance is a relative concept, that what we call "crime" and "criminals" are more or less arbitrarily defined classes of acts and actors rather than clear-cut distinctions implied by the labels "criminal" and "noncriminal." Although people and behaviors are viewed as one or the other, in reality the classifications of criminal and noncriminal shade into each other with no sharp lines of demarcation. The distinctions made between them are arbitrary but apparently not random; criminal labels are usually dispensed in ways that uphold the established order and do not threaten the lives and life styles of the classes or groups with power and influence.[46]

---

[46] Doleschal and Klapmuts, "Toward a New Criminology," p. 623. The term "new criminology" first appeared in Taylor, Walton, and Young, *The New Criminology*.

Doleschal and Klapmuts were on the mark in their characterization of shifts in criminological thinking that have occurred during the past two decades. However, they have described a revised rather than a new criminology. The theoretical shift in the direction of pluralistic conceptions of society and conflict theory has been gradual rather than abrupt, which is also true of the growth of labeling viewpoints. But, even more important, what these commentators had in mind as the new criminology is a blander version of theorizing than the radical or Marxist viewpoints to be examined in the next chapter. These latter arguments are in fact more deserving of the title "new criminology."

Gresham Sykes has also drawn attention to major revisions in criminological thought, arguing that "in the last ten to fifteen years, criminology in the United States has witnessed a transformation of one of its most fundamental paradigms for interpreting criminal behavior." [47] Sykes indicated that some people have identified the newer thoughtways as radical criminology, but he held that "the term is misleading since it suggests a particular ideological underpinning that probably does not exist. I think 'critical' criminology is a somewhat better term." [48]

Sykes's explication of critical criminology involved the following major elements. First, critical criminology is more concerned about why some people and not others are singled out for criminal labeling and stigmatization, rather than with queries about "Why do they do it?" Second, critical criminology involves negative views about the motivations behind the actions of social control agencies, arguing that these operations function as tools of the ruling class or that they promote their own organizational ends rather than the welfare of offenders. A third feature is emphasis on laws as the product of conflict and interest-group activities, rather than as being supported by widespread societal consensus. Finally, crime rates are seen as indicators of police behavior rather than crime levels.

Sykes offered a summary description of critical criminology, indicating that

> at the heart of this orientation lies the perspective of a stratified
> society in which the operation of the criminal law is a means of con-
> trolling the poor (and members of minority groups) by those in power
> who use the legal apparatus to (1) impose their particular morality
> and standards of good behavior on the entire society; (2) protect their
> property and physical safety from the depradations of the have-nots,
> even though the cost may be high in terms of the legal rights of those

[47] Sykes, "The Rise of Critical Criminology," p. 206.
[48] *Ibid.,* p. 208.

it perceives as a threat; and (3) to extend the definition of illegal or criminal behavior to encompass those who might threaten the status quo. The middle classes or the lower middle classes are drawn into this pattern of domination either because (1) they are led to believe they too have a stake in maintaining the status quo; or (2) they are made a part of agencies of social control and the rewards of organizational careers provide inducements for keeping the poor in their place.[49]

Sykes perceived both positive and negative aspects in critical criminology. On the positive side, these newer views have forced criminologists to pay more attention to variations in social support for particular criminal laws, the actual as opposed to the idealized operations of the legal-correctional machinery, and interrelations between criminality and the political order. Sykes scored critical criminologists for their frequently encountered tendency to convert latent functions of laws and the legal machinery into manifest ones, as, for example, when they argue that legislators deliberately draft laws in order to repress and victimize lower-class people or contend that prisons are designed explicitly for the purposes of warehousing troublesome minority group members. Sykes also argued that critical criminology involves an oversimplified or ambiguous conception of social stratification and power relationships and apparently opted for a pluralistic account of social power and interest groups in American society.

Sykes's account of critical criminology closely paralleled the description of new criminology by Doleschal and Klapmuts. There is little question that a considerable number of criminologists and students of deviance do embrace propositions of this variety. Also, Sykes may have been correct in criticizing the portrayal of the stratification system as made up of the ruling class, a broad middle class, and the lower-class victims of repression and oppression. At the same time, his analysis was off the mark in claiming that radical or Marxist criminology does not exist. An identifiable body of Marxist-radical criminology has sprung up in the past dozen years, containing themes that are not captured in Sykes's portrayal of critical criminology. It is to this set of ideas that attention now turns.

[49] *Ibid.*, p. 210.

NEW DIRECTIONS IN CRIMINOLOGICAL THEORY, Conclusion

7

THE ORIGINS OF RADICAL–MARXIST CRIMINOLOGY

Although conflict-oriented perspectives in criminology that stress the pluralistic nature of American society have existed at least in rudimentary form for some decades, only within the past ten years has a thoroughly radical, Marxist version of criminological thought emerged. For the most part, this new brand of theorizing has been an American invention, for there is little in the way of contemporary Marxist criminology elsewhere.[1]

What has produced the radicalization of criminologists and the development of radical brands of criminological thought? Why have Marxist views of crime and its causes captured the attention of many criminologists, particularly relatively young ones? Is it because existing explanatory paradigms have persistently failed to deal with new empirical facts that have emerged? The role of new facts in the rise of radical criminology cannot be gainsaid. But these new facts have arisen from the world of social events outside the discipline of sociology,[2] not from criminological research studies that have turned up puzzling results. Gresham

---

[1] However, see Erich Buchholz, Richard Hartmann, John Lekschas, and Gerhard Stiller, *Socialist Criminology,* translated by Ewald Osers (Lexington, Mass.: Lexington Books, 1974). This volume was produced by East German scholars and presented a socialist interpretation of crime, both in capitalist and socialist countries. Criminality in socialist nations was attributed to various "survivals" and "relics" of capitalism. For example, at one point (p. 73) they asserted that: "criminality in socialist society is no longer a product of objectively insoluble situations. Instead, it is an individual's specific conflict—conditioned by certain social and personal circumstances—with society, with the state, with minor collectives or with other individuals, a conflict in which the lawbreaker violates the elementary norms of social behaviour."

[2] For some commentary on the emergence of radical sociology, see David Horowitz, ed., *Radical Sociology* (San Francisco: Canfield Press, 1971).

Sykes has argued that "it does not appear that this new viewpoint in criminology simply grew out of the existing ideas in the field in some sort of automatic process where pure logic breeds uncontaminated by the concerns and passions of the times." [3]

The Spring-Summer 1974, issue of *Crime and Social Justice,* billed as a "radical journal for a people's criminology," contained an editor's comment that asserted that "radical criminology appeared on the crest of the final surges of social protest by women, blacks, the poor, students, and many others whose rage has scoured American institutions throughout the previous decade." [4] Peter Garabedian and I noted that the first murmurings of radical criminology appeared in radical and New Left publications such as *The Berkeley Barb,* while Francis Allen linked its emergence to the Vietnam War and the political turmoil that it generated, black militancy, and the development of youth culture.[5] Similarly, Sykes offered a catalogue of factors that included the Vietnam War and growing citizen cynicism regarding the government, the development of a youth counterculture, widespread brutality and illegality in police responses to political dissidents and the Black Panthers, and growing evidence of the ubiquity of white-collar crime carried on with impunity by upper-class individuals.[6] Finally, Anthony Platt has asserted that

> in the United States, we are presently witnessing and practicing a radical criminology which has been developing in its latest form since the early 1960s and has begun to challenge the hegemonic domination of the field by liberal scholars. The roots of this radicalism are to be found in political struggles—the civil rights movement, the anti-war movement, the student movement, Third World liberation struggles inside as well as outside the United States—and in the writings of participants in these struggles—George Jackson, Angela Davis, Eldridge Cleaver, Tom Hayden, Sam Melville, Bobby Seale, Huey Newton, Malcolm X, and Ruchell Magee, to name a few.[7]

Interpretations of the precise linkage of these events to radical criminology vary somewhat, but nearly all of these commentators agree

[3] Gresham M. Sykes, "The Rise of Critical Criminology," *Journal of Criminal Law and Criminology,* 65 (June 1974):211.

[4] Editorial, *Crime and Social Justice,* 1 (Spring–Summer 1974):1.

[5] Don C. Gibbons and Peter G. Garabedian, "Conservative, Liberal, and Radical Criminology: Some Trends and Observations," in Charles E. Reasons, ed., *The Criminologist: Crime and the Criminal* (Pacific Palisades, Calif.: Goodyear, 1974), pp. 51–65. Francis A. Allen, *The Crimes of Politics* (Cambridge, Mass.: Harvard University Press, 1974), pp. 9–10.

[6] Sykes, "Rise of Critical Criminology," pp. 210–12.

[7] Anthony Platt, "Prospects for a Radical Criminology in the United States," *Crime and Social Justice,* 1 (Spring–Summer 1974):2–10.

that the role of the state in the oppression of masses of the citizenry through criminal law and a variety of other devices has been exposed by these tumultuous happenings. Also, the overriding importance of corporate capitalism and class relationships in criminality has been revealed with great clarity, producing a crisis in the old criminology favored by mainstream criminologists.

THE OLD AND THE NEW CRIMINOLOGY

In Chapter 3 and elsewhere in this book, I have already drawn attention to the major ingredients of mainstream criminology. However, it would be well to examine Anthony Platt's description of liberal criminology, to which radical criminological thought is said to be a challenge. Although his account was an unintended caricature of mainstream criminology, it does provide a useful indicator of some of the viewpoints of radical criminologists. To begin with, Platt charged mainstream criminologists with unthinking acceptance of the state's definition of crime, because they take legal codes as given and lend support to the corrective or rehabilitative thrust of social control efforts directed at garden-variety offenders. According to Platt, liberal criminologists deliberately avoid the study of forms of behavior that are not currently defined as crime, such as imperialism, exploitation, racism, and sexism.[8] Platt also charged that liberal criminologists ignore violations of the criminal law that are not typically prosecuted, such as tax evasion, price fixing, consumer fraud, and police violence. Platt was correct in arguing that the humanistic conception of crime, centered around exploitation and the like, has not been widely accepted. However, his second claim was less accurate, for Sutherland's work on white-collar crime and the research studies of a number of other mainstream criminologists have dealt with price fixing, consumer

---

[8] *Ibid.,* p. 2. The most well-known essay urging the adoption of a humanistic definition of crime, centering on racism, exploitation, and the like, is Herman Schwendinger and Julia Schwendinger, "Defenders of Order or Guardians of Human Rights?" *Issues in Criminology,* 5 (Summer 1970):123–57. They would have criminologists study all violations of basic human rights, defined in the following manner (p. 144): "All persons must be guaranteed the fundamental prerequisites for well-being, including food, shelter, clothing, medical services, challenging work and recreational experiences, as well as security from predatory individuals or repressive and imperialistic social elites." For additional debate over legalistic versus humanistic definitions of crime, see Clayton Hartjen, "Legalism and Humanism: A Reply to the Schwendingers," *Issues in Criminology,* 7 (Winter 1972):59–69; Herman Schwendinger and Julia Schwendinger, "The Continuing Debate on the Legalistic Approach to the Definition of Crime," *Issues in Criminology,* 7 (Winter 1972):71–81; Austin T. Turk, "Prospects and Pitfalls for Radical Criminology: A Critical Response to Platt," *Crime and Social Justice,* 4 (Fall–Winter 1975):41–42.

fraud, and other rarely prosecuted offenses that are carried on by members of the upper classes.

Platt also contended that liberal criminology "supports the extension of state capitalism and gradualist programs of amelioration, while rejecting radical and violent forms of social and political change." [9] Mainstream criminologists were also held to be at fault for embracing behaviorism, pragmatism, and social engineering and for rejecting macrocosmic theory and historical analysis. The consequence, according to Platt, is that

> the liberal emphasis on pragmatism, short-range solutions and amelioration reveals an attitude of cynicism and defeatism concerning human potentiality and the possibility of far-ranging changes in society. This focus serves to exclude or underestimate the possibility of a radically different society in which cooperation replaces competition, where human values take precedence over property values, where exploitation, racism and sexism are eliminated, and where basic human needs are fulfilled. Liberal cynicism served to reinforce the malevolent view that radical change is utopian and visionary, thereby helping to impede the development of revolutionary social and political movements.[10]

It is difficult to know quite what to say about this commentary. Doubtless it is true that liberal criminology has a cynical or pessimistic cast. At the same time, the reluctance of most criminologists to embrace radical and violent measures directed at racism, sexism, and exploitation is surely understandable in the light of great uncertainty about the efficacy of such tactics, when no one knows which particular strategies might hold promise, and when the vision of an alternate workable society is so evanescent. Radical criminologists have themselves been almost entirely silent on these questions.[11] No blueprint of a new society has been drafted, nor have radical criminologists even been able to describe the general outlines of this new social pattern.

Platt would have criminologists abandon their supposed role as scholar-technicians, which requires them to do agency-determined research and thus to share complicity with the state for the oppression of its citizens. He advocated a new criminology, oriented around a conception of crime centered on violations of egalitarian rights to decent food and shelter, human dignity, and self-determination. For Platt, the proper role of criminology is to aid in the revolutionary transformation of society and elimination of economic and political systems of exploitation.

---

[9] Platt, "Prospects for a Radical Criminology," p. 3.
[10] *Ibid.*, p. 4.
[11] One serious attempt to explicate the outlines of an alternative political-economic system, revolving around regional socialism, can be found in William Appleman Williams, *The Contours of American History* (Chicago: Quadrangle Books, 1966).

These recommendations have not gone unchallenged. In one re-joinder, Austin Turk argued that there is no need to reject the legalistic conception that defines crimes as violations attributed to those against whom the agents of legal control take, or propose to take, action.[12] Such a definition would be preferable to the political slogan, "crimes against the people," which is open to countless interpretations, at the same time that it would alert criminologists to study abuses of power by the state. Turk agreed that criminologists must deal with imperialism, racism, sex-ism, and other aspects of state-crime linkages, but he also contended that criminology must retain its legalistic focus if it is to continue to be a distinct, identifiable field of study.

Turk also disagreed with Platt's fulminations on liberalism, for he held that, while criminologists have indeed supported welfare-state capi-talism, those ameliorative and corrective efforts have produced positive accomplishments. Additionally, Turk declared that, "I find no intrinsic necessity for liberal reformism to stop short of calling for radical social changes insofar as it becomes demonstrably clear that further improve-ments require them, including improvements in terms of the technical effectiveness of legal control ('criminal justice') systems." [13]

Turk averred that the real quarrel between radicals and liberals is over means, not ends. Perhaps, but it is not entirely clear whether the "evolutionary socialism" or "evolutionary capitalism" about which Turk offered only a few hints actually parallels the kind of socialist and egali-tarian society that is envisioned in hazy form by Platt and other radicals.

Turk offered one judgment about much of the radical criminology that has emerged to date with which it is difficult to disagree.

> There is no gain over "cynicism, hipsterism, trivia, and dry technical jargon," assuming these to be as Platt sees them, if we simply move to macroscopic theorizing that never gets down to details of stating and testing descriptive and explanatory notions in particular instances, and is characterized mainly by passionate diatribes that invoke but do not creatively *use* certain theoretical views, propositions, and terms.[14]

The most comprehensive critique of mainstream criminology has been produced by Ian Taylor, Paul Walton, and Jock Young, who ex-amined in depth a variety of lines of theorizing, beginning with classical criminology and the early positivists such as Lombroso and Ferri.[15] Taylor,

---

[12] Turk, "Prospects and Pitfalls."

[13] *Ibid.,* p. 41.

[14] *Ibid.,* p. 42.

[15] Ian Taylor, Paul Walton, and Jock Young, *The New Criminology* (London: Routledge & Kegan Paul, 1973). Also see George B. Vold, *Theoretical Criminology* (New York: Oxford University Press, 1958), for an earlier comprehensive critique of criminological theories.

Walton, and Young also dissected the writings of Durkheim, Marx, Engels, and Bonger, as well as many of the recent statements by labeling theorists and by advocates of pluralistic conflict perspectives on criminality. Their book, *The New Criminology,* provoked an abundance of responses, some positive and others negative in tone.[16] One major complaint of some of the critics was that this volume was a *tour de force* in which straw men were laboriously constructed and then demolished by these authors.[17] That is, theoretical positions attributed to various people were outlined, but these lacked fidelity to the theorists' actual arguments. The distorted characterizations were then subjected to vigorous critical attacks.

However, the major defect of Taylor, Walton, and Young's book was that it was misbranded. There was preciously little "new criminology" contained in it, in spite of its title. Only about a dozen pages near the end of the volume were devoted to an outline of the elements that are required in this new version of criminological thought. Taylor, Walton, and Young asserted that the new criminology "must be able to cover, and sustain the connections between

1. The wider origins of the deviant act . . .
2. Immediate origins of the deviant act . . .
3. The actual act . . .
4. Immediate origins of social reaction . . .
5. Wider origins of deviant reaction . . .
6. The outcome of the social reaction on deviant's further action . . .
7. The nature of the deviant process as a whole." [18]

Few would disagree that the sociogenic conditions that generate criminality need to be identified, along with the more specific learning processes through which criminality is generated. The elements in societal reactions and their impact on lawbreakers must also be incorporated into explanatory frameworks. But, relatively few new insights on these issues were contained in Taylor, Walton, and Young's book.[19]

Some significant gains in radical criminology have been made in the half-dozen or so years since these first stirrings were observed. Some of these contributions to the emerging radical criminology are presented in the next section.

[16] For example, see "Feature Review Symposium" on *The New Criminology* in *Sociological Quarterly,* 14 (Autumn 1973):589–99, involving reviews by Richard Quinney (pp. 589–95), Paul Rock (pp. 594–96), and Anthony Platt (pp. 597–99). Also see Jim Hackler, "The New Criminology: Ideology or Explanation," *Canadian Journal of Criminology and Corrections,* 19 (April 1977):192–95.
[17] For example, see Rock, "Feature Review Symposium," pp. 594–96.
[18] Taylor, Walton, and Young, *The New Criminology,* pp. 270–78.
[19] Some progress toward filling in the details of a new criminology can be seen in Ian Taylor, Paul Walton, and Jock Young, eds., *Critical Criminology* (London: Routledge & Kegan Paul, 1975).

VARIETIES OF RADICAL CRIMINOLOGY

David M. Gordon

One relatively early and quite moderate statement on radical criminology was made by economist David M. Gordon. His basic thesis was captured nicely in the following excerpt.

> Capitalist societies depend, as radicals often argue, on basically competitive forms of social and economic interaction and upon substantial inequalities in the allocation of social resources. Without inequalities, it would be much more difficult to induce workers to work in alienating environments. Without competition and a competitive ideology, workers might not be inclined to struggle to improve their relative income and status in society by working harder. Finally, although rights of property are protected, capitalist societies do not guarantee economic security to most of its individual members. Individuals must fend for themselves, finding the best available opportunities to provide for themselves and their families. At the same time, history bequeaths a corpus of laws and status to any social epoch which may or may not correspond to the social morality of that epoch. Inevitably, at any point in time, many of the "best" opportunities for economic survival open to different citizens will violate some of those historically-determined laws. Driven by the fear of economic insecurity and by a competitive desire to gain some of the goods unequally distributed throughout the society, many individuals will eventually become "criminals."

> ... In that respect, therefore, radicals would argue that nearly all crimes in capitalist societies represent perfectly rational responses to the structure of institutions upon which capitalist societies are based. Crimes of many different varieties constitute functionally similar responses to the organization of capitalist institutions, for those crimes help provide a means of survival in a society within which survival is never assured.[20]

The key term in this argument was *economic precariousness*, engendered by the structure of capitalist institutions. In the remainder of his discussion, Gordon took up ghetto crime, organized crime, and corporate or white-collar crime, and endeavored to indicate how each is a rational response to economic precariousness, and each differs from the others because of the circumstances surrounding it.

Gordon's interpretation of ghetto crime was straightforward. For

---

[20] David M. Gordon, "Class and the Economics of Crime," *Review of Radical Political Economics,* 3 (Summer 1971):51–75. See also Gordon, "Capitalism, Class, and Crime in America," *Crime and Delinquency,* 19 (April 1973):163–86.

people who are faced either with chronic unemployment, underemployment, or low-paying and demeaning jobs, ghetto crime represents an attractive and rational means of making money. Similarly, organized crime constitutes an illegal form of business that fulfills demands for illicit goods and services. White-collar crimes arise in response to the pressures from owners and stockholders that the businesses and financial organizations continue to show an inexorable accumulation of profits.

Gordon also argued that ghetto crime takes its relatively gross, crude, and violent form because of the deprived backgrounds of ghetto residents which prevent them from engaging in the more sophisticated offenses available to upper-class citizens. He maintained that the class biases of the police, courts, and prisons also explain much of the relative violence of garden-variety crimes by ghetto residents and the internecine violence among organized crime groups. Ghetto criminals and syndicate gangsters are moved to violent acts in order to avoid apprehension and conviction. In contrast, corporate crime is nonviolent "because it is ignored by the police; corporate criminals can safely assume they do not face the threat of jail and do not therefore have to cover their tracks with the threat of harming those who betray them." [21]

Why does the state ignore crimes by corporations and upper-class citizens, but come down hard on garden-variety criminals? Why is white-collar crime ignored by federal regulatory agencies or dealt with administratively or in civil court proceedings, while conventional offenders are pursued vigorously by the police and punished severely when convicted in criminal courts? According to Gordon, this occurs because the government in capitalist societies exists primarily to protect the interests of the owners of capital. As long as corporate offenses tend to harm only members of other classes such as consumers, the state will not normally move to prevent such violations from occurring.

Gordon drew on a variety of sources to support his contentions about crime in the United States. Some might object that part of this supporting evidence was anecdotal or inconclusive, while others might take issue with certain of his contentions, such as his claim that a manifest function of prisons is to remove blacks from the job market and prevent them from organizing with others in attempts to change the oppressive economic system through revolutionary actions. Also, Gordon meant his piece to be more of a dramatic essay than a tightly structured theoretical exposition, so he was relatively silent on a number of points. For example, it is unclear how rape and a number of other relatively common offenses would be interpreted within his framework. Also, he had little to say about why some ghetto residents go about "income redistribution" through armed

[21] *Ibid.*, p. 58.

robbery while others manage to avoid these criminal tactics. This last criticism could also be applied to the majority of radical criminologists, who are oriented toward social classes rather than toward individuals.

Many of the themes voiced by Gordon were not marked departures from the viewpoints contained in mainstream criminology. Indeed, Gordon's argument derived most of its radical thrust from his conclusion that significant reductions in crime and fundamental reform in the criminal justice system can only be achieved insofar as the capitalist system in the United States undergoes radical changes in the direction of socialism.

Other Voices

A number of expositions of radical criminology parallel Gordon's perspective to a considerable degree. For example, Barry Krisberg maintained that the lawbreaking of various social classes and the responses to those offenses reflect the markedly unequal distribution of power and privilege that grows out of capitalist social-political-economic relationships. In the course of his discussion, he put forth some contentious claims. For example, "police decision making is loaded heavily with class and status considerations." [22] However, the major problem with Krisberg's statement was that it was overly descriptive and discursive, making it difficult to evaluate critically. As Krisberg himself acknowledged, "this book does not represent a full-blown new theory of crime or social control." [23]

Another venture into radical theorizing can be found in an essay by Raymond Michalowski and Edward Bohlander, which centered principally on social control rather than crime causation. These authors took issue with theories that hold that criminal law is a reflection of normative consensus within a society or that the justice process exists as a collectively supported, impartial arena in which conflicts arising out of the pluralistic nature of society are resolved in the interests of the whole society. Instead, Michalowski and Bohlander opted for a conflict model of criminal law and its enforcement, arguing that the legal basis of the state is created by those who occupy positions of social power and is used to maintain this power differential. They held that the criminal law is an instrument of

[22] Barry Krisberg, *Crime and Privilege: Toward a New Criminology* (Englewood Cliffs, N.J.: Prentice-Hall, 1975), p. 24. At least one of the studies cited by Krisberg in support of this claim does not, in fact, provide corroborrating evidence. See Irving Piliavin and Scott Briar, "Police Encounters with Juveniles," *American Journal of Sociology*, 70 (September 1964):206–14. For a review of a number of studies of discriminatory law enforcement, which indicates that this is a complex phenomenon that is not easily captured in unequivocal assertions, see Don C. Gibbons, *Delinquent Behavior*, 2nd ed. (Englewood Cliffs, N.J.: Prentice-Hall, 1976), pp. 37–48.

[23] Krisberg, *Crime and Privilege*, p. 168.

repression that operates to thwart certain individuals and groups in society from achieving their organic interests, that is, fulfillment of their basic interests such as health, happiness, and a sense of personal worth.

Who are the people who enjoy positions of social power and whose interests are incorporated into the criminal law? According to Michalowski and Bohlander, "in a modern capitalist society this power group is comprised of owners, controllers, and managers of the means of production." [24] The law and its administration was viewed by these theorists as a device through which the corporate ruling class attempts to shape society in its own image. However, they equivocated somewhat on this point, conceding that the relationship between power and the administration of justice is not always clear cut. Advocates for the underclasses and disadvantaged can sometimes force compromises in the law, while, on other occasions, the ruling class may sponsor reforms that seemingly run counter to its own basic interests. While these concessions are probably in order, they also damaged their general thesis considerably, because Michalowski and Bohlander were not able to indicate the circumstances under which each of these outcomes is most likely.[25]

If, as Michalowski and Bohlander alleged, the legal order in the United States serves the interests of the capitalist ruling class and is utilized for the repression of the economically and politically disadvantaged classes, how is it that the underclasses lend their support to the laws and the criminal justice machinery? Why do working-class citizens tolerate the crimes that are carried on with relative impunity by corporations? Why does there appear to be social consensus regarding the legal order, in the face of ruling-class repression? Michalowski and Bohlander's answer, in brief, was that the power-advantaged control the social definition of crime.

> The powerful class shapes a definition of crime which supports their capitalist interests by insuring that the bulk of offenses from which individuals will acquire the meaning of crime bear no resemblance to the harmful acts of corporate profiteers, and that the majority of offenders—by the example of whom we learn to identify who is the criminal—bear no resemblance to members of the capitalist ruling class.[26]

In another broad sketch of radical theory, Steven Spitzer outlined a Marxian theory of deviance.[27] He faulted a variety of existing theories on

[24] Raymond J. Michalowski and Edward W. Bohlander, "Repression and Criminal Justice in Capitalist America," *Sociological Inquiry*, 46, No. 2 (1976):99.
[25] A parallel and similarly imprecise argument about criminal laws and ruling class interests is John R. Hepburn, "Social Control and the Legal Order: Legitimate Repression in a Capitalist State," *Contemporary Crises*, 1 (January 1977):77–90.
[26] Michalowski and Bohlander, "Repression and Criminal Justice," p. 104.
[27] Steven Spitzer, "Toward a Marxian Theory of Deviance," *Social Problems*, 22 (5:1975):638–51.

the grounds that they attempt to understand deviance apart from examination of historically specific forms of political-economic organization. By contrast, he provided an account of the processes of "deviance production," examining the development and changes in societal definitions of deviance, the sorting processes that produce problem behaviors and problem populations, and the development and operation of control systems at different points in history. His discussion dealt with a variety of forms of deviance and was not restricted to criminality.[28]

Spitzer advanced a Marxian argument about deviance production involving core contentions derived from Marx, holding that the capitalist mode of production forms the foundation of American society, that this productive system contains contradictions that are fundamental accompaniments of capitalism, and that the social and political superstructure serves to preserve the power position of capitalists and corporate managers.

Problem populations arise in capitalist societies, composed of people who threaten the social relations of production. Spitzer asserted that

> populations become generally eligible for management as deviant when they disturb, hinder or call into question any of the following:
>
> 1. The capitalist modes of appropriating the product of human labor (e.g., when the poor "steal" from the rich)
> 2. The social conditions under which capitalist production takes place (e.g., those who refuse or are unable to perform wage labor)
> 3. Patterns of distribution and consumption in capitalist society (e.g., those who use drugs for escape and transcendence rather than sociability and adjustment)
> 4. The process of socialization for productive and nonproductive roles (e.g., youth who refuse to be schooled or those who deny the validity of "family life")
> 5. The ideology which supports the functioning of capitalist society (e.g., proponents of alternative forms of social organization).[29]

The difficulty with this inventory of potential problem populations is relatively obvious. It is broad and general enough to provide a place for nearly everyone. It is not entirely helpful to learn that nearly everyone *might* become a target of the control machinery under unspecified circumstances.

[28] In centering attention both upon deviant behavior and social attributions of deviance status, Spitzer steered clear of vulgar labeling theory, which implies that deviant labels are applied to persons quite apart from whether they engage in nonconforming acts.

[29] *Ibid.*, p. 642.

Spitzer presented some insightful commentary on the production in capitalist societies of a relatively surplus population from which recruits to deviance, or problem populations, are drawn. For example, large segments of the black population have become economically redundant as a result of the growth of technology and mass production in American society. As a result, these people are economically marginal, faced with chronic underemployment or, in many cases, permanent unemployment. Groups of this kind create grave problems for capitalist societies, because they must be maintained through funds that could otherwise be used for capital investment. Moreover, surplus populations constitute potential recruits to political organizations that may endeavor to overthrow the capitalist system.

Other contradictions of capitalism generate problem populations. For example, mass education in the United States was originally developed in order to provide a means by which the young would first be withheld from the labor market and then later assimilated into wage-laborer niches in the capitalist economy. But mass education may also provide the masses with insights into the oppressive and alienating character of capitalist institutions, thereby creating individuals who are hostile to the status quo and who may become mobilized in resistance to it.

Spitzer dealt at some length with the conditions under which problem groups are likely to be responded to as deviants and enumerated seven general categories of variables, such as the availability of alternative control mechanisms and the like. He also distinguished between problem groups who constitute "social junk" and those who represent "social dynamite." Skid Row alcoholics come to mind in the first category, as they are relatively passive nonparticipants in the economic order who must be maintained but who pose no threat to the ruling class. Social dynamite, on the other hand, is represented by such groups as the Black Panthers who are widely believed by the authorities to be activists and revolutionaries and are consequently likely to be dealt with much more harshly. A variety of illegal attacks on such groups has been made by the police, but these have often been dealt with tolerantly, owing to the public fears that surround certain putatively revolutionary groups.

Spitzer's analysis ended on an extremely gloomy note. He pointed to the inexorable pressures of capitalism toward substitution of machine labor for manual labor, in order to raise profits by decreasing costs. This process generates increasingly larger numbers of superfluous people and a growing division between useful and useless individuals. In turn, these trends demand more state resources devoted to controlling surplus groups, involving the management of social junk and the incarceration of social dynamite.

Spitzer's essay was a provocative and carefully thought-out preliminary statement of Marxist theory regarding deviance and crime. A less impressive explication of Marxist theory regarding criminality has been offered by William Chambliss, who was at an earlier time an exponent of a pluralistic conflict perspective. Chambliss began his exposition by setting out nine propositions derived from Marxist theory.

A. On the content and operation of criminal law
  1. Acts are defined as criminal because it is in the interests of the ruling class to so define them.
  2. Members of the ruling class will be able to violate the laws with impunity while members of the subject classes will be punished.
  3. As capitalist societies industrialize and the gap between the bourgeoisie and the proletariat widens, penal law will expand in an effort to coerce the proletariat into submission.
B. On the consequences of crime for society
  1. Crime reduces surplus labor by creating employment not only for the criminals but for law enforcers, locksmiths, welfare workers, professors of criminology and a horde of people who live off of the fact that crime exists.
  2. Crime diverts the lower classes' attention from the exploitation they experience, and directs it toward other members of their own class rather than toward the capitalist class or the economic system.
  3. Crime is a reality which exists only as it is created by those in the society whose interests are served by its presence.
C. On the etiology of criminal behavior
  1. Criminal and non-criminal behavior stem from people acting rationally in ways that are compatible with their class position. Crime is a reaction to the life conditions of a person's social class.
  2. Crime varies from society to society depending on the political and economic structures of society.
  3. Socialist societies should have much lower rates of crime because the less intense class struggle should reduce the forces leading to and the functions of crime.[30]

These propositions are similar to the contentions of Spitzer and others that have already been examined. But Chambliss's discussion was weak in terms of supporting arguments and elaborations on these propositions. For example, after enunciating the view that criminal laws do not arise out of societal consensus, but serve ruling-class interests, Chambliss went on to take note of some studies of the origins of criminal laws. He concluded that

> in all of these studies there is substantial support for the Marxian theory. The single most important force behind criminal law creation

[30] William Chambliss, "Toward a Political Economy of Crime," *Theory and Society*, 2 (Summer 1975):152–153.

is doubtless the economic interest and political power of those classes which either (1) own or control the resources of the society, or (2) occupy positions of authority in the state bureaucracies. It is also the case that conflicts generated by the class structure of a society act as an important force for legal innovation. These conflicts may manifest themselves in an incensed group of moral entrepreneurs (such as Gusfield's lower middle class, or the efforts of groups such as the ACLU, NAACP or Policemen's Benevolent Society) who manage to persuade courts or legislators to create new laws. Or the conflict may manifest itself in open riots, rebellions or revolutions which force new criminal law legislation.[31]

Taken together, the studies of criminal law origins on which Chambliss drew, suggest that some statutes reflect societal support, many of them foster the goals of specific interest groups of various kinds, and some directly serve the interests of the most powerful groups in American society.[32] But, it surely is debatable that the goals of the Women's Christian Temperance Union, the NAACP, the ACLU, or the Policemen's Benevolent Society and which are promoted by these laws are identical with "the interests of the ruling class" in Chambliss's first proposition.

At another point Chambliss asserted that "in actual practice, however, class differences in rates of criminal activity are probably negligible. What difference there is would be a difference in the type of criminal act, not in the prevalence of criminality."[33] Although there is much unreported crime on the part of middle- and upper-class citizens, including white-collar offenses and a variety of other forms of lawbreaking, the available evidence also points to class differences in rates of criminal activity. At the very least, Chambliss should have confronted the available data before offering conclusions of this sort.

The same point holds for another of Chambliss's contentions: "I have the impression that such a series of comparisons [of crime rates for different nations] would strongly support the Marxist hypothesis of crime rates being highest in the capitalist societies."[34] This free-floating speculation is unwarranted. There is existing evidence that could have been brought to bear on this issue.[35] Thus, it need not be dealt with solely as a matter of one's impressions.

[31] *Ibid.*, p. 154.
[32] Don C. Gibbons, *Society, Crime, and Criminal Careers,* 3rd ed. (Englewood Cliffs, N.J.: Prentice-Hall, 1977), pp. 31–36, 207.
[33] Chambliss, "Toward a Political Economy of Crime," p. 166.
[34] *Ibid.*, p. 167.
[35] See, for example, Gibbons, *Delinquent Behavior,* pp. 202–20; Walter D. Connor, "Juvenile Delinquency in the U.S.S.R.: Some Quantitative and Qualitative Indicators," *American Sociological Review,* 35 (April 1970):288–97; Mark G. Field, "Alcoholism, Crime, and Delinquency in Soviet Society," *Social Problems,* 3 (October 1955):100–109; Valery Chalidze, *Criminal Russia: Essays on Crime in the Soviet Union,* translated by P. S. Falla (New York: Random House, 1977).

Chambliss's article also contained an examination, based on his own research, of organized crime in Seattle and crime and law enforcement in Nigeria. This material is interesting, but it lends only anecdotal support, at best, to the Marxian argument.

Richard Quinney

The most prolific and prominent spokesman for radical criminology in the United States has been Richard Quinney, who holds a Ph.D. degree from the University of Wisconsin. His earlier publications were in the mainstream genre, but he has become increasingly more radicalized over the years. His mainstream scholarly products included a study of prescription violations by pharmacists, a form of white-collar crime; research on social area analysis and delinquency rates; and an essay on criminological theory. Quinney also co-edited one of the better-known anthologies on criminal typologies.[36]

Quinney's venture into conflict theory, represented by his *The Social Reality of Crime,* was featured in Chapter 6. Although he had shifted noticeably away from mainstream criminology by the early 1970s, Quinney did co-author a revised version of his typological volume in 1973.[37] However, this book stood as a holdover from his past work, in that Quinney turned out a strident attack on liberal criminology and a call for Marxist thought in 1974, in the form of *Critique of Legal Order.* He also edited a vigorous, radical anthology on the criminal justice system in 1974, followed by a radically oriented criminology textbook in 1975.[38]

Quinney's output of published work continued in 1977 with a revised version of *The Problem Crime,* but his most important book that year was *Class, State, and Crime,* which is his most well-developed exposition of Marxist criminology.[39] That book endeavored to address some of the criticisms that had been directed at his earlier *Critique of Legal*

---

[36] Richard Quinney, "Occupational Structure and Criminal Behavior: Prescription Violations by Retail Pharmacists," *Social Problems,* 2 (Fall 1963):179–85; "Crime, Delinquency, and Social Areas," *Journal of Research in Crime and Delinquency,* 1 (July 1964):149–54; "A Conception of Man and Society for Criminology," *Sociological Quarterly,* 6 (Spring 1965):115–27; and Marshall B. Clinard and Quinney, eds., *Criminal Behavior Systems* (New York: Holt, Rinehart and Winston, 1967).

[37] Marshall B. Clinard and Richard Quinney, *Criminal Behavior Systems,* 2nd ed. (New York: Holt, Rinehart and Winston, 1973). While the 1967 version of this work was a text-reader, the second edition is a fairly heavily revised textbook without readings.

[38] Richard Quinney, *Critique of Legal Order* (Boston: Little, Brown, 1974); Quinney, ed., *Criminal Justice in America* (Boston: Little, Brown, 1974); and Quinney, *Criminology* (Boston: Little, Brown, 1975).

[39] Richard Quinney and John Wildeman, *The Problem of Crime,* 2nd ed. (New York: Harper & Row, 1977); Quinney, *Class, State, and Crime: On the Theory and Practice of Criminal Justice* (New York: McKay, 1977).

Order and at versions of Marxist criminology that had been put forth by others.

The claim that Quinney has become radicalized is not solely an inference drawn from his books. He himself has offered some observations on the shifts in his views. In 1973, he declared that conflict theory as found in his *The Social Reality of Crime* was "misguided at best, and perhaps at worst a mistake." He argued that his early sociological training failed him and that he was not initially able to accurately comprehend the social events of the 1960s about which the opening section of this chapter spoke. The liberal blind spots which he detected in his sociological perspective and his earlier exposure to Midwestern populism led him first to a relatively unfocused kind of pluralistic conflict theory. However, he later came to the opinion that "conflict failed to be viewed in terms of the dynamics and contradictions of concrete historical conditions and processes. Conflict theory as thus formulated was merely another bourgeois academic enterprise." [40] That conclusion moved him to take up Marxist theory.

Quinney's *Critique of Legal Order* included an explicit set of propositions that formed the version of radical criminological thought which he endeavored to elaborate throughout the book.

1. American society is based on an advanced capitalist economy.
2. The state is organized to serve the interests of the dominant economic class, the capitalist ruling class.
3. Criminal law is an instrument of the State and ruling class to maintain and perpetuate the existing social and economic order.
4. Crime control in capitalist society is accomplished through a variety of institutions and agencies established and administered by a governmental elite, representing ruling class interests, for the purpose of establishing a domestic order.
5. The contradictions of advanced capitalism—the disjunction between essence and existence—require that the subordinate classes remain oppressed by whatever means necessary, especially through the coercion and violence of the legal system.
6. Only with the collapse of capitalist society and the creation of a new society, based on socialist principles, will there be a solution to the crime problem. [41]

A number of observations come quickly to mind. First, the Marxist perspective contained in these six claims was extremely sketchy. As a result, Quinney's book is vulnerable to a number of criticisms of radical theory which are taken up later in this chapter. Consider for example, the arguments about the domination exercised by a ruling class

[40] Quinney, "Feature Review Symposium," p. 592.
[41] Quinney, *Critique of Legal Order*, p. 16.

in the United States. Much of Quinney's commentary implied the existence of a very small, monolithic collectivity of corporate heads who engage in malevolent schemes to oppress the entire citizenry, with particular focus on the underdogs in American society: blacks, other minorities, and working-class groups. To the extent that these writings conjure up this kind of imagery, they are subject to the critic's charge of oversimplification of the real world.

However, in at least one place in this book, Quinney put forth quite another definition of the ruling class: "What, then, is the nature of this ruling class as reflected in criminal matters? It is composed of (1) members of the upper economic class (those who own or control the means of production) and (2) those who benefit in some way from the present capitalist economic system." [42] The second category could easily be interpreted to include a sizable portion of the total American population.

Quinney's book suffered in other places from inadequate scholarship, substitution of hyperbole for hard evidence, and kindred defects. For example, he dwelled at some length on the Law Enforcement Assistance Administration and the research funded by the National Institute of Criminal Justice within that agency. After enumerating some studies funded by that institute, he concluded that "the above research can best be regarded as counterinsurgency research." [43] But it is highly debatable that the institute administrators, the people who carried on these investigations, or many neutral observers would agree with this characterization. More generally, Quinney's discussion of the Law Enforcement Assistance Administration was superficial and misleading, for it failed to describe the confused history or the complexity, internal contradictions, and other organizational features of that agency. [44]

Quinney's *Class, State, and Crime* was an attempt to confront some of the criticisms and objections of those who rejected radical criminology. In that book, Quinney expanded on many of the themes already encountered in the writings of Spitzer, Gordon, and others. Quinney's central thesis was in effect a contemporary version of Marxism. Quinney argued that the productive relationships of capitalism produce a relative surplus population, some of the members of which turn to crime as an adaptive response to their predicament.

Class, State, and Crime was not devoid of defects. For one thing,

---

[42] *Ibid.*, p. 55.

[43] *Ibid.*, p. 43.

[44] A good deal of the published commentary on LEAA, much of it quite properly critical of that agency, is reviewed in Don C. Gibbons, Joseph L. Thimm, Florence Yospe, and Gerald F. Blake, Jr., *Criminal Justice Planning* (Englewood Cliffs, N.J.: Prentice-Hall, 1977), p. 12–27.

such terminology as "capitalist hegemony" and "dialectic" was used in undefined ways. A criticism of a more serious nature is the lack of supporting evidence for much of the argument, coupled with frequent references to other theorists and their speculations, as well as some distortions of the writings of other scholars.[45] For example, consider the claim that all levels of government in the United States are currently involved in the planning and implementation of an apparatus to secure the existing capitalist order. This contention is an exaggerated one, at best.[46]

Quinney started off with an extraordinarily sweeping generalization: "A Marxist analysis of crime begins with the recognition that crime is basically a material problem." [47] This was followed, however, with a more detailed attempt to indicate how the developments in modern capitalism have led to various forms of crime and responses to them. He presented a relatively straightforward explication of the nature of capitalist political-economy, contending that the basic relations of production are the foundations on which the superstructure of social relations are created. More directly relevant to crime, capitalist production involves fundamental contradictions, particularly those centered on a growing army of relative surplus individuals and alienated laborers, which generates recruits to crime and potential participants in class struggle and revolutionary action.

In one section of his book, Quinney outlined a classification that apparently is the pioneering version of a Marxist typology of crime.[48] Two broad categories were identified—crimes of domination and crimes of accommodation and resistance—along with a number of subtypes.

1. Crimes of domination
   a. Crimes of control
   b. Crimes of government

---

[45] For example (*Class, State, and Crime*, p. 15), Quinney charged those researchers currently involved in studies of deterrence with seeking to "establish the importance of 'certainty' and 'swiftness' of punishment in deterring crime." This claim implies that these persons are handmaidens of the existing social control system and involved in advocacy, rather than more objective inquiry into deterrence. Such an implication is unwarranted. Along the same line (*Ibid.*, p. 17), Norval Morris was characterized as an advocate and apologist for prisons, which is not entirely accurate, while on another page (*Ibid.*, p. 20) Jack Gibbs was incorrectly identified as an advocate of deterrence and punishment.

[46] For counterevidence, pointing to the *lack* of planning and coordination, see Gibbons, Thimm, Yospe, and Blake, *Criminal Justice Planning*, pp. 19–27; or, on this same point, (pp. 107–17) Quinney drew attention to the markedly increased federal funding of the Law Enforcement Assistance Administration between 1969 and 1977, concluding that this fact demonstrates the growing role of the federal government in legal control. But what he failed to note is that LEAA has come under increased fire from members of Congress, its most recent budgets have been cut, and it is being threatened with extinction through Congressional unwillingness to refund it.

[47] Quinney, *Class, State, and Crime*, p. 31.

[48] *Ibid.*, pp. 43–62.

   c. Crimes of economic domination
2. Crimes of accommodation and resistance
   a. Predatory crime
   b. Personal crimes
   c. Crimes of resistance

     Crimes of control, according to Quinney, involve such things as illegal police violence and other violations carried on by agents of legal control. Crimes of government have to do with such matters as the Watergate crimes, illegal acts carried on by the Federal Bureau of Investigation, Central Intelligence Agency, and other agencies. Crimes of economic domination include white-collar offenses, organized crime, and social injuries. "Social injuries" refers to phenomena that fall outside the existing statutes, having to do with violations of basic human rights of citizens. Taken together, the crimes of domination are those offenses engaged in with relative impunity by overdogs and members of the ruling class.

     By contrast, crimes of accommodation and resistance are violations carried on by underdogs—members of the lower class. Predatory crimes arise out of the economic deprivation suffered by those at the bottom of the economic heap, while personal crimes arise "in immediate situations that are themselves the result of more basic accommodations to capitalism." [49] The third form within this category, crimes of resistance, involves various deliberate and calculated threats to the state in the form of revolutionary acts, in contrast to predatory and personal offenses, which usually express only inarticulate opposition.

     One positive feature of Quinney's book is his attempt to deal in some detail with the nature of class relations in capitalist America, moving somewhat beyond gross assertions about the machinations of the ruling class. He claimed that, although advanced capitalism continued to be characterized by a basic class division between the owners of property and the laboring class, it had also given rise to a number of *fractions* or subgroups within the two basic classes. Quinney's discussion also spelled out some of the relationships between the state and the capitalist ruling class, going beyond overly simple statements about the former being a tool of the latter. Finally, he elaborated on some of the central problems of the modern state as it tries to provide governmental support for capital accumulation, through regulating and supporting financial affairs and industrial development, including the utilization of governmental funds in order to buttress the economy; and manage the growing problems of capitalism through the welfare state. The modern capitalist state faces an insoluble problem centered around the inexorable expansion of the relative

---

[49] *Ibid.,* p. 54.

surplus population which requires increased state management through welfare and other management and control programs, on the one hand, and the unwillingness and/or inability of the capitalist economy to provide the requisite funding, on the other. There is in all of this commentary a degree of sophistication that is lacking in some of his earlier writings and in much of the theorizing of other radical criminologists.[50]

Quinney's book avoided some of the romanticizing about garden-variety criminals that marred earlier Marxist-radical writings in criminology. Much of the earlier commentary portrayed these individuals as political prisoners or modern-day Robin Hoods, ignoring the fact that many of them were engaged in crude assaults and serious depradations directed at other disadvantaged individuals, as well as the fact that the political prisoner ideology is foreign to many of these lawbreakers.

A closely related proposition that has surfaced in radical criminology is that garden-variety offenders represent available raw material to be recruited to the cause of revolutionary change. That contention is at variance with the observation that revolutionary movements in the past have rarely been successful in employing common criminals.[51] Quinney avoided this romantic image of offenders who are regarded as political figures because they violate bourgeois rules and acknowledged that, at best, most conventional crime is a crude and unconscious reaction to oppression. His conclusion seemed to be that criminologists have the responsibility of raising the political consciousness of garden-variety lawbreakers. However, it is doubtful that criminologists in large numbers will accept that mandate.

Juvenile Delinquency and Radical Criminology

Nearly all the versions of radical criminology that have been developed so far have taken a panoramic view of crime and the political-economic order, with the theorists speaking of ruling-class oppression, state-administered repressive actions, crime, and other sweeping concepts. Radical criminologists have had very little to say about the specific mechanisms by which capitalism produces crime and have not offered theories that provide explanations for the involvement or noninvolvement of specific individuals in lawbreaking. In addition, most radical criminologists have

[50] In this regard, Quinney's commentary is in the direction worked out in even greater detail, precision, and sophistication in such works as Charles H. Anderson, *The Political Economy of Social Class* (Englewood Cliffs, N.J.: Prentice-Hall, 1974); and James O'Connor, *The Fiscal Crisis of the State* (New York: St. Martin's Press, 1973).

[51] For some evidence on this point, see R. Kelly Hancock and Don C. Gibbons, "The Future of Crime in American Society." Paper presented at the Pacific Sociological Association meeting, Victoria, Canada, April 1975.

virtually ignored juvenile delinquency, even though crimes by adolescents make up much of the garden-variety lawbreaking in capitalist societies.[52]

One ambitious attempt to provide a Marxist interpretation of juvenile delinquency in capitalist societies has been made by David Greenberg, who drew together a large collection of research evidence on youthful misconduct. His general argument was that the disproportionate involvement of juveniles in major crimes is a product of the historically changing position of youth in industrial societies.

Greenberg's starting point was with the available evidence concerning age relationships in delinquency. He argued that subcultural theories, including those discussed in Chapter 4, cannot account for the fact that involvement in serious delinquency reaches a peak at about age 15–16 and then declines in magnitude. If the thrust of the subcultural arguments—that delinquent activities are valued positively by juveniles—is correct, then subcultural members ought to continue in those endeavors beyond age 16.

The formulation proposed by Greenberg emphasized the strains experienced by many youngsters in the transition period from childhood to adolescence. During this period, attachments to parents become weakened at the same time that youths become highly sensitive to peer judgments and peer standards. This peer group culture places pressures on adolescents to engage in a hedonistic social life, but increasing numbers of these youths are incapable of financing those activities because of the decline of teenage employment opportunities in capitalist societies. According to Greenberg, "adolescent theft then occurs as a response to the disjunction between the desire to participate in social activities with peers and the absence of legitimate sources of funds needed to finance this participation."[53] However, as these adolescents get older, they become less vulnerable to peer evaluations at the same time that legitimate opportunities to earn money increase, with the consequence that adolescent theft declines among older youths.

The status problems of many juveniles in modern societies are exacerbated by school experiences. Greenberg emphasized the restraints imposed on the autonomy of youngsters by modern schools, along with the stigmatizing and degrading experiences to which many adolescents are exposed while in school. Those who have a reduced stake in conformity rebel against these negative experiences by engaging in hostile acts directed at the schools and school personnel.

---

[52] For one exception, see Herman Schwendinger and Julia Schwendinger, "Delinquency and the Collective Varieties of Youth," *Crime and Social Justice*, 5(1976): 7–12.

[53] David F. Greenberg, "Delinquency and the Age Structure of Society," *Contemporary Crises*, 1 (April 1977):197.

A third, related source of delinquent motivation identified by Greenberg results from the lack of employment for adolescents, which creates anxiety about one's prospects for attaining masculine status in American society. In Greenberg's view of things, these three pressures on juveniles account for most of the delinquency in capitalist societies. Exclusion from the world of work deprives adolescents of opportunities to finance the intensive leisure activities that are emphasized in peer norms. Stigmatizing school experiences directed particularly at low-status, unemployed youths provoke hostile and aggressive responses from those juveniles. Finally, fear of failure to achieve adult male status positions, which is common among juveniles in the late adolescent period, results in violent, status-defining acts on their parts.

Greenberg was not the first sociologist to point to exclusion of juveniles from the labor market as a major factor in delinquency. But, contrary to most interpretations that regard this situation as a recent and short-range one created by the invasion of women into the labor market, teenage preferences for part-time work, and the like, Greenberg argued that it "may more plausibly be explained in terms of the failure of the oligopoly-capitalist economy to generate sufficient demand for labor, than to these recent developments." [54] Greenberg's argument comes down to the view that juvenile delinquency in industrialized nations rests on the disadvantaged structural position of adolescents in advanced capitalist economies. If he is correct, juvenile delinquency is not likely to be reduced markedly by the kinds of remedies that have been proposed in the United States, such as job training for youths. Job training in a situation in which jobs for teenagers are limited or nonexistent is likely to be of little avail.

RESPONSES TO RADICAL CRIMINOLOGY

Responses to radical criminology have been markedly varied, ranging from studied indifference or mild hostility expressed by some of the leading figures of mainstream criminology to enthusiastic approval by other criminologists. Those who have embraced these themes have done so more because those views resonate with the prevailing mood of the country than from the force of supporting evidence.

One positive evaluation of radical criminology was made by Karl Schumann who contended that, while radical criminology is to be applauded, its major limitation is that it is too limited in scope.[55] He would have Marxist or radical criminological thought extended further, with more

[54] *Ibid.*, p. 213.
[55] Karl F. Schumann, "Theoretical Presuppositions for Criminology as a Critical Enterprise," *International Journal of Criminology and Penology,* 4 (August 1976): 285–94.

attention being given to criminalization processes. According to Schumann, more work is required on the question of why certain social conflicts and not others are brought within the scope of the criminal law in some societies and not in others. He would also broaden the search for a comprehensive, analytic account of societal conflicts which would include sexual and racial discrimination and other conflicts besides those that arise out of class relations. Finally, he maintained that radical criminology ought to strive toward the development of an alternative societal model in which social conflicts would no longer be regulated by criminal law.

Another view of radical criminology has been expressed by Robert Meier, who declared that there is little that is really new in "the new criminology." [56] He claimed that, rather than evolving new insights into lawbreaking and responses to it, radical criminology has taken many established viewpoints from mainstream criminological thought and re-phrased them in political terms. More specifically, he charged that radical criminology contains elements drawn from the social pathology tradition, as well as Chicago criminology, functionalism, and labeling arguments.

Where the older social pathology notions dealt with alleged defects of individuals, the new criminology stresses the political pathology of capitalism. The new criminology also resembles the Chicago tradition of the 1930s in that both are concerned with normative conflict. Moreover, the Chicago researchers also examined the repressive operations of the criminal justice system. Meier noted that Sutherland's studies of white-collar crime implied the need for a redefinition of crime. Finally, radical criminology is functionalist in form insofar as it implies that the criminal justice system operates to maintain the privileges of the ruling class.

Meier's characterization of the key elements of radical criminology centered on the claim that a ruling-class elite controls the law-making processes and thus the definitions of criminality. The legal and social control agencies operate in complicity with the ruling-class elite. Also, according to Meier, radical criminology advocates new definitions of criminality centering around violation of inherent human rights, along with revolutionary change designed to remove the criminogenic conditions associated with capitalism.

Paul Hirst and Stephen Mugford, among others, have charged that contemporary Marxist criminology is not drawn in any direct fashion from the writings of Marx, who in fact had little to say about criminality. Thus, radical criminology presents a distorted version of Marxist thought.[57]

[56] Robert F. Meier, "The New Criminology: Continuity in Criminological Theory," *Journal of Criminal Law and Criminology,* 67 (December 1976):461–69.
[57] Paul Q. Hirst, "Marx and Engels on Law, Crime, and Morality," *Economy and Society,* 1 (February 1972):28–56; and Stephen K. Mugford, "Marxism and Criminology: A Comment on the Symposium on 'The New Criminology,'" *Sociological*

But, in a rejoinder to Hirst, Ian Taylor and Paul Walton enumerated a number of connections between the writings of Marx and radical criminologists.[58] The most prudent conclusion on this debate parallels Anderson's position regarding the application of Marxist insights to the analysis of contemporary social class relationships in the United States.[59] Rather than emphasizing "dead Marxism," that is, slavish attention to the original writings of Marx, contemporary analysts of social behavior ought to deal in "plain Marxism," working openly and flexibly with Marx's general social theory in an attempt to develop theoretical propositions that are relevant to criminality in contemporary societies.

One of the major complaints by critics of Marxist criminology is a counterclaim to the charge by radicals that mainstream criminology is involved in "mystification" of the real world, through promulgation of consensus views of the criminal law that disguise the role of the ruling class in criminal law making and its implementation. Radical criminologists have often defined their task as involving "demystification," that is, the stripping away of these false accounts of the real world offered by liberal theorists. A good many critics have asserted that radical criminologists are even more guilty of mystification through the portrayals they offer of a monolithic ruling class that determines which acts are to be criminalized. Opponents of radical criminology contend that these accounts oversimplify the nature of social power and class relations in modern societies,[60] fail to acknowledge that many criminal statutes are the product of myriad forces and interests, and overlook the large number of laws that are supported by societal consensus.[61]

Quarterly, 15 (Autumn 1974):591–96. Also see Zenon Bankowski, Geoff Mungham, and Peter Young, "Radical Criminology or Radical Criminologist?" *Contemporary Crises,* 1 (January 1977):37–51.

[58] Ian Taylor and Paul Walton, "Radical Deviancy Theory and Marxism: A Reply to Paul Q. Hirst's 'Marx and Engels on Law, Crime, and Morality,'" in Taylor, Walton, and Young, *Critical Criminology,* pp. 233–37. See also Paul Q. Hirst, "Radical Deviancy Theory and Marxism: A Reply to Taylor and Walton," in Taylor, Walton, and Young, *Critical Criminology,* pp. 283–43.

[59] Anderson, *Political Economy of Social Class,* pp. 2–5.

[60] For example, see the commentary, (pp. 180–81) on the conception of the ruling class and its activities contained in Quinney's *Critique of Legal Order.*

[61] This observation appeared in Meier, "The New Criminology," p. 463, among other places. A point made in Chapter 6 ought to be reiterated, namely that the dividing line between pluralistic conflict views and radical-Marxist versions of criminology is not clean cut. Critics have sometimes focused upon alleged deficiencies in these kinds of theories and have tended to blend the two in their analyses. More specifically, some of the criticisms that discuss the oversimplified views of the origins of criminal laws appear to be directed both at conflict and at radical arguments or are not entirely clear on the identity of the targets of criticism. One essay that seemed to be most heavily concentrated on the shortcomings of conflict perspectives is Andrew Hopkins, "On the Sociology of Criminal Law," *Social Problems,* 22 (5:1975):608–19. Much of his commentary focused on such works as Quinney's

Paul Rock has written at some length about the inarticulate and inchoate conceptualization of social structure and the moral order contained in radical theorizing regarding the nature and origins of criminal laws.

> Although there are exceptions, it is most difficult to discover in the writings on deviance a description of legislation and rule-making which embodies more than an anthropomorphic conspiracy theory. There is little conception of history. If the social contract was not imposed today, it was certainly imposed in the recent past. The contract conceived by the deviancy theorists contains a pristine set of vested interests which have not lost their immediate connections with a dominating elite. The perspective offers no understanding of law as a complex and variegated rule-system whose origins are frequently as mysterious to elites as to governed. It offers no vision of a legal system as a series of constraints upon law-giver and ruled alike. It does not refer to legitimacy and authority other than in the context of manipulation and mystification. It does not provide for the elaborate patterns of accommodation that characterize many situations of social control. The law-giver is an Olympian figure endowed with a rationality, an innocence of unintended consequences, and a clear self-interestedness.[62]

Much the same assessment of radical and conflict hypotheses about the origins of criminal laws has been made by Peter Manning. He detected much oversimplification in arguments that have been advanced regarding the development of laws, illustrated specifically by contentions about the origins of full-time police in England in the early 1800s. Conflict and radical theorists have opined that police organizations were invented to defend the propertied classes from the "dangerous classes," that is, the lower-class, unpropertied victims of industrialization. The police

---

The Social Reality of Crime, rather than on his radical-Marxist writings. Hopkins made a number of pithy observations about conflict views. Speaking of the controversy over consensus versus conflict arguments, he observed (pp. 613–14): "However, it seems to me that much of the recent effort to adjudicate between the two models of criminal law is misconceived. Neither model has been formulated unambiguously by its proponents and neither is sufficiently specific in its predictions to be falsifiable. Indeed, the outcome of the debate depends more on definition and the way terms are used than it does on empirical research. For example, if we allow that the interests of the powerful may on occasion coincide with the interests of less powerful groups or alternatively that the community itself is a powerful interest group, then even laws which reflect widespread consensus can be interpreted as expressions of the interests of the powrful." Hopkins would avoid the advocacy of trivial or circular claims holding that laws are created by groups who enjoy social power and would move on to inquiries about the relative powerfulness of particular interest groups, the interplay between opposing interest groups, and kindred issues.

[62] Paul Rock, "The Sociology of Deviance and Conceptions of Moral Order," *British Journal of Criminology,* 14 (April 1974):139–49.

were meant to serve as a buffer between the oppressed underclass and the capitalist elite. But, according to Manning.

> closer attention to historical facts and additional investigation would have revealed, however, that the origins of the civil police in England can be attributed to a variety of "factors" or "causes," some in combination with each other. For example, there are at least five distinct arguments with supporting evidence which can be formulated to explain the "interests" which "lay behind" the conceptualization and passage of the Metropolitan Police Act of 1829. They may be enumerated in a very brief form. (1) A *Marxist interest* theory seeing the elites as key backers of the police idea as a means of attempting repression of the working classes; (2) a *reformist* conception or interpretation which links elites, scholar-intellectuals, and administrators in a broadly conceived effort to reform the penal code, judicial structure and function, and law enforcement organization and practice; (3) a *middle-class* "growth of respectability" argument which claims that elites, bourgeoisie and working-class "tories" or loyalists united to create mechanisms to control social disorder in burgeoning cities; (4) a view which saw the development of the police as a logical outgrowth of the utter *failure of the army* to control domestic disorders—a pragmatic bargain struck between the elites, the army, and rural landed gentry; (5) a *counterrevolutionary* explanation which portrays large segments of the population, supported in their beliefs by Methodism and responding to Jacobin sentiments and activities of urban artisans and labourers, as working through mob action and demands upon politicians to seek to repress democratic or revolutionary strivings. Each of these views is defensible: a repressive elite argument; a responsible elite argument; a modernisation argument; a pragmatic centered argument; and a counter-revolutionary anti-Jacobin argument; but none adopts the rigid simplicity of the crude interest theory implied by Quinney and others.[63]

Some parallel objections to radical criminology and its views regarding the criminal law have been made by David Greenberg. He charged that radical theorists have ignored the existence of a substantial consensus among members of the general public concerning many categories of crime.[64] He also took them to task for failing to acknowledge

---

[63] Peter K. Manning, "Deviance and Dogma," *British Journal of Criminology*, 15 (January 1975):14.

[64] David F. Greenberg, "On One-Dimensional Criminology," *Theory and Society*, 3 (1976):610–21. One study, cited by Greenberg, that showed a marked degree of public agreement on the relative seriousness of different crimes is Peter H. Rossi, Emily Waite, Christine E. Bose, and Richard E. Berk, "The Seriousness of Crimes: Normative Structure and Individual Differences," *American Sociological Review*, 39 (April 1974):224–37; see also Don C. Gibbons, "Crime and Punishment: A Study in

that members of the working class are frequently the victims of crimes carried on by other underprivileged individuals from low-income backgrounds, so that they have a stake in current laws and their enforcement.

Greenberg also judged the radical views of social power and class relations to be immature. "Powerful groups are generally portrayed as operating virtually without constraint, never as being forced to make concessions to challenging groups or as being forced to act contrary to short-run interests so as to maintain legitimacy by responding to the expectations of a public." [65]

A number of incisive comments were offered by Greenberg concerning the radical thesis that criminality, the product of capitalism, could be virtually eradicated through the substitution of socialism as the basis of societal structure. Greenberg contended that crime will be present in any populous and socially differentiated society, although the amount and nature may vary from one society to another.[66] Also, he suggested that efforts to drastically reduce crime in modern societies would probably require the use of exceedingly repressive or Draconian tactics by the state, which is a possibility that is rarely mentioned in the utopian speculations of some radical theorists.

One effort to rescue radical criminology from these charges that it is "unable to explain the existence of those laws which provide equal protection to all members of society, the existence of those laws seen to be irrelevant to the interests of the capitalist elite, and those laws inimical to the interests of the capitalist elite" has been made by John Hepburn.

Hepburn conceded that laws against burglary, assault, murder, and other garden-variety crimes may serve to protect many citizens, but he then argued that these statutes could not have been enacted or enforced if not for the fact that these behaviors are potentially or actually threatening to the capitalist elite group, the membership of which was not made clear by Hepburn. He also asserted that many crimes were invented to meet the needs of the state rather than to protect the rights of citizens. In particular,

---

Social Attitudes," *Social Forces,* 45 (June 1969):391–97; Graeme Newman, *Comparative Deviance: Perception and Law in Six Cultures* (New York: Elsevier, 1976); Charles W. Thomas, "Public Opinion on Criminal Law and Legal Sanctions: An Examination of Two Conceptual Models," *Journal of Criminal Law and Criminology,* 67 (March 1976):110–16. The radical rejoinder to this observation has been presented in Michalowski and Bohlander, "Repression and Criminal Justice."

[65] Greenberg, "On One-Dimensional Criminology," p. 612.

[66] On this point, Greenberg commented (p. 619): "In view of the persistence of crime in state and market socialist economies, it is plausible to assume that all societies contain contradictions that will be perceived as sufficiently threatening and sufficiently reprehensible to warrant punitive intervention, and that in *modern* societies this intervention will at least some of the time take the form of criminalization. Indeed, under socialism, the expansion of the public sphere into traditionally private realms may create a strain toward an expanded use of the criminal sanctions."

many laws have been created in order to safeguard private property. "In short, the criminal laws emerged to protect the capitalist institutions of entrepreneurship, private property and the market system." [67]

There is a considerable measure of truth in these observations, but they are not entirely consistent with a literal reading of much radical criminological theorizing, which implies that a single, identifiable ruling elite has been able to have its interests enacted into law. Many critics of radical criminology would agree that many laws in Western societies do serve to protect the institution of private property, but agreement with that contention does not require that one also concur with radical hypotheses about a national ruling class. Also, laws that protect private property benefit large numbers of citizens, as well as wealthy capitalists.

The rejoinders offered by Hepburn to the argument that the criminal laws provide equal protection to all citizens were also strained. For example, he argued that equal protection of citizens from homicides would exist only if such death-producing acts as the production of defective merchandise, maintenance of unhealthy work conditions, or violations of "abstract moral laws" (e.g., malnutrition, starvation, and exposure) were also included in homicide statutes. While most would agree that deaths from these causes are indeed regrettable, at least some of these represent acidental deaths that could not have been prevented and can thus be fairly removed from culpable killings. Then too, it is a non sequitur to contend, as Hepburn did, that because not all harmful acts are prohibited by criminal laws, existing criminal statutes do not provide relatively equal protection to citizens.

Hepburn acknowledged that some criminal laws arise that are irrelevant to ruling-class interests, but then argued that these statutes only occurred "because the interests of the capitalist elite are not threatened." [68] Leaving aside the point that this curious proposition seems to say that irrelevant laws arise because they are irrelevant, this concession that some statutes develop out of sources other than ruling-class actions constitutes a major qualification that has often been absent from radical theorizing. [69]

The arguments advanced by Hepburn concerning laws that appear

[67] Hepburn, "Social Control and the Legal Order," p. 79.

[68] *Ibid.*, p. 83. Hepburn did not find the evidence of widespread societal consensus on many laws to be persuasive.

[69] Hepburn was probably correct in arguing that some irrelevant laws have the latent function of conveying an impression of pluralism rather than elite domination in capitalist societies, *Ibid.*, pp. 83–84, for, in fact, they are indicators of pluralism that actually exists. Hepburn was able only to account for the appearance of laws that are irrelevant to the interests of a capitalist elite, rather than being able to demonstrate that existing radical arguments that attribute nearly all laws to ruling class interests are correct.

to be inimical to elite interests are not entirely convincing. He acknowledged that the powerless are not totally without power and that statutes such as those regulating business and financial activities may function to placate the powerless. Also, he declared that regulatory statutes can be seen as vehicles designed to protect elite interests by restricting the reckless, harmful, or rapacious activities of some elite members which might alienate a large section of the powerless. But the question arises, why is it necessary to placate the powerless or to prevent them from becoming alienated? And, if the capitalist elite and the state are sometimes compelled to attend to concerns such as these, does that not indicate that existing radical theorizing gives exaggerated emphasis to the power and influence of a single ruling elite? [70]

CRIMINOLOGY: PAST, PRESENT, AND FUTURE

So far, we have examined the earliest awakenings of criminological thought in the United States, the rise of mainstream perspectives over a forty-year period from 1930 to 1970, and a number of conflict and radical-Marxist viewpoints which have recently appeared, accompanied by much fanfare and uncritical applause. Attention has been drawn to a number of deficiencies that detract markedly from the force of these recent arguments. But, at the same time, many of the mainstream versions of criminology also show serious flaws that render them increasingly inadequate as explanations of lawbreaking in contemporary society. It is by no means the case that the entire body of criticisms of mainstream criminology that have been advanced by radical theorists is without substance, nor is it true that radical-Marxist criminological writings can be rejected in their entirety, on the basis of the criticisms that have been examined in this chapter. For example, even though most radical arguments contain crude, monolithic, and misleading claims about a ruling class and its domination of economic and social life in American society, it does not follow that ruling-class arguments are entirely wide of the mark.

Radical claims represent a major challenge to mainstream criminology. Criminologists will ultimately have to embark on the task of

---

[70] Hepburn was on much more solid ground in arguing that many of these regulatory statutes are weakened through differential enforcement, in which business violations are ignored, handled administratively or in civil court, and receive light penalties. All of this points to the fact that corporations, business groups, and financial institutions enjoy considerably more social power than do other citizen groups. At the same time, regulatory statutes have been enacted and some criminal convictions have been obtained, so that it can hardly be argued that the existence of such laws is entirely inconsequential to a ruling elite.

extracting the most crucial elements of Marxist-radical criminology from this body of literature. In the process, the mainstream criminological perspective of the future may come to differ in important ways from criminology of the 1970s. Chapter 8 offers some relatively brief observations on the future of criminological theory.

THE FUTURE
OF CRIMINOLOGICAL
THEORY

8 INTRODUCTION

Where is criminology going? What will be the shape of criminological theory in the next few decades and beyond? Is a distinct brand of new criminology going to spring up, making mainstream criminology obsolete? Some of the answers to these queries may have already been provided, at least implicitly, in the preceding pages.

It is unlikely that mainstream criminology will soon be declared dead and that a new radical or Marxist criminology will be ushered in as the dominant paradigm for criminology. Radical criminologists are too few in number to be able to bring about such a result. Even more important, as Chapter 7 indicated, many of the major themes of radical criminology are ambiguous, overly simple, or inchoate, so that Marxist criminological theory is not sufficiently robust to capture the allegiance of most criminologists.

The most likely development in the criminology of the future is one in which a modified brand of mainstream criminology will develop, informed by many of the themes that have appeared in recent years in the social labeling and deviance literature, in conflict versions of criminological thought, and in radical-Marxist analysis. Indeed, Sykes, Doleschal and Klapmuts, and a number of other observers have already drawn attention to some indications that many of these newer hypotheses are being coopted by mainstream criminology, so that the transformation of criminological thought is already underway.[1]

---

[1] Gresham M. Sykes, "The Rise of Critical Criminology," *Journal of Criminal Law and Criminology,* 65 (June 1974):206–13; and Eugene Doleschal and Nora Klapmuts, "Toward a New Criminology," *Crime and Delinquency Literature,* 5 (December 1973):607–26.

Although Chapter 7 contained a good many critical remarks concerning Marxist criminology, it ended on an appreciative note, arguing that radical theorists have made a valuable contribution to criminological thought by emphasizing the normality of crime and the social-structural roots of deviance. Crime is no less a normal and natural product of societal organization than are various forms of socially applauded activity.

Many sociological students of criminality might be quick to take issue with this statement, arguing that mainstream criminology also emphasizes these core contentions about the normality of crime and about its social-structural origins. Those propositions can certainly be found in the writings of Sutherland and many other theorists. Even so, many of the sociological formulations about criminality that have been favored in the past have shown some kinship with psychogenic arguments holding that lawbreaking is an individual aberration attributable to psychological flaws or pressures of one kind or another. Sociologists have substituted a conceptualization of criminality as a social aberration for the psychologist's hypothesis of individual pathology.

The differences between radical theorizing and mainstream criminology are a matter of degree as far as the social origins of crime are concerned. Still, liberal mainstream criminology has often contained arguments that imply that criminality is a transitory and socially abnormal form of behavior that can be markedly reduced through various kinds of tinkering with the existing social-economic order. By contrast, radical-Marxist theorists have insisted that high rates of predatory crime and other lawbreaking are the inevitable products of a capitalist social-economic structure. Although the radical view may be overdrawn, it seems on the mark in stressing the social-structural sources that make this activity much less tractable than mainstream criminologists have supposed.

Now, what are some of the unfinished tasks in criminological theorizing? What directions need to be pursued in the decades ahead, as the transformation of criminological perspectives continues? First, criminological thought needs to be linked more closely to history, economics, political science, and sociology. More attention to the historical shifts and changes in criminality and responses to it in American society is called for, along with closer examination of the interrelationships between crime and economic organization. Additionally, the crude insights of radical criminologists concerning the role of the ruling class in the creation and promulgation of criminal laws demand further development. Also, more work is required on the criminological implications of labeling theory and other perspectives on social deviance. The psychological issue in causal analysis, which has troubled each generation of criminologists, must ultimately be faced. Those who have argued that sociologists must "bring men back in" have identified a fundamental theoretical problem that will not simply go away if it is ignored. In all of this, criminological theorizing ought to be centered around certain broad categories of lawbreaking, rather than on "crime" on the one hand or an extremely detailed offender taxonomy on the other. These are interrelated theoretical problems, all centering around the development of a historically grounded political-economic account of crime in modern society.[2]

MAJOR FORMS OF CRIME

Radical theorists in criminology have usually put forth broad arguments about lawbreaking without attempting to specify the particular forms of criminality that are most adequately accounted for by those claims. This tendency to speak of crime in general terms without paying attention to the varied forms that it takes in modern societies has been common among mainstream criminologists as well. But common sense and a moment's reflection indicate the inadequacy of this approach. Certain kinds of crime probably ought to be separated from other patterns, and causal formulations specific to them probably should be pursued.

A large number of attempts have been made over the past two or three decades to develop elaborate classifications or typologies of offenders (see Chapter 4). These efforts have been relatively fruitless.[3] The accumulated evidence seems incontrovertible that offender-oriented typological schemes are overly clinical in character and assume a good deal more uniformity of behavior and social-psychological characteristics among lawbreakers than in fact exists.

There is not much warrant for further poking about in attempts to pigeonhole offenders into types, but there is something to be said for a scheme that would meaningfully distinguish a few major forms of crime. David Gordon's classification comes quickly to mind. Gordon argued that ghetto crime, organized crime, and white-collar criminality constitute the major forms of lawbreaking.[4]

Garden-variety crime is perhaps a better term than ghetto crime. Garden-variety crime refers to those offenses that make up the FBI Crime Index, namely, murder, forcible rape, robbery, aggravated assault, burglary, larceny, and auto theft. Gordon was correct in suggesting that the lion's share of these offenses is carried on by ghetto residents, often against other ghetto dwellers. Garden-variety crimes are frequently the crimes of the

---

[2] A prototype of this kind of criminological analysis is Charles H. Anderson, *The Political Economy of Social Class* (Englewood Cliffs, N.J.: Prentice-Hall, 1974).

[3] Don C. Gibbons, "Offender Typologies—Two Decades Later," *British Journal of Criminology,* 15 (April 1975):140–56.

[4] David M. Gordon, "Class and the Economics of Crime," *Review of Radical Political Economics,* 3 (Summer 1971):51–75.

underclass, but at the same time, these crimes, most of which are criminally unsophisticated, situationally induced, and regarded as "real crime" by citizens, are also engaged in by people from more comfortable social circumstances. What makes them garden-variety offenses is their ubiquity, crudity, and directness.

There is no need to allocate much attention in this book to garden-variety crime. The radical charge that mainstream criminologists have devoted inordinate attention to this activity while downplaying the significance of white-collar or corporate crime rings true, even though the companion indictment that criminologists have been the knowing lackeys of the ruling class is less compelling.[5]

Although there have been some significant contributions to criminological knowledge regarding business and corporate lawbreaking since Edwin Sutherland's pioneering research on white-collar crime, it is also fair to say that much of the most useful data has appeared in the pages of *Consumer's Reports* or in the work of investigative journalists, rather than in the pages of sociological publications.[6]

Organized crime is a form of lawbreaking that cries out for more sociological scrutiny. Public attention has been captured by Mafia or Cosa Nostra imagery which contends that organized criminality throughout the United States is tightly controlled by a syndicate made up of a dozen crime families, headed up by individuals of Sicilian extraction. This same Mafia hypothesis often argues that American racketeers and organized criminals are part of an international crime cartel. In addition, this portrayal of organized crime is often contained in criminological writings and in the pages of textbooks.[7]

Many of these themes regarding the Mafia or Cosa Nostra do not ring true. For one thing, closer attention to the evidence concerning the Mafia structure in Italy casts grave doubt on the argument that American organized crime has been simply transplanted from Sicilian soil.[8] A number of people have presented persuasive arguments indicating that the

---

[5] A large share of the evidence on garden-variety crime is summarized in Don C. Gibbons, *Society, Crime, and Criminal Careers,* 3rd ed. (Englewood Cliffs, N.J.: Prentice-Hall, 1977).

[6] For example, see Warren G. Magnuson and Jean Carper, *The Dark Side of the Marketplace* (Englewood Cliffs, N.J.: Prentice-Hall, 1968); and Howie Kurtz, "The Real Problem with the FDA," *The Washington Monthly* (July–August 1977):59–62.

[7] For example, see Donald R. Cressey, *Theft of the Nation* (New York: Harper & Row, 1969). A large share of the mass media and sociological writings on organized crime is presented in Gibbons, *Society, Crime and Criminal Careers,* pp. 407–23.

[8] Dwight C. Smith, Jr., *The Mafia Myth* (New York: Basic Books, 1975); Francis A. J. Ianni, with Elizabeth Reuss-Ianni, *A Family Business* (New York: Russell Sage Foundation, 1972); Humbert S. Nelli, *The Business of Crime* (New York: Oxford University Press, 1976); Giovanni Schiavo, *The Truth about the Mafia* (New York: Vigo Press, 1962).

picture of a national criminal conspiracy is overdrawn and that what exists in this country is a number of loosely coordinated regional crime syndicates, not some octopus-like crime structure.[9] Several studies of organized crime in particular communities have shown these activities to be localized and not part of a large-scale criminal structure.[10] It should not be surprising to find that organized criminality in Chicago or New York differs markedly in scale and seriousness from the less-developed structures of organized crime to be found in Portland, Wichita, or Nashville.

There is much work that remains to be accomplished in unraveling the tangled web of facts regarding organized crime. In particular, historically grounded inquiries are called for, along with probing studies that zero in on the complex interweaving of local politics, police corruption, and criminal interests that often comprise organized crime in particular communities.

CRIMINOLOGY AND HISTORICAL ANALYSIS

American criminology is about eight decades old. By and large, criminological inquiry in this country has rarely looked backward to law-breaking in the 1800s or before. Criminology has suffered from historical impoverishment, although some exceptions to this generalization exist, as, for example, in the studies on the varied societal responses that have been directed at juvenile offenders.[11] There is also a body of evidence concerning the social forces that produced particular instances of criminal legislation.[12] Even so, a better-developed historical perspective would enrich

[9] Joseph L. Albini, *The American Mafia: Genesis of a Legend* (Englewood Cliffs, N.J.: Prentice-Hall, 1971); Gordon Hawkins, "God and the Mafia," *The Public Interest,* 14 (Winter 1969):24–51.

[10] Ianni and Ianni, *A Family Business*; Francis A. J. Ianni, *The Black Mafia* (New York: Simon & Schuster, 1974); John A. Gardiner, *The Politics of Corruption: Organized Crime in an American City* (New York: Russell Sage Foundation, 1970); William J. Chambliss, "Vice, Corruption, Bureaucracy, and Power," *Wisconsin Law Review,* 4 (1971):1130–55.

[11] Robert M. Mennel, *Thorns and Thistles: Juvenile Delinquents in the United States, 1825–1940* (Hanover, N.H.: The University Press of New England, 1973); Anthony M. Platt, *The Child Savers* (Chicago: University of Chicago Press, 1969); J. Lawrence Schultz, "The Cycle of Juvenile Court History," *Crime and Delinquency,* 19 (October 1973):457–76; Edwin M. Lemert, *Social Action and Legal Change: Revolution within the Juvenile Court* (Chicago: Aldine, 1970).

[12] William Chambliss, "A Sociological Analysis of the Law of Vagrancy," *Social Problems,* 12 (December 1964):67–77; Jerome Hall, *Theft, Law and Society,* 2nd ed. (Indianapolis: Bobbs-Merrill, 1952); Leon Radzinowicz, *A History of English Criminal Law and Its Administration from 1750,* 3 vols. (New York: Macmillan, 1948–1957); Edwin H. Sutherland, "The Sexual Psychopath Laws," *Journal of Criminal Law and Criminology,* 40 (January–February 1950):543–54; Sutherland, "The Diffusion of Sexual Psychopath Laws," *American Journal of Sociology,* 56 (September 1950):142–48; Joseph Gusfield, *Symbolic Crusade* (Urbana, Ill.: Uni-

criminological analysis. For example, as the preceding section noted, historical accounts of the Mafia structure in Sicily have generated a good deal of skepticism about hypotheses that organized crime is a foreign weed that has taken root in American soil.

A recent example of the kind of research from which much can be learned is William Nelson's investigation of changes in criminal law and procedure in the Massachusetts colony from 1760 to 1830.[13] Nelson rummaged through court records to uncover the nature of law and prosecution during that period and discovered drastic changes in that system. In the pre-Revolutionary period, juries were empowered to determine law as well as fact. The laws functioned to enforce the Puritan morality of a tightly knit community. Property and contract law restrained people from pursuit of wealth and financial speculation. But that legal system became anachronistic in post-Revolutionary America. The emerging economy required new legislation that would reduce the restrictions on economic activity and the pursuit of financial success. Ultimately, property and contract laws were revised to focus on the protection of private property. Nelson concluded that this transformation of the Massachusetts legal system both mirrored the changing nature of American society and also helped to speed up the growth of an entrepreneurial society.

There are some other recent historical investigations toward which one can point.[14] A particularly useful one is by John Hagan and Jeffrey Leon involving the development of Canadian juvenile delinquency legislation.[15] Hagan and Leon examined the Marxist perspective that holds that criminal legislation, including delinquency statutes, served the basic interests of the ruling class. Contrary to Marxist claims, they found that the Canadian delinquency legislation did not lead to increased incarceration of

---

versity of Illinois Press, 1963); Howard S. Becker, *Outsiders* (New York: Free Press, 1963), pp. 121–46; Troy Duster, *The Legislation of Morality* (New York: Free Press, 1970); Pamela A. Roby, "Politics and Criminal Law: Revision of the New York State Penal Law on Prostitution," *Social Problems,* 17 (Summer 1969): 83–109. Some of these studies are summarized in Gibbons, *Society, Crime, and Criminal Careers,* pp. 27–36.

[13] William E. Nelson, *Americanization of the Common Law: The Impact of Legal Change on Massachusetts Society, 1760–1830* (Cambridge, Mass.: Harvard University Press, 1975); also see Kai T. Erikson, *Wayward Puritans* (New York: Wiley, 1969).

[14] For example, see Eric H. Monkkonen, *The Dangerous Class: Crime and Poverty in Columbus, Ohio, 1860–1885* (Cambridge, Mass.: Harvard University Press, 1975); Samuel Walker, *A Critical History of Police Reform* (Lexington, Mass.: Lexington Books, 1977); Sidney L. Harring, "Class Conflict and the Suppression of Tramps in Buffalo," *Law and Society Review,* 11 (Summer 1977):873–911.

[15] John Hagan and Jeffrey Leon, "Rediscovering Delinquency: Social History, Political Ideology and the Sociology of Law," *American Sociological Review,* 42 (August 1977):587–98. Also see Hagan, Edward T. Silva, and John H. Simpson, "Conflict and Consensus in the Designation of Deviance," *Social Forces,* 56 (December 1977): 320–40.

juveniles and did not result in the development of new categories of delinquency. They uncovered little support for related arguments to the effect that delinquency laws were designed to create a specialized labor market or to discipline unruly urban youths. No evidence turned up indicating that the ruling class played a dominant role in the rise of delinquency laws. Instead, these statutes were the work of a few charismatic figures. Although the Hagan and Leon study did not entirely disconfirm Marxist hypotheses about the origins and latent purposes of statutes, those claims contribute little to the understanding of the particular legislation which they scrutinized.

THE RULING CLASS, LEGISLATION, AND CRIME

Contemporary Marxist criminologists have been taken to task for the gross claims they have offered concerning an alleged ruling class whose interests presumably determine the nature of criminal statutes and social responses to those who violate these class-biased legal rules. A number of critics have castigated the theorists of radical criminology for their crude conspiratorial characterizations of a ruling elite, which are devoid of specifics that reveal either the composition of this ruling class or the nature of the social power exercised by that shadowy group.

This discussion on the shortcomings of ruling-class hypotheses in criminology is part of a larger dialogue in sociology regarding social power and influence in modern societies.[16] On one side of the debate are those who favor pluralistic models that hold that social power is exercised in a variable and shifting fashion by a multiplicity of groups that compete for influence in modern communities.[17] According to this perspective, no single group of individuals occupies a position of power sufficient to dominate in almost all decisions of significance.

The alternative elitist portrayal of social power owes much to the writings of C. Wright Mills, who advanced this view at a time when pluralistic notions reigned almost unchallenged.[18] Mills contended that a "power elite," made up of corporate officials, governmental figures, and military leaders, exercises nearly all of the real power in American society.

More recently, William Domhoff has carried on the legacy of Mills in a number of books seeking to limn the contours of power in the United

---

[16] This debate is reviewed briefly in William J. Chambliss and Thomas E. Ryther, *Sociology* (New York: McGraw-Hill, 1975); and Anderson, *Political Economy of Social Class*, pp. 216–33.

[17] For example, see Robert Dahl, *Who Governs? Democracy and Power in an American City* (New Haven, Conn.: Yale University Press, 1961).

[18] C. Wright Mills, *The Power Elite* (New York: Oxford University Press, 1956).

States.[19] His methodology was described as involving the "sociology of leadership," in which the social backgrounds of those who occupy positions of putative leadership were probed, rather than a decision-making approach centered on the study of the actual exercise of power and influence. Domhoff found that most of the presumed leaders come from similar, privileged backgrounds. For example, most were listed in the *Social Register* in their community and belonged to private prestigious men's clubs. These observations led him to assert that

> we conclude that the income, wealth, and institutional leadership of what Baltzell calls the "American business aristocracy" are more than sufficient to earn it the designation "governing class." As Sweezy would say, this "ruling class" is based upon the national corporate economy and the institutions that economy nourishes. It manifests itself through what the late C. Wright Mills called the power elite.[20]

Those who have been critical of Domhoff's conclusions and those of Mills before him argue that the sociology-of-leadership strategy only turns up plausible rather than definitive evidence of a ruling elite. For example, it is conceivable that although a relatively small cadre of socially advantaged individuals may occupy a number of seemingly strategic decision-making positions, those individuals may not actually control the influence processes. Moreover, even if it can be demonstrated that a ruling elite does exist, it does not necessarily follow that such a group will always be motivated toward action that maximizes its own interests to the disadvantage of other competing groups or that it will always be successful in overcoming opposition from other groups. The critics maintain that crucial findings on the exercise of social power can only come from an abundance of studies of actual decisions. The decision-making approach would pinpoint the composition of the group or groups exerting influence, and the interests and values that are being served by those acts of power.

Although written some years ago, Nelson Polsby's small book on power structures and power relationships at the local community level contained a number of trenchant and still relevant criticisms of studies that have purported to find a single ruling elite that pursued its own interests unimpeded by any effective opposition in the communities studied.[21] These research investigations also reported that the ruling class was pitted in con-

---

[19] G. William Domhoff, *Who Rules America?* (Englewood Cliffs, N.J.: Prentice-Hall, 1967); *The Higher Circles: The Governing Class in America* (New York: Random House, 1970); *The Bohemian Grove and Other Retreats: A Study in Ruling Class Cohesiveness* (New York: Harper & Row, 1974).

[20] Domhoff, *Who Rules America?* p. 156.

[21] Nelson W. Polsby, *Community Power and Political Theory* (New Haven: Yale University Press, 1963).

flict with other social class groups in the community, but it virtually always prevailed over these other strata.

Polsby indicated that the studies in question actually contained a good deal of evidence that pointed toward pluralism, diffuse power, and shifting power relationships, but these findings, which undermined the power elite argument, were usually explained away or ignored by the researchers. One device employed to rescue elite theories has been the "false consciousness" argument, which holds that when a social class group acts in ways counter to its real interests (as identified by the theorist) that group is said to have acted irrationally. Another ploy has been to invoke the "and-also" argument, which claims that those instances in which community power has been influenced in a fashion that departs from the power elite model are trivial or irrelevant. Still another device has been the "lump of power" assumption that denies that power can be exercised by groups that are not at the apex of the socioeconomic structure. This assumption has led researchers to argue that lower- or middle-class groups are without effective social power, in spite of contrary evidence in community studies that indicated that these groups have prevailed over the socioeconomic elite in important community issues.

According to Polsby, researchers in community power have also claimed that although seemingly powerless groups sometimes appear to be exercising influence in the community, real power is wielded covertly by the ruling class operating behind the scenes. Powerless groups (as defined by the researcher) only *seem* to be exercising influence. Still another stratagem has been to argue that an apparently powerless elite is powerful because of its strategic position among community groups. That argument is less than persuasive in that the strategic influence of the putative elite group has rarely been demonstrated. Finally, some theorists have offered a "power potential" claim, holding that while the economic elite may sometimes appear to be inactive, it could exercise decisive power if it were interested in so doing.

Polsby's own conclusions about community power, which were derived from a number of research investigations, were that

> rulership . . . is often characterized by (1) relatively wide sharing of powers among leaders specialized to one or a few issue areas, calling upon many different resources and techniques for applying resources to influencing outcomes, (2) constraints upon decision-making applied by nonelites and by elites themselves, (3) conditions of all kinds imposed by impersonal outside forces, and (4) uncertainty about the of modern American local life, some people attain their ends more distributions of payoffs of political actions. But given these conditions frequently than others, and a theory of community power might rea-

sonably be expected to explore "rulership" in this rather more limited sense of the term.[22]

Polsby and others have made a strong case for pluralistic conceptions of power at the local level. Accordingly, the burden of proof rests with those who favor national ruling elite arguments. While there is no serious disagreement with the proposition that wealth and prestige are concentrated in the hands of a relatively few people in American society, it is still far from clear that this group constitutes a unified ruling class. And, if a ruling class in some sense does exist, much remains to be learned regarding how and under what circumstances that elite manages to exercise its influence.

Radical criminological theorists would do well to examine other recent discussions of class power and state power in the United States, including Roberta Garner's observations on this matter.[23] She has argued that the conspiratorial view of a small powerful elite clique running the nation is an entirely too crude characterization of power relationships. She also questioned the accuracy of the "overlap of power" view of Domhoff and others, which assumes that this arrangement in which ruling class members man the machinery of the state is the major device through which ruling class interests are protected by the state. Her own portrayal of ruling class-state linkages is a much more finely-grained one, calling attention to a variety of direct and indirect organizational links between the managers of the capitalist economy and the government. Furthermore, state support for corporate class interests often comes about even though specific organizational links between capitalist elites and officials of the state have not been forged. She likened the situation to that of a luxury cruise ship, in which the passengers (rulers) and the crew (the state) all move in the same direction, even though they do not directly collaborate in running the ship.

> The crew is committed to smooth sailing for several reasons. At its upper levels, the crew's officers have a tradition of service to passengers, a love of the sea that is shared with the passengers, a sense of accomplishment at running a tight ship, and a substantial remuneration. At the bottom levels, pay is less, but it is the major incentive because the sailors must make a living. The crew does not openly question its passengers' desires to enjoy the cruise and arrive at a certain destination.[24]

Given the unsettled nature of this issue in sociological analysis, it is no wonder that the ruling-class argument regarding criminal laws and

[22] *Ibid.,* p. 136.
[23] Roberta Ash Garner, *Social Change* (Chicago: Rand McNally, 1977), pp. 252–59.
[24] *Ibid.,* p. 258.

their enforcement is empirically shaky. Most of the assertions of radical criminology about a ruling elite have contained one or another of the specious defenses of power elite formulations noted in this discussion. Some specific instances of criminal law making to which ruling class hypotheses seem inapplicable were noted in Chapter 7. Additionally, the Hagan and Leon study discussed in this chapter failed to turn up findings congruent with radical claims about ruling-class interests. Enough evidence has already accumulated to indicate that a richer, more finely crafted theory and considerably more research on interest groups and legislation are required in a criminological perspective that captures the complexity of the real world.

ECONOMIC STRUCTURE, ECONOMIC CHANGE, AND CRIMINALITY

The articulation of economic analysis with the study of criminality is another difficult task facing criminologists. Part of this assignment involves sorting out the claims of Marxist-radical criminologists regarding the linkages between the political-economic order and lawbreaking, but it includes other theoretical and research chores as well.

American sociology grew out of the American Social Science Association in the late 1800s. In the process, the discipline of economics fractured off from the parent social science organization and went its own way, while, somewhat later, the American Sociological Society arose and proceeded in a different direction. As a number of commentators have indicated, the infant field of sociology initially represented little more than "the study of everything else," in which sociologists concerned themselves with leftovers that had not already been seized on by one of the older, established fields of social science.

American sociology outgrew its disorderly and inchoate beginnings and ultimately became a coherent discipline with a unique and identifiable focus. However, it seems fair to say that the rupture between sociology and economics has never been repaired satisfactorily. Economic factors continue to be regarded as of only tangential interest in much sociological analysis, while many sociologists have been economic illiterates.[25] One guage of the importance attached to economic factors in social life is that

[25] Some attempts to spell out linkages between economics and sociological analysis are Neil J. Smelser, "The Sociology of Economic Life," in Talcott Parsons, ed., *American Sociology* (New York: Basic Books, 1968), pp. 143–55; Smelser, *The Sociology of Economic Life* (Englewood Cliffs, N.J.: Prentice-Hall, 1963); Parsons and Smelser, *Economy and Society* (New York: Free Press, 1956). Regarding economic factors and sociology, Smelser remarked: "Economic Sociology is rather a perspective in the process of emergence." (Smelser, *The Sociology of Economic Life*, p. 145.)

they are usually assigned to a single chapter in the back of introductory sociology textbooks, along with other institutions such as education and religion.

Although current diagnoses of the health of the economic system of corporate capitalism run in a variety of directions, the unbridled optimism characteristic of the first few years following World War II has disappeared from contemporary American society. In those halcyon days, many people believed that the United States was on the threshold of a permanent state of economic well-being, in which poverty would be entirely banished at home at the same time that American largesse would be used to improve the lot of the less fortunate elsewhere in the world. By contrast, gloomy portrayals of an economically troubled nation have been presented in abundance in recent years.

One example of economic pessimism recently appeared in a feature article on "The American Underclass." [26] A depressing litany of facts regarding the underclass was voiced in that essay, indicating that this social-economic stratum contains an inordinate concentration of delinquents, school dropouts, drug users, welfare recipients, criminals, and other forms of "social junk" or "social dynamite." This report also argued that there are now two basic classes of black citizens: upwardly mobile, successful blacks, and a much larger group of underclass members. The seething resentment or sense of relative deprivation of those who are at the bottom of the economic heap is fueled by this situation, for the underclass citizens compare themselves with these few, highly visible cases of success. The *Time* essay also indicated that the underclass is heavily populated with people for whom there are no jobs. These individuals have been rendered economically superfluous or obsolete because they lack special skills or abilities in an economy in which machines have replaced unskilled laborers.

This commentary on the American underclass is anchored on a foundation of facts. For example, Wayne Villemez and Alan Row examined a number of studies that claimed that there were substantial black economic gains in the 1960s.[27] They concluded that most of the apparent narrowing of the gap between black and white income is a misleading artifact of research methodology. They argued that, although there has been some relative gain in affluence for a small portion of blacks, most black citizens continue to show significantly lower incomes, with no nar-

[26] "The American Underclass," *Time Magazine* (August 29, 1977):14–27.
[27] Wayne J. Villemez and Alan R. Row, "Black Economic Gains in the Sixties: A Methodological Critique and Reassessment," *Social Forces,* 54 (September 1975): 181–93; see also Anderson, *Political Economy of Social Class,* pp. 76–115; Sidney Willhelm, *Who Needs the Negro?* (Cambridge, Mass.: Schenkman, 1970); Edna Bonacich, "Advanced Capitalism and Black/White Race Relations in the United States: A Split Labor Market Interpretation," *American Sociological Review,* 41 (February 1976):34–51.

rowing of the black-white differential. For example, the median income for employed white males in the United States in 1970 was approximately $9,000, while the figure for blacks was only $5,900. This income gap becomes even more pronounced when the higher proportion of unemployed blacks is taken into account and when acknowledgement is given to the fact that the entire income distribution from highest to lowest income status shows blacks to be disadvantaged when compared to whites.

There is also a body of research evidence on crimes of the underclass. In a study carried out a number of years ago, Daniel Glaser and Kent Rice showed that crime among 18- to 35-year-old adults in the United States is most frequent during periods of widespread unemployment. More recently, James Levine reported a very high correlation between robbery rates and the number of out-of-school and unemployed males in the 16- to 20-year-old age category in the 26 largest American cities in 1970. Still another recent inquiry turned up evidence that crime rates for larceny, robbery, burglary, and auto theft are particularly pronounced among young adult males who have dropped out of the labor force.[28]

Recent commentators on crime among lower-class groups have drawn attention to the role of relative deprivation in exacerbating the sting of poverty and unemployment and in fueling a sense of resentment that may impel many people from this segment of the population into lawbreaking.[29] Those who have been left behind in the economic struggle, particularly during a time of expanding affluence for the majority of the population, may well come to perceive themselves to be victims of an unjust society.

The relative deprivation hypothesis has received support from a number of studies. For example, economists Sheldon Danziger and David Wheeler have explored a complex econometric model dealing with certain garden-variety crimes and measures of income inequality and relative deprivation.[30] Their findings were consistent with the relative deprivation argument.

So much for the facts. What remedies can be directed at the economic ills that appear to generate garden-variety crime? The American liberal tradition that has flourished for many decades has centered on the

[28] Daniel Glaser and Kent Rice, "Crime, Age, and Unemployment," *American Sociological Review*, 24 (October 1959):671–86; James P. Levine, "The Ineffectiveness of Adding Police to Prevent Crime," *Public Policy*, 23 (Fall 1975):136; Llad Phillips, Harold L. Votey, Jr., and Darold Maxwell, "Crime, Youth, and the Labor Market," *Journal of Political Economy*, 80 (May–June 1972):491–503.

[29] *Time*, "The American Underclass"; C. Ronald Chester, "Relative Deprivation as a Cause of Property Crime," *Crime and Delinquency*, 22 (January 1976):17–30.

[30] Sheldon Danziger and David Wheeler, "The Economics of Crime: Punishment or Income Redistribution," *Review of Social Economy*, 33 (October 1975):113–30.

implicit assumption that these social and economic flaws will gradually but inexorably shrink in magnitude and importance through the efforts of an enlightened state that will secure the cooperation of the economic sector in programs of social and economic reform. Liberal optimism regarding crime control was mirrored in a major recommendation of the President's Commission on Law Enforcement and Administration of Justice: "First, society must seek to prevent crime before it happens by assuring all Americans a stake in the benefits and responsibilities of American life, by strengthening law enforcement, and by reducing criminal opportunities." [31] Similarly, *Time* prescribed a liberal nostrum as a partial cure for the economic doldrums and the crime and other problems that grow out of them, asserting that "a most crying long-range need is to improve public education." [32]

But there are mounting indications that the liberal vision may be obsolete and that the social and economic problems of American society run deeper and are markedly more intractable. Bleak assessments of the current economic state of American society and the future prospects for this nation have been put forth in quantity in recent years. For example, Daniel Bell has complained that modernism—the unfettered pursuit of self, along with values stressing unrestrained mass hedonism that are commonplace in contemporary America—threatens to undermine the capitalist system. [33] Bell perceived great danger to the existing system in the form of masses of citizens who demand more from the state than it can provide.

A different diagnosis of the problems of modern capitalism and the state can be found in the writings of Marxist theorists. [34] Charles Anderson, James O'Connor, and a number of others have directed scrutiny at the fiscal problems of the state in capitalist societies. [35] The modern capitalist state is faced with ever-increasing demands for financial supports to be extended to a faltering economy in the form of governmental subsidies, purchases of military hardware, and the like. At the same time, the state must provide economic assistance to a growing army of displaced workers, welfare recipients, and other casualties of industrial-corporate capitalism. In an economic system that is plagued with severe and ever-increasing

---

[31] The President's Commission on Law Enforcement and Administration of Justice, *The Challenge of Crime in a Free Society* (Washington, D.C.: U.S. Government Printing Office, 1967), p. *vi*.

[32] *Time,* "The American Underclass," p. 27.

[33] Daniel Bell, *The Cultural Contradictions of Capitalism* (New York: Basic Books, 1976).

[34] For example, see Harry Magdoff, *The Age of Imperialism* (New York: Monthly Review Press, 1969); Paul M. Sweezy and Magdoff, *The Dynamics of U.S. Capitalism* (New York: Monthly Review Press, 1972).

[35] Anderson, *Political Economy of Social Class*; James O'Connor, *The Fiscal Crisis of the State* (New York: St. Martin's Press, 1973).

strains of this kind, relatively few state resources are likely to be available for economic and social reforms. On this matter, Anderson has argued that

> monopoly capitalism requires for its prosperity an economically active state, something which the majority of the ruling class failed to fully comprehend until the 1940s. . . . On its own corporate capitalism cannot keep the economy running; it needs the taxation and spending powers of the state. . . . Through purchases and transfer payments the government creates effective demand, which enables the capitalist state not only to survive, but to reap profits in traditional and new government-subsidized areas. In advanced technological society, government taxation and spending does not subtract from the private sector; quite the contrary: it adds to the economy an amount of surplus which would never appear otherwise.

> With all levels of U.S. government currently accounting for between one-fourth and one-third of economic activity and employment, no one can seriously question the state's indispensibility to corporate capitalism. . . . Given the extravagant economic needs of the ruling class, their control of the tax system and the enormous financial demands upon the state, government faces serious fiscal problems. The capitalist class demands billions in subsidies, systematically evades taxes, and unloads the burden of financing state operations upon the working class—all of which creates mounting fiscal pressures upon the public purse.

> The state thus finds itself as a buffer for capitalist contradictions and irrationality, desperately trying to preserve the integrity of the capitalist class and its major institutions while at the same time trying to preserve a simulacrum of social stability and well-being for the masses. . . .

> The combination of emphasis on military production and the inflation of U.S. currency has contributed to yet another serious structural problem of U.S. capitalism: an unprecedented (in this century) trade deficit of growing proportions, as productivity in consumer industries declined vis-à-vis world leaders and as inflated U.S. prices placed exports in unfavorable and imports in favorable selling positions. The Vietnam War rapidly hastened these symptoms of economic illness. This, together with the costs of maintaining the empire (the "free world"—as in Brazil, Greece, South Vietnam, South Korea, and dozens of other places), has led to the balance-of-payments problem and devaluations of the dollar—more of which are sure to come, even given continued superprofits taken by U.S. corporations around the world. Thus, the U.S. ruling class, in its actions through the state, is pitted not only against its own working class as it strives to limit wages and increase productivity through speed-ups and automation in order to make its

goods more competitive on the world market (and also as it milks the
working class for taxes to pay the costs of empire), but also against
the bourgeoisie of other advanced nations in the struggle for markets
and profits. . . .

The consequence of state manipulation of available economic variables,
whatever combination might be selected for action, is almost uni-
versally destined to be unfavorable to the working class. All actions
are calculated to maximize corporate profits, for it is corporate profits
which make the system run in the way it does. However, the calcula-
tions now current are approaching an impasse: profits cannot be
maintained or increased without flagrant violations of the working
class and without risking serious destabilizing political unrest and
political upheaval. Temporarily, scapegoats and rationalizations have
bought additional time, but the day of more fundamental reckoning
cannot be long postponed.[36]

In the years since these prophetic words were written, the problems of state capitalism in the United States have worsened. The emergence
of the Organization of Petroleum Exporting Countries (OPEC) has resulted in drastically increased costs for petroleum exports into the country.
Trade deficits have risen as American products have been priced out of
world markets because of inflated prices that put them at a disadvantage
to the industrial output of countries such as Japan, South Korea, or West
Germany. Meanwhile, the federal government has been unable to make
any serious impact on economic stagnation or high unemployment rates.
It has become increasingly more difficult to sustain the spirit of optimistic
liberalism in the face of these ominous trends in American society.

This commentary centers on the current difficulties of capitalist
economies. Another pessimistic analysis has been provided by economist
Robert Heilbroner, who took a longer view on these matters. He argued
that capitalist and socialist nations are both modern and industrialized
and, therefore, both face a number of external challenges that threaten to
produce an extremely bleak long-range future for them. These external
challenges include the continued demographic crisis in the Third World
nations, which produces runaway population growth that consumes any
economic surplus that might be generated in those countries. Another
challenge arises from the threat of nuclear and other forms of warfare,
including attempts by Third World countries to bring about redistribution
of wealth. Finally, even if these two challenges are dealt with successfully,
environmental exhaustion looms ahead, particularly in the form of eleva-
tion of atmospheric heat levels as a result of increased industrial use of
energy as well as the depletion of world resources such as petroleum.

[36] Anderson, *Political Economy of Social Class*, pp. 242–45.

The inexorable push for ever-increasing economic growth under capitalism or industrial socialism has other consequences as well. Heilbroner contended that people became dehumanized as a result of those productive arrangements that accommodate people to machines rather than attending to the psychic needs of workers. Heilbroner concluded that if modern societies are to survive, a stationary, no-growth economy will have to be developed. Income will have to be distributed more equitably. In both capitalist and socialist countries, people will have to become reconciled to markedly lower levels of living. He asserted that

> whether we are unable to sustain growth or unable to tolerate it, there can be no doubt that a radically different future beckons. In either eventuality it seems beyond dispute that the present orientation of society must change. In place of production must come its careful restriction and long-term dimunition within society. In place of prodigalities of consumption must come new frugal attitudes. In these and other ways, the "post-industrial" society of the future is apt to be as different from present-day industrial society as the latter was from its pre-industrial precursor.[37]

How can industrial deceleration and lowered materialistic expectations be brought about? According to Heilbroner, this kind of reordered future will require massive state planning, carried on within the structure of an authoritarian social order. He acknowledged that these would be highly unpalatable changes in societal structure, but insisted that they represent the only hope for the future. Even then, Heilbroner noted that "if . . . we ask whether it is possible to meet the challenges of the future without the payment of a fearful price, the answer must be: No, there is no such hope."[38]

What are the implications of these varied diagnoses as far as crime levels and patterns in the future are concerned? There is enough validity to these judgments that the American economy is in deep trouble and moving toward a state of permanent debility and disarray to raise doubts about the adequacy of mainstream criminological explanations and perspectives. Changes in the structure of American society may not inevitably lead to increased criminality on the part of the underclass. Nor do these changes mean that revolutionary movements will arise, carried on by people who see themselves as having no hope for economic security. It is possible that the masses of citizens will reconcile themselves without protest to life in the altered social order of the future. What does seem clear is that crime levels and responses to lawbreaking will be influenced

---

[37] Robert L. Heilbroner, *An Inquiry into the Human Prospect* (New York: Norton, 1974), p. 94.
[38] *Ibid.,* p. 136.

by these economic changes now underway in ways that will need to be divined by a new generation of criminologists. The American economy can no longer be treated as a given that needs no special attention. As criminologists go about ferreting out the causal dimensions of crime, they must include economics in their study of social factors.

PSYCHOLOGICAL FACTORS IN CRIMINALITY

Sociological criminology has not succeeded in resolving the issue of psychological forces and personality factors in crime and delinquency. That criminology has been deficient in this regard should come as no surprise, given the fact that the psychological question is a perennial and nagging one that has not been solved in sociology.

Alex Inkeles, the most insistent and articulate spokesman for the place of psychological variables in sociological analysis, has argued that "the study of social systems can often be much more incisive if one element in the analysis is a psychological theory, that is, a theory of the person as a system." [39] Inkeles identified three major ways in which psychological theory can make important contributions to sociological analysis. First, institutional or social-structural patterns are mediated through personalities. Hence, a general theory of psychological functioning is required if sociologists are to comprehend the ways in which psychological patterns operate as intervening variables in social behavior. Reckless's argument that the self-concept can be an "insulator" against criminogenic social influences is a criminological example of the kind of formulation suggested by Inkeles, because it contends that certain kinds of personality structures largely determine whether youngsters will be drawn into delinquency or will be able to resist the harmful influences of their environment (see Chapter 5).

A second proposition advanced by Inkeles was that the functioning of the social system is often influenced by the kinds of personality patterns, personality needs, and other psychological characteristics of the individuals who are found within a social system. Social organizations do not usually draw their members randomly from the population at large. Instead, people with particular personality configurations or individual qualities are often disproportionately common in particular social systems. If there is an allocation of personality types into particular organizations, sociological analyses that speak only of social roles and role performances

[39] Alex Inkeles, "Sociological Theory in Relation to Social Psychological Variables," in John C. McKinney and Edward A. Tiryakian, eds., *Theoretical Sociology* (Englewood Cliffs, N.J.: Prentice-Hall, 1970), p. 406. Also see Inkeles, "Personality and Social Structure," in Talcott Parsons, ed., *American Sociology* (New York: Basic Books, 1968), pp. 3–18.

will fail to provide a full account of system functioning. As Inkeles put it, "role performance obviously also depends on possession of the knowledge or skills a role requires and on the motivation to perform the role. In addition, there may be 'qualities' in the person which hinder or facilitate his role performance because they make it intrinsically rewarding or repugnant to him, quite apart from the formal system of sanctions." [40] For example, criminological inquiries into American penitentiaries have attributed much of the violence in prisons to the number of people in the prison population with volatile personalities. Because such individuals are much less frequently encountered in European prisons, those institutions are not wracked by the assaultive episodes and collective outbursts by prisoners characteristic of American prisons.

The third contribution that psychological theory can make to sociological analysis, according to Inkeles, is through the special fields of psychological theory such as cognition and learning processes. Chapter 3 took note of some efforts by criminologists to introduce principles of learning theory into criminological analysis.

Criminologists have not been totally unaware of psychological or psychiatric theory and research on psychic forces in lawbreaking. Most criminology textbooks have contained a section dealing with the psychological literature on criminality. For example, consider the chapter on "Personality" by Sutherland and Cressey. That discussion reviewed claims that mental retardation is involved in crime, along with data on psychosis as a factor in lawbreaking. It also examined the evidence for psychopathy as a correlate of criminality and found that hypothesis wanting. Other emotional patterns were also rejected as important in etiology, as were psychoanalytic theories of crime. Sutherland and Cressey concluded their review with the assertion that "the explanation of criminal behavior, apparently, is to be found in social interaction, in which both the behavior of a person and the overt or prospective behavior of other persons play their parts." [41]

Sutherland and Cressey's treatment of psychogenic arguments is representative of the stance taken by most criminologists and found in most criminology textbooks.[42] Most of these discussions have drawn at-

[40] Inkeles, "Sociological Theory in Relation to Social Psychological Variables," p. 414.

[41] Edwin H. Sutherland and Donald R. Cressey, *Criminology*, 9th ed. (Philadelphia: Lippincott, 1974), p. 170.

[42] For example, see Gibbons, *Society, Crime, and Criminal Careers*, Chapter 7, "Psychogenic Approaches," pp. 155–83. That chapter judged psychoanalytic theories of crime to be hopelessly ambiguous and incapable of empirical verification. Nearly all the studies on emotional problems and psychological maladjustment among offenders have either failed to discover differences between offenders and noncriminals or have been methodologically flawed. The argument that many criminals suffer from psychopathy or sociopathy was also judged to be without merit.

tention to a number of crippling flaws in the theoretical claims that have been put forth by psychologists and psychiatrists. Criminological critiques have made it abundantly clear that little confidence can be placed in most of the research that has been conducted on psychological variables in criminality.[43] These investigations have been plagued by a variety of methodological problems that make any conclusions that psychological correlates of lawbreaking have been discovered highly suspect.

Sociological criminologists have been on solid ground in concluding that no convincing evidence of psychological forces, particularly in the form of aberrant personality patterns and the like, has yet been uncovered. At the same time, it is clearly a non sequitur to imply, as many criminologists have done, that research results demonstrate that personality factors play no part in criminality. It is entirely conceivable that there are important psychological forces that have yet to be uncovered.[44]

Criminologists and theorists concerned with deviant behavior have also occasionally acknowledged that more work needs to be done in bringing psychological elements into etiological explanations. For example, George Vold reviewed a large collection of research findings on the relationship between mental and emotional disorders and crime and delinquency and reached the common sociological conclusion that no convincing evidence of a relationship had been produced by the studies. But, he also examined a body of material on drunkenness, vagrancy, gambling, prostitution, and drug offenses and concluded that "some kind of eclectic syncretism of theories of individual characteristics, and of theories of social and economic influences, is in order." [45]

---

[43] One illustrative case of a complex psychological theory which has lead to considerable research, but in which methodological problems render the findings unconvincing, is the theory and research of the English psychologist, Hans Eysenck who argued that extraverted individuals are less likely to develop a social conscience through conditioned learning, due to autonomic nervous system characteristics that accompany extraversion. As a result, extraverted people, particularly those who also exhibit neuroticism or psychoticism, are likely to be inordinately common in the population of offenders. This theory appeared in Hans J. Eysenck, *Crime and Personality* (London: Granada Press, 1970). Supporting evidence has been reported in Sybil B. G. Eysenck and H. J. Eysenck, "Crime and Personality: An Empirical Study of the Three-Factor Theory," *British Journal of Criminology*, 10 (July 1970):225–39. General critiques of Eysenck's theory and methodology include Ian Taylor, Paul Walton, and Jock Young, *The New Criminology* (London: Routledge & Kegan Paul, 1973), pp. 47–61; Richard Christie, "Some Abuses of Psychology," *Psychological Bulletin*, 53 (1956):439–51. Also see M. S. Hoghughi and A. R. Forrest, "Eysenck's Theory of Personality," *British Journal of Criminology*, 10 (July 1970):240–54; and P. K. Burgess, "Eysenck's Theory of Personality: A New Approach," *British Journal of Criminology*, 12 (January 1972):74–82.

[44] For further discussion of this point, see Gibbons, *Society, Crime, and Criminal Careers*, pp. 177–82.

[45] George B. Vold, *Theoretical Criminology* (New York: Oxford University Press, 1958), p. 155.

More recently, Clarence Schrag included social learning theory as one of the elements needed in a comprehensive theory of crime, although his commentary had little to say about personality patterns and personality characteristics. In a similar vein, Edwin Lemert's critical essay on Merton's anomie argument contained a relatively brief acknowledgment that psychic processes must be taken into account in explanations of deviant behavior.[46]

A much more detailed and comprehensive discussion of socio-psychological factors in lawbreaking has been provided by Gwynn Nettler. He examined a number of control arguments, including containment theory and Hirschi's views on social control (see Chapter 5). He also surveyed a number of social training or social learning formulations and studies, including the work of Eysenck, Gordon Trasler, and Albert Bandura and Richard Walters.[47] Nettler offered an assessment of the significance of these studies that was sympathetic to psychogenic viewpoints.

> Both developmental and comparative studies yield the same description of what makes us the way we are. If we grow up "naturally," without cultivation, like weeds, we grow up like weeds—rank. If our nurturing is defective—unappreciative, inconsistent, lax, harsh, and careless—we grow up hostile, and the hostility seems as much turned inward as turned outward. The nurturing environments that produce this denigration of self and others are the same ones that breed criminality.[48]

Most of the criminological effort directed at the merging of sociological and psychological elements has been of the third variety identified by Inkeles, the application of special fields of psychological theory such as operant conditioning and modeling to criminology. Criminologists have had relatively little to say about qualities such as anxiety over masculine identity, passivity, dependency, extroversion, or other personality characteristics that may operate as intervening variables in crime, delinquency, and deviancy.

---

[46] Clarence Schrag, *Crime and Justice: American Style* (Rockville, Md.: National Institute of Mental Health, 1971), pp. 32–52; Edwin M. Lemert, *Human Deviance, Social Problems, and Social Control,* 2nd ed. (Englewood Cliffs, N.J.: Prentice-Hall, 1972), pp. 45–46.

[47] Eysenck, *Crime and Personality*; Gordon Trasler, *The Explanation of Criminality* (London: Routledge & Kegan Paul, 1962); Albert Bandura and Richard H. Walters, *Adolescent Aggression* (New York: Ronald Press, 1959); Bandura and Walters, *Social Learning and Personality Development* (New York: Holt, Rinehart and Winston, 1963). For a treatment of deviant behavior from a social learning perspective, see Ronald L. Akers, *Deviant Behavior: A Social Learning Approach,* 2nd ed. (Belmont, Calif.: Wadsworth, 1977).

[48] Gwynn Nettler, *Explaining Crime,* 2nd ed. (New York: McGraw-Hill, 1978), p. 332.

Lemert's research involving dependency as an intervening factor in alcoholism is illustrative of the kind of sociopsychological theory and research that needs to be pursued.[49] He examined the hypothesis that alcoholics frequently have dependent personalities prior to the onset of alcoholism. He found behavioral and psychological indicators of dependency in a sizable portion of the cases he studied.

There is little more that can be said about psychological correlates in criminality at the present time, given the paucity of attention that this question has received in criminology. But, there are hints contained in some of the personal accounts of crime careers that have been provided by actual offenders that these "qualities," as Inkeles termed them, do play a role in lawbreaking. Also, the criminological literature includes indications that dependency may be a frequently encountered psychological characteristic of naïve check forgers, and that certain sex offenders may exhibit relatively atypical sexual attitudes and motives that are the product of unusual patterns of sexual socialization which they have undergone. Sociological criminologists have often ignored or slurred over sexual criminality, partly because it does not seem to fit within such perspectives as anomie and differential association, and partly because of the lack of a satisfactory social-psychological theory of sexual socialization which might be used to account for sexual deviance. One important effort to fill in that gap has been made by John Gagnon and William Simon.[50] More such linkages between social conditions and psychological states are likely to be uncovered if and when criminologists begin the task of "bringing men back in."

CONCLUDING REMARKS

American sociological criminology has grown impressively in theoretical sophistication and empirical validity over the three-fourths of a century since 1900. The eclectic, atheoretical arguments of early criminologists have been replaced by a number of rich and elegant sociological formulations that stand as some of the more impressive products of modern American sociology.

At the same time, a number of additions and revisions are in order in criminology. There are a host of unfinished tasks that cry out for atten-

---

[49] Edwin M. Lemert, "Dependency in Married Alcoholics," *Quarterly Journal of Studies on Alcohol*, 23 (December 1962):590–609.

[50] For example, see Malcolm Braly, *False Starts* (Boston: Little, Brown, 1976); and Bruce Jackson, *A Thief's Primer* (New York: Macmillan, 1969). For some comments on naïve check forgers, see Gibbons, *Society, Crime, and Criminal Careers*, pp. 304–8. For a discussion of sexual offender patterns, see *Ibid.*, pp. 369–409; and John H. Gagnon and William Simon, *Sexual Conduct* (Chicago: Aldine, 1973).

tion. In particular, the recent conflict and radical arguments have posed some thorny problems for criminological theory.

The major figures who now make up the criminological establishment in sociology, many of whose works are discussed in this book, will have passed from the scene by the turn of the century. The key contributors to criminological inquiry in the year 2000 have not yet made their appearance. Perhaps those individuals, whoever they turn out to be, will succeed in accomplishing much of the unfinished business of criminology.

INDEX